# 1002
# FASCINATING
# FACTS
## AND
# FIGURES

# 1002 FASCINATING FACTS AND FIGURES

**the Diagram Group**

BONANZA BOOKS
New York

**The Diagram Group**

Authors    Susan Bosanko, David Lambert, Ruth Midgley
Artists    Joe Bonello, Mark Evans, Brian Hewson, Richard Hummerstone, Philip Patenall, Graham Rosewarne, Jerry Watkiss

**US Edition**

Managing Editor    Reet Nelis
Editor    Ellen Sarewitz
Assistant    Annabel Else

This 1986 edition is published by Bonanza Books, distributed by Crown Publishers, Inc., 225 Park Avenue South, New York, New York 10003, by arrangement with Diagram Visual Information Limited 1985.

Originally published as *Illustrated Encyclopedia of Facts and Figures*

A Diagram Book first created by Diagram Visual Information Limited of 195 Kentish Town Road, London NW5 8SY, England.

Printed and Bound in the United States of America

Library of Congress Cataloging-in-Publication Data

Bosanko, Susan.
  1002 fascinating facts and figures.

  Originally published as: Illustrated encyclopedia of facts and figures / Diagram Group. 1985.
  Includes index.
  1. Encyclopedias and dictionaries.   I. Lambert, David, 1932–
II. Midgley, Ruth.    III. Illustrated encyclopedia of facts and figures.
IV. Title.   V. Title: One thousand two fascinating facts and figures.
AG6.B67    1986     031      86-9740
ISBN 0-517-61933-4

hgfedcba

# Contents

# Section 3
# THE HUMAN BODY

# Section 4
# SCIENCE

# Section 5
# NUMBERS

# Section 6
# SPACE

# Section 1
# The Earth

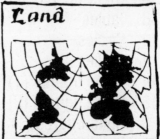

# Earth profile

**The Earth in space**  Of the nine known planets that orbit the Sun to form our solar system, the Earth is the third nearest the Sun and the fifth largest. The average distance between the Earth and the Sun is roughly 93,000,000 mi. The average distance between the Earth and the Moon is roughly 238,840 mi.

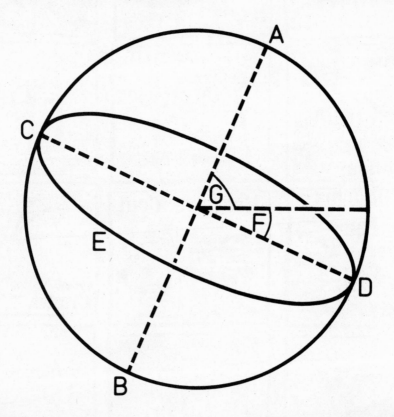

**Earth measurements** (above) Because the Earth is not a true sphere, its diameter varies from place to place. The distance between the Poles, called the polar diameter (**A–B**), is 7,900 mi. The equatorial diameter (**C–D**) is 7,926 mi. The distance around the Equator, called the equatorial circumference (**E**), is 24,902 mi.

The Earth has a surface area of 196,940,000 sq.mi and a volume of 259,875,300,000 cu.mi. Also shown is the Earth's tilt or angle of inclination. There is 23½° (**F**) between the plane of the Equator and the plane of the Earth's orbit around the Sun, and 66½° (**G**) between the plane of the orbit and the polar axis.

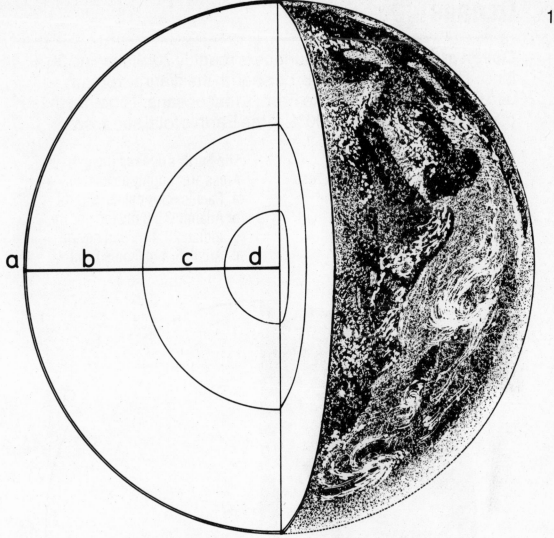

**The Earth's interior** (above)
This diagram shows the different
layers that make up the Earth. Much
of our information comes from
studies of earthquake waves as they
pass through the Earth. (The depths
listed here are only approximate.)

a  Crust (under oceans): 3.1 mi
   deep; made of basalt (a type of
   rock) Crust (continental): average
   24.8 mi deep; made of granite

b  Mantle: 1,798 mi deep; probably
   containing peridotite (a
   heavy, dark rock), dunite
   (olivine rock) and ecologite
   (a dense form of basalt)

c  Outer core: 1,243 mi deep;
   probably liquid iron with some
   dissolved sulfur and silicon

d  Inner core: 851 mi deep;
   probably solid iron

**Oceans**

**Ocean areas** The Earth's surface is roughly 70% sea and 30% land. These proportions can be seen in the diagram below, as can the relative areas of the Earth's four oceans. Together these oceans account for over 90% of the Earth's total sea area.

**Sea and land** (below)
Here we give the approximate areas of sea and land that make up the Earth's surface.
☐ Sea 140 million sq. mi
■ Land 57 million sq. mi

**The Earth's oceans** (below)
Areas are roughly as follows.
**a** Pacific 63.8 million sq. mi
**b** Atlantic 31.8 million sq. mi
**c** Indian 28.4 million sq. mi
**d** Arctic 5.4 million sq. mi

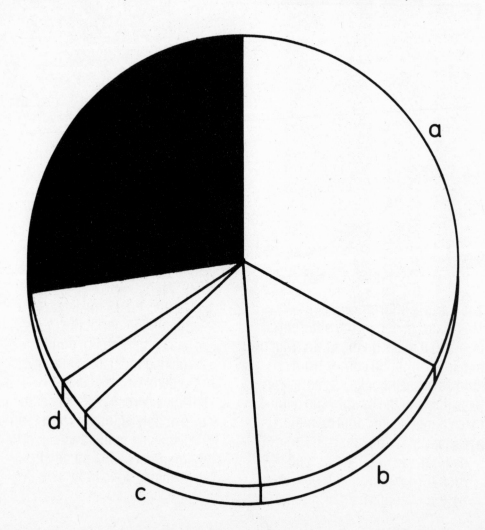

## Greatest ocean depths

| | | | |
|---|---|---|---|
| **a** | Pacific | Marianas Trench | 36,198 ft |
| **b** | Atlantic | Puerto Rico Trench | 27,498 ft |
| **c** | Indian | Diamantina | 26,400 ft |
| **d** | Arctic | (Unnamed location) | 17,850 ft |

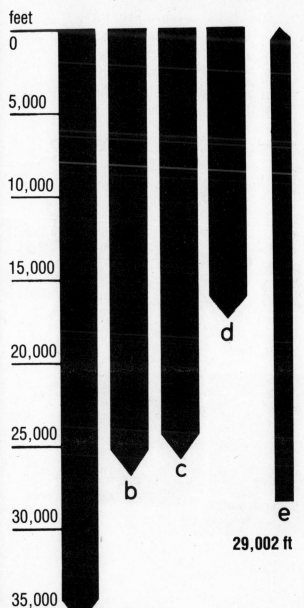

**Down and then up** (left)
This diagram compares the depth of the deepest known point in each ocean with the height of Mount Everest (**e**). Deeper than any other sea depth in the world, the Pacific's Marianas Trench is at its deepest point 7,196 ft deeper than Mount Everest (29,002 ft) is high.

**Sailing the oceans** (above)
Illustrated here is Magellan's *Victoria*, the first ship to sail around the world. The expedition left Spain in 1519 and crossed the Atlantic, Pacific and Indian Oceans before reaching home again in 1522.

© DIAGRAM

# Continents

**The continents** The Earth's total land area of roughly 57 million square miles is divided geographically into seven continents. Here we compare the shapes and sizes of the continents and show how some are joined in huge landmasses.

**Shapes and sizes** (below)
These maps show the seven continents in order of size but not to the same scale. The areas of the continents are listed right and shown diagrammatically by the squares below the maps.

**a** Asia 17 million sq. mi
**b** Africa 11.7 million sq. mi
**c** N. America 9.4 million sq. mi
**d** S. America 6.9 million sq. mi
**e** Antarctica 5.1 million sq. mi
**f** Europe 3.8 million sq. mi
**g** Oceania 3.3 million sq. mi

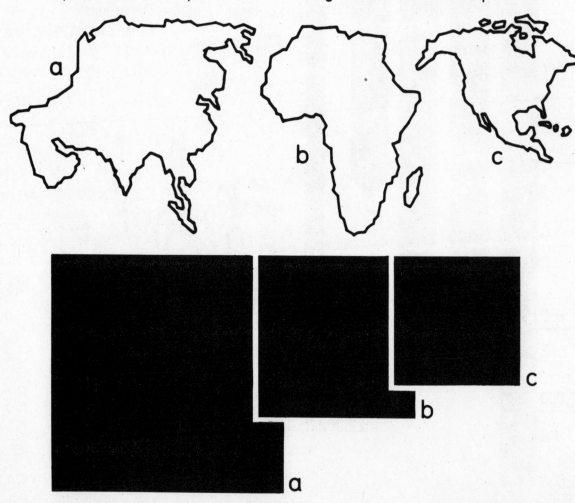

**Two great landmasses** (right)
This map shows the two great
landmasses that together account
for roughly 80% of the Earth's total
land area. The Asia-Africa-Europe
landmass is roughly twice as big as
the North America-South America
landmass. The landmass of the
Americas has a slightly smaller area
than the continent of Asia on its
own.

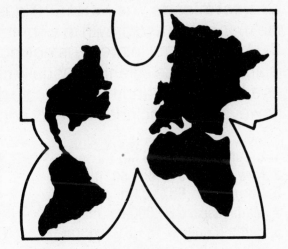

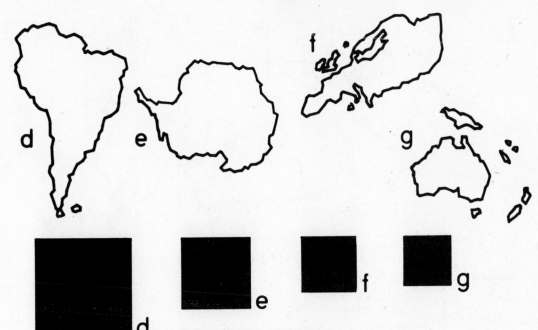

# Islands

**Largest islands** The world's 10 largest islands are located on the map below and drawn to a common scale right. Australia – 2,941,526 sq. mi in area – is not included in our list of largest islands because scientists usually classify it not as an island but as a continental landmass. A scale drawing of Australia has, however, been included here for comparison.

**1** Greenland 840,000 sq. mi
**2** New Guinea 316,856 sq. mi
**3** Borneo 286,967 sq. mi
**4** Madagascar 227,000 sq. mi
**5** Baffin (Canada) 183,810 sq. mi

**6** Sumatra 182,866 sq. mi
**7** Honshu (Japan) 88,930 sq. mi
**8** Great Britain 88,756 sq. mi
**9** Victoria (Canada) 82,119 sq. mi
**10** Ellesmere (Canada) 81,930 sq. mi

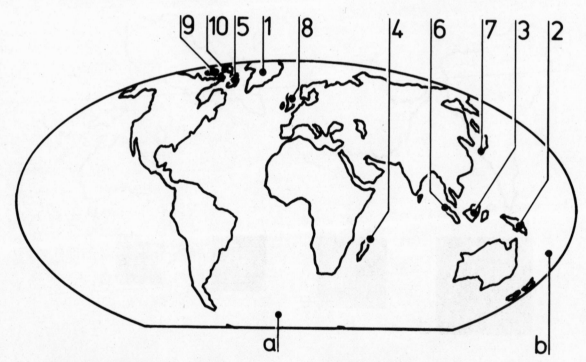

**Remotest island**
The world's remotest uninhabited island is Bouvet Øya in the South Atlantic – (**a**) on our map. It is approximately 1.054 mi from any other land.

**Newest island**
The world's newest island is Lateiki Island – (**b**) on our map. First sighted in 1979, it rose above the sea after a volcanic eruption. It belongs to Tonga.

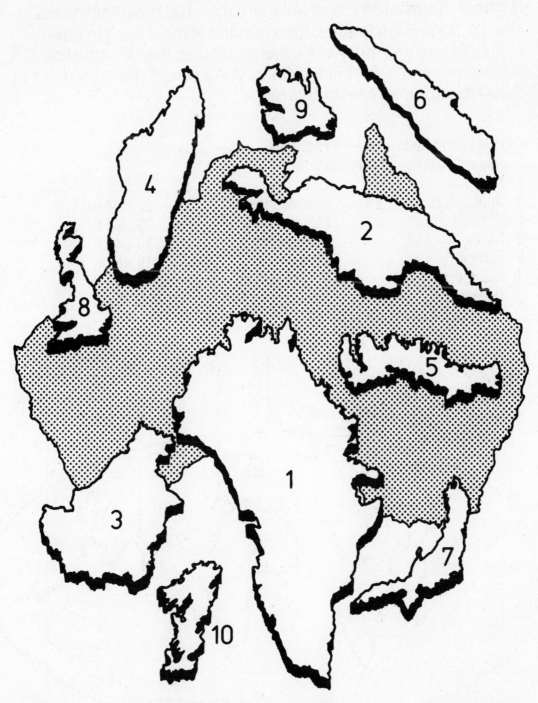

©DIAGRAM

# Mountains (1)

**Highest mountains** There are more than 100 mountain peaks over 22,000 ft high in Asia, mainly in the Himalayas. No other continent has any mountain peak as high as this. N. America's highest mountain, Mount McKinley in Alaska, is more than 8,000 ft lower than Mount Everest.

**The highest mountain in each continent**
See the map below and diagram right.

| | | | |
|---|---|---|---|
| a | Asia | Everest | 29,002 ft |
| b | South America | Aconcagua | 22,834 ft |
| c | North America | McKinley | 20,320 ft |
| d | Africa | Kilimanjaro | 19,340 ft |
| e | Europe | Elbrus | 18,480 ft |
| f | Antarctica | Vinson Massif | 16,863 ft |
| g | Oceania | Jaya | 15,967 ft |

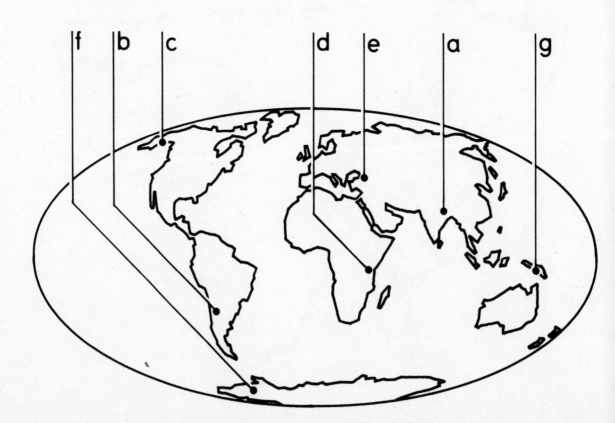

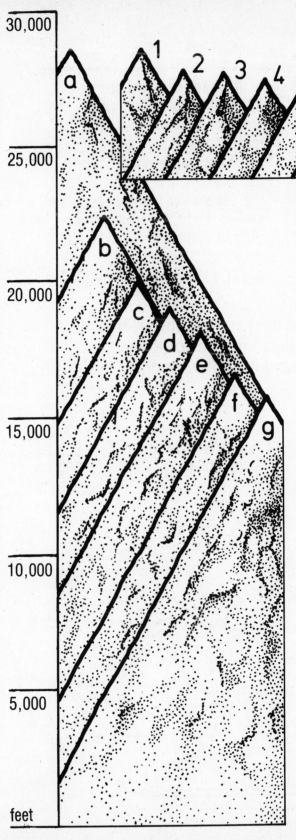

## The world's top ten (above)

All are in the Himalayas.

1. Everest 29,002 ft
2. K2 (Godwin Austen) 28,250 ft
3. Kanchenjunga 28,208 ft
4. Lhotse 27,831 ft
5. Yalung Kang 27,801 ft
6. Makalu 27,733 ft
7. Dhaulagiri 26,722 ft
8. Manaslu 26,670 ft
9. Cho Oyu 26,660 ft
10. Nanga Parbat 26,572 ft

## Mount Everest

The world's highest mountain is on the border between Nepal and Tibet (China). Its old Tibetan name was Chomolungma, meaning Goddess Mother of the World.

## Highest in the Americas

The highest American peaks are in the southern continent, in the Andes mountains.
1. Aconcagua 22,834 ft
2. Ojos del Salado 22,572 ft
3. Bonete 22,546 ft

The highest N. American peaks are in Alaska, Canada and Mexico.
1. McKinley 20,320 ft
2. Logan 19,847 ft
3. Chitlatepetl 18,697 ft

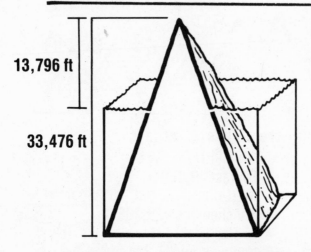

13,796 ft

33,476 ft

**Taller than Everest?** (left)
Although Mount Everest is the world's tallest mountain when measurements are made in the usual way from sea level, Mauna Kea in Hawaii is taller from base to top. Mauna Kea has its base on the seabed, and although it extends only 13,796 ft above sea level it measures 33,476 ft from base to top (4,448 ft more than Everest).

**Longest mountain ranges** The longest mountain range in the world is under the sea, in the Indian and Pacific Oceans. It is shown on the map below together with the four longest mountain ranges above sea level.

| | | | |
|---|---|---|---|
| **a** | Indian-Pacific Oceans submarine range | | 19,100 mi |
| **b** | Andes | South America | 4,500 mi |
| **c** | Rocky Mountains | North America | 3,750 mi |
| **d** | Himalaya – Karakoram – Hindu Kush | Asia | 2,400 mi |
| **e** | Great Dividing Range | Oceania | 2,250 mi |

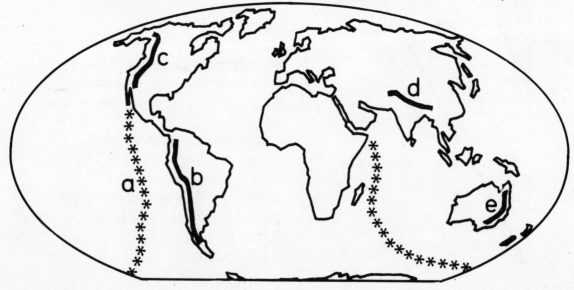

**Climbing achievements** Mountaineering as a sport began in the late 18th century in the Alps of Southern Europe. Mont Blanc, the tallest Alpine peak at 15,730 ft, was first climbed in 1786. By 1870 all the major Alpine peaks had been conquered and mountaineers began to make major climbs in other parts of the world.

**Conquering Everest** (right)
This diagram shows the top heights reached by climbing expeditions on Mount Everest in different years. The summit was first reached by Hillary and Tenzing in 1953.
**A** About 27,206 ft (1922)
**B** 28,024 ft (1924)
**C** 28,024 ft (1933)
**D** 28,119 ft (1952)
**E** 28,933 ft (1953)

**Continental firsts**
The highest mountain in every continent has been climbed. Here we list the dates when the summits were first reached.
Everest 1953
Aconcagua 1897
McKinley 1913
Kilimanjaro 1889
Elbrus 1874
Vinson Massif 1966
Jaya 1962

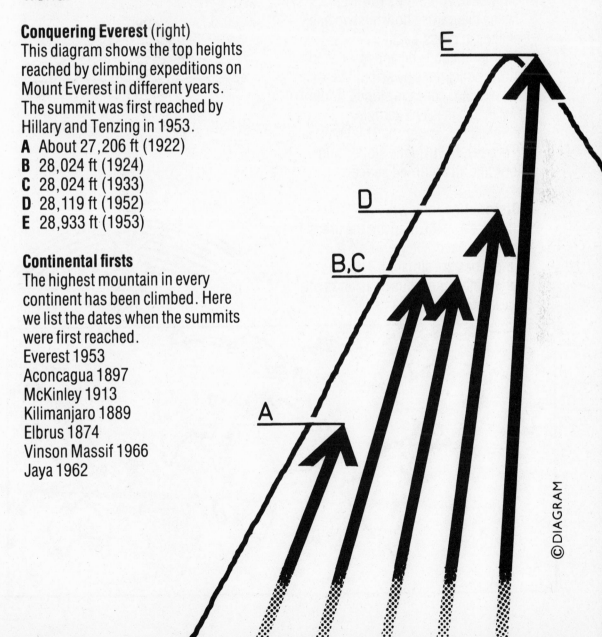

©DIAGRAM

# Volcanoes

**Activity** Estimates of the number of active volcanoes on the Earth range from about 500 to over 800. The number that erupt in any one year is much smaller – probably between 20 and 30. A very few volcanoes, for example Stromboli in Italy and several volcanoes in Hawaii, erupt almost continuously.

### Shapes of volcanoes (right)

These diagrams show the two basic shapes in cross section.
**1** Cone-shaped volcanoes – called strato-volcanoes by scientists – have steep, concave slopes. Mount Fuji in Japan is an example.
**2** Shield volcanoes, like Mauna Loa (Hawaii), have gentle slopes and look like an upturned saucer.

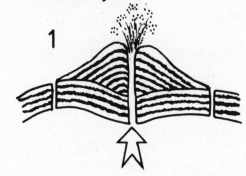

### Distribution (below)

Indicated on the map are the areas where most of the world's volcanoes are situated. They are especially numerous on islands off the landmass of Asia.

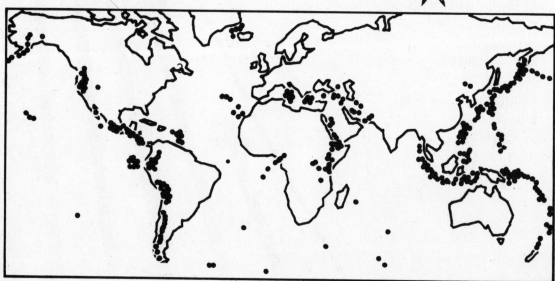

## Dormant or extinct

An inactive volcano may be either dormant ("sleeping") or extinct. A dormant volcano is capable of future eruptions, an extinct volcano is not.

## Comparative heights (right)

**A** Antofalla (S. America), the highest volcano that is claimed to be active, 21,092 ft

**B** Llullaillaco (S. America), the highest dormant volcano, 22,057 ft

**C** Aconcagua (S. America), the highest extinct volcano, 22,834 ft

**D** Everest, the highest non-volcanic mountain, 29,002 ft

## Greatest eruption

The greatest volcanic eruption known was that of Tambora in Indonesia in 1815. The total release of energy during this eruption was equivalent to 20,000 megatons of TNT. As a result of the eruption, Tambora's height was reduced from 13,400 ft to 8,175 ft.

## Explosive power (right)

The greatest single volcanic explosion in the last 3,000 years was during the eruption in 1883 of Krakatoa (Indonesia). This explosion (**a**) was equivalent to 1,500 megatons of TNT, making it 25 times more powerful than the biggest ever nuclear explosion (**b**).

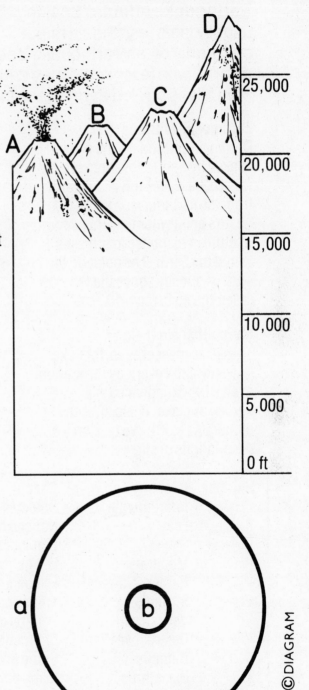

© DIAGRAM

# Earthquakes

**Earthquake effects**  Shaking of the ground in an earthquake usually lasts less than a minute. The damage caused depends only partly on an earthquake's severity. A severe earthquake in an area with few people may cause less damage and loss of life than a less severe earthquake in a city.

### Earthquake features

During an earthquake the ground is shaken by a series of shock-waves (**a**). These waves travel outward from the earthquake's focus (**b**), i.e. the point where the rocks first fracture in response to stresses within the Earth. The point on the surface directly above the focus is called the epicenter (**c**).

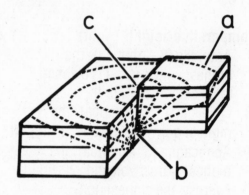

### Mercalli Scale (below)

This scale measures earthquake intensity and describes the amount of shaking experienced at a particular place. It uses Roman numerals I to XII. We give only brief descriptions of effects.

### Richter Scale

This scale is used to record an earthquake's "magnitude". It provides an estimate of the total energy released and is based on readings from instruments called seismographs.

| Number | Intensity | Effects |
|---|---|---|
| I | Instrumental | Detected by seismographs and some animals |
| II | Feeble | Noticed by a few sensitive people at rest |
| III | Slight | Similar to vibrations from a passing truck |
| IV | Moderate | Felt generally indoors; parked cars rock |
| V | Rather strong | Felt generally; most sleepers wake |
| VI | Strong | Trees shake; chairs fall over; some damage |
| VII | Very strong | General alarm; walls crack; plaster falls |
| VIII | Destructive | Chimneys, columns, monuments, weak walls fall |
| IX | Ruinous | Some houses collapse as ground cracks |
| X | Disastrous | Many buildings destroyed; train tracks bend |
| XI | Very disastrous | Few buildings survive; bad landslides and floods |
| XII | Catastrophic | Total destruction; ground forms waves |

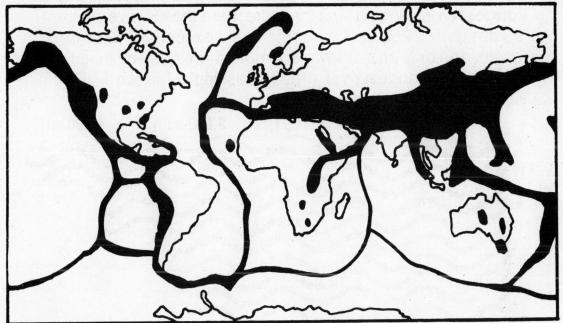

## Distribution (above)
This map shows the world's major earthquake zones. Earthquakes are commonest around the margins of the Pacific Ocean and along or near the mountain belt running from the Alps to the Himalayas.

## Severest this century
Each of these earthquakes exceeded 8 on the Richter Scale.
1906 Colombian coast 8.6
1906 San Francisco 8.3
1920 Kansu Province, China 8.6
1923 Kwanto Plain, Japan 8.3
1950 Assam, India 8.6
1952 Kamchatka, USSR 8.5
1957 Aleutian Islands 8.3
1960 Lebu, Chile 8.3
1964 Anchorage, Alaska 8.5
1976 Tangshan, China 8.2

## Historic earthquakes
The Lisbon earthquake of 1755 would probably have rated between 8.75 and 9 on the Richter Scale. The earthquake in Shensi Province, China in 1556 is said to have killed 830,000 people.

## Loss of life
Of the earthquakes this century these have killed the most people.
1908 Messina, Italy 80,000
1915 Avezzano, Italy 29,970
1920 Kansu, China 180,000
1923 Kwanto Plain, Japan 142,807
1932 Kansu, China 70,000
1935 Quetta, India 60,000
1939 Erzincan, Turkey 30,000
1970 Northern Peru 66,800
1976 Tangshan, China 242,000
1978 Tabas, Iran 25,000

# Rivers

**Longest rivers** Worldwide there are more than 50 rivers with lengths over 1,250 mi. Only three rivers exceed 3,700 mi in length, and only another two are more than 3,000 mi long. N. America's longest river – the Mississippi – Missouri – Red Rock – ranks third in the world.

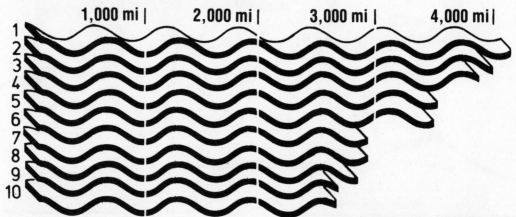

**World's longest rivers**
Shown to scale in the diagram above and listed below are the world's 10 longest rivers.

1 Nile (Africa) 4,132 mi
2 Amazon (S. America) 3,900 mi
3 Mississippi – Missouri – Red Rock (N. America) 3,860 mi
4 Ob-Irtysh (Asia) 3,461 mi
5 Yangtze (Asia) 3,430 mi
6 Huang Ho (Asia) 2,903 mi
7 Congo (Africa) 2,900 mi
8 Amur (Asia) 2,802 mi
9 Lena (Asia) 2,653 mi
10 Mackenzie (N. America) 2,635 mi

**Nile and Amazon** (right)
The Nile (**1**) is longer than the Amazon (**2**), but the Amazon drains a larger area – 2,722,000 sq. mi compared with 1,293,000 sq. mi.

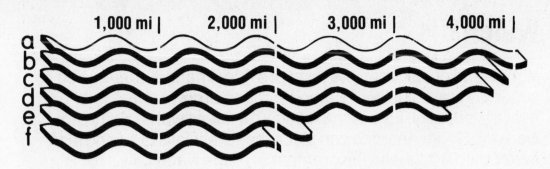

| 1,000 mi | 2,000 mi | 3,000 mi | 4,000 mi |

a
b
c
d
e
f

## Longest in its continent

Shown to scale in the diagram above and listed right are the longest rivers in six continents (icy Antarctica is not included). Africa's Nile is more than twice as long as Oceania's longest river, the Murray in Australia.

**a** Africa: Nile 4,132 mi
**b** S. America: Amazon 3,900 mi
**c** N. America: Mississippi – Missouri – Red Rock 3,860 mi
**d** Asia: Ob-Irtysh 3,461 mi
**e** Europe: Volga 2,293 mi
**f** Oceania: Murray 2,000 mi

## Longest in N. and S. America

The Rio Grande stretches the entire length of the border between Texas and Mexico. The Amazon has over 1,000 tributaries, including the 2,000-mi-long Madeira. The Orinoco, only 1,337 mi long, loops around Colombia and Venezuela to form the second largest S. American river system.

**1** Amazon (Brazil, Peru) 4,050 mi
**2** Mississippi – Missouri (USA) 3,740 mi
**3** Paranà – (Argentina) 2,800 mi
**4** Mackenzie (Canada) 2,640 mi
**5** Yukon (Alaska, Canada) 1,980 mi
**6** St Lawrence (Canada, USA) 1,900 mi
**7** São Francisco (Brazil) 1,800 mi
**8** Rio Grande (USA, Mexico) 1,785 mi
**9** Paraguay (Paraguay, Brazil) 1,615 mi

## Biggest river bore

A river bore (or tidal bore) is a large wave that sea tides cause to travel up some rivers. Bores occur on about 60 rivers worldwide. The biggest is on the Ch'ient'ang'kian in China. In spring it reaches a height of 24.5 ft , much taller than a greyhound bus.

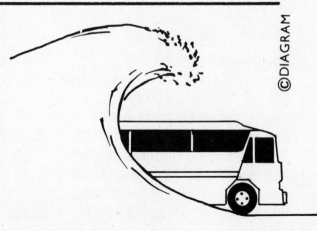

©DIAGRAM

# Waterfalls

**Waterfalls** occur when the level of a river channel changes so suddenly that the flow of water is caused to drop vertically or almost vertically. Five of the world's 10 tallest waterfalls are in Norway. South America can claim the tallest falls of all and also five of the 10 falls with the greatest average water flow.

### Tallest waterfalls

Shown to scale in the diagram right and listed below are the heights of the world's 10 tallest waterfalls. All the heights included here refer to the total drop from the top to the bottom of the waterfalls. In some cases the total drop is made up of several smaller, separate drops.

1  Angel (Venezuela) 3,212 ft
2  Tugela (S. Africa) 3,110 ft
3  Utigård (Norway) 2,625 ft
4  Mongefossen (Norway) 2,540 ft
5  Yosemite 2,425 ft
6  Østre Mardøla (Norway) 2,154 ft
7  Tyssestrengane (Norway) 2,120 ft
8  Kukenaom (Venezuela) 2,000 ft
9  Sutherland (New Zealand) 1,904 ft
10 Kjellfossen (Norway) 1,841 ft

### Angel Falls

Measuring about 0.5 mi from top to bottom, the world's tallest falls are situated on a tributary of the R. Caroni. They are named after James Angel, a U.S. pilot who crash-landed nearby in 1937. The greatest single drop measures 2,639 ft, and the width at the base is about 490 ft.

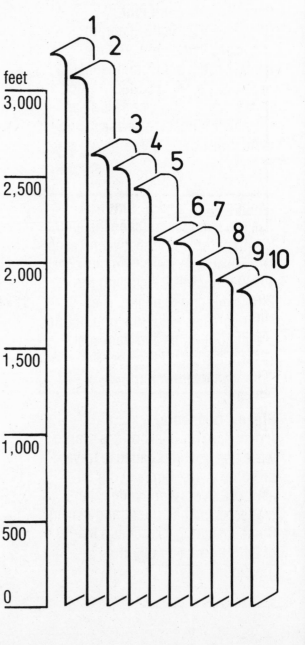

## Widest waterfalls

The world's widest falls are the Khône Falls on the Mekong River in Laos, southeast Asia. Only 49.74 ft high, these falls are some 6.7 mi wide.

| | | | |
|---|---|---|---|
| 1 | Boyoma | Zaire | 600,372 cu. ft/sec |
| 2 | Guaíra | Brazil/Paraguay | 459,108 cu. ft/sec |
| 3 | Khône | Laos | 406,134 cu. ft/sec |
| 4 | Niagara | Canada/USA | 211,896 cu. ft/sec |
| 5 | Paulo Afonso | Brazil | 98,885 cu. ft/sec |
| 6 | Urubupungá | Brazil | 95,353 cu. ft /sec |
| 7 | Cataratas del Iguazú | Brazil/Paraguay | 60,037 cu. ft/sec |
| 8 | Patos-Maribondo | Brazil | 59,974 cu. ft/sec |
| 9 | Victoria | Zimbabwe | 38,848 cu. ft/sec |
| 10 | Churchill | Canada | 35,316 cu. ft/sec |

## Greatest volume of water (above)

Included in this list are the 10 waterfalls with the greatest average flow of water over them. Measurements are in cubic feet per second (sometimes called cusecs). First in the list are the Boyoma Falls, formerly known as the Stanley Falls, on the Lualaba River in Zaire.

## Filling bathtubs

The average flow of water over the Boyoma Falls (600,372 cu. ft/sec) would be sufficient in 1 second to provide bath water for 149,582 people (using a typical 59.5 gal each)!

©DIAGRAM

# Lakes and seas

**Lakes and seas** The word lake is used to describe slow-moving or standing water occupying an inland basin. Some large lakes containing saltwater are known as seas, e.g. the Dead Sea and the Caspian Sea. The word sea is also used to name areas of water around the margins of the oceans.

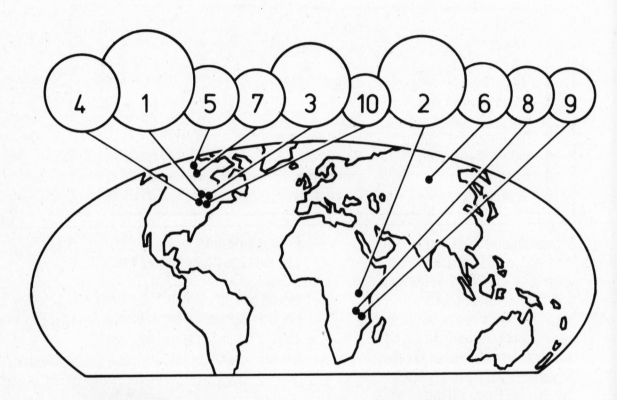

### Largest freshwater lakes
Listed right are the areas of the world's 10 largest freshwater lakes. These lakes – of which six are in North America, three in Africa and one in Asia – are also located on the map above. The circles drawn above the map represent the comparative areas of the lakes.

**1** Superior 31,820 sq. mi
**2** Victoria 28,828 sq. mi
**3** Huron 23,010 sq. mi
**4** Michigan 22,400 sq. mi
**5** Great Bear 12,275 sq. mi
**6** Baykal 12,159 sq. mi
**7** Great Slave 10,980 sq. mi
**8** Tanganyika 10,965 sq. mi
**9** Malawi 10,900 sq. mi
**10** Erie 9,940 sq. mi

## The Great Lakes
North America's Great Lakes – Superior, Huron, Michigan, Erie and Ontario – have a combined area of roughly 114,000 sq. mi. This is bigger than the area of Ecuador (106,000 sq. mi).

## Lake Baykal
Lake Baykal in the USSR is deeper than any other freshwater lake in the world, and contains more water. It has a depth of 6,382.6ft and contains an estimated 5,500 cubic miles of water.

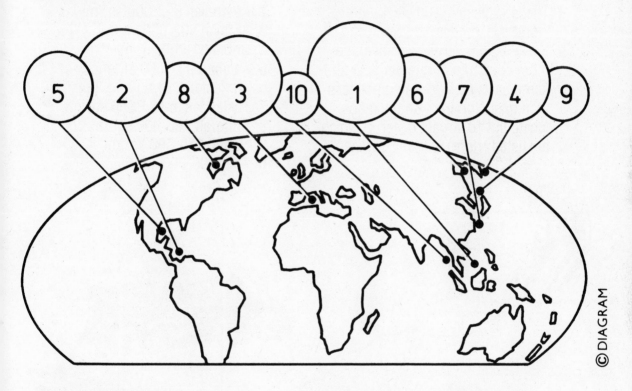

© DIAGRAM

## Largest seas (above)
The areas of the world's 10 largest seas are listed right and shown diagrammatically by circles above this location map.

## Largest inland sea
The world's largest inland sea or saltwater lake is the USSR's Caspian Sea. It has an area of 144,000 sq. mi.

1 South China Sea 1,148,656 sq. mi
2 Caribbean Sea 1,063,000 sq. mi
3 Mediterranean Sea 967,000 sq. mi
4 Bering Sea 876,000 sq. mi
5 Gulf of Mexico Sea 596,000 sq. mi
6 Sea of Okhotsk 590,000 sq. mi
7 East China Sea 482,000 sq. mi
8 Hudson Bay 476,000 sq. mi
9 Sea of Japan 389,000 sq. mi
10 Andaman Sea 308,000 sq. mi

# Deserts

**Desert regions** Deserts are very dry areas where there is little or no vegetation. Some people include the Polar regions as deserts because they lack vegetation and receive less than 10in of rain or snow per year, but the term desert tends to be reserved for the relatively hot, dry regions described here.

**Major deserts** (below)
These maps show (in black) the world's major deserts. None of these regions receives on average more than 10in of rain per year and some parts receive very much less than this. Numbers on the maps locate the 10 largest deserts, which are listed (right) with their areas.

1 Sahara 3,242,000 sq. mi
2 Australian 598,000 sq. mi
3 Arabian 502,000 sq. mi
4 Gobi 401,000 sq. mi
5 Kalahari 201,000 sq. mi
6 Turkestan 139,000 sq. mi
7 Takla Makan 124,000 sq. mi
8 Sonoran 120,000 sq. mi
9 Namib 120,000 sq. mi
10 Thar 100,000 sq. mi

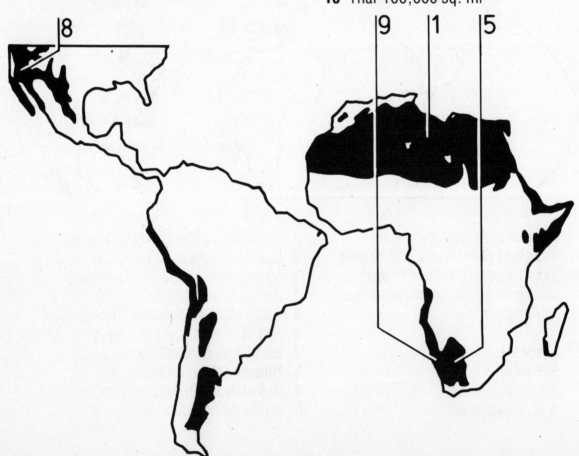

## Desert areas compared (below)

These squares show the relative areas of the world's 10 largest deserts (listed opposite page). Together they make up roughly 10% of the world's total land area.

## The Sahara Desert

Easily the largest of all the world's deserts, the Sahara accounts for approximately 6% of the world's total land area and 28% of the area of Africa. It covers parts of Morocco, Western Sahara, Mauritania, Algeria, Mali, Niger, Chad, Tunisia, Libya, Egypt and Sudan.

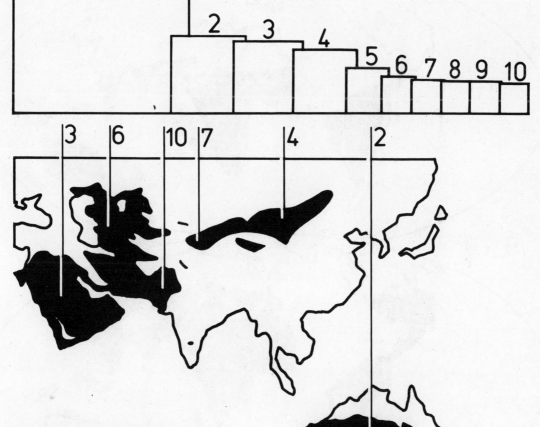

## The Australian Desert

The second largest desert in the world, the Australian Desert, is larger (598,000 sq. mi) than Alaska (586,400 sq. mi).

©DIAGRAM

# Temperature (1)

**Temperature distribution** Temperatures depend on latitude (places nearer the Equator are generally hotter than places nearer the Poles), on the season (summer temperatures are higher), on distance from the sea (which moderates temperature extremes) and on altitude (temperatures decrease with height).

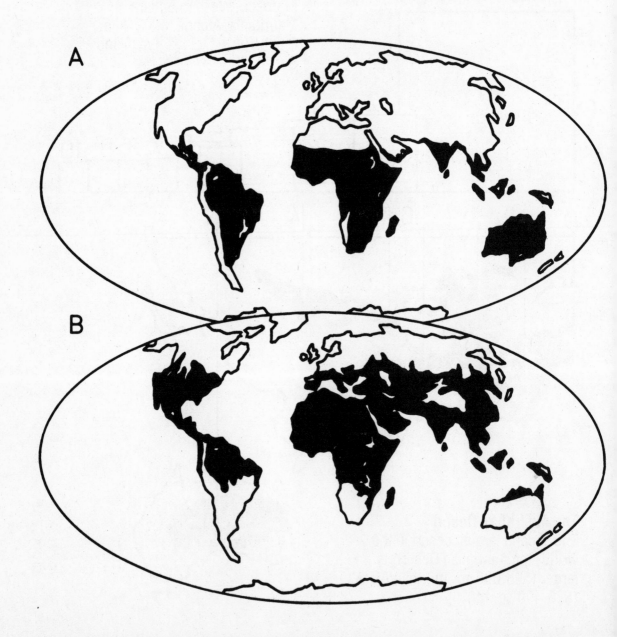

A

B

**Hot areas** (left)
Marked in black on these two maps are areas where the hottest temperature each day averages more than 68°F during the months of January (**A**) and July (**B**).

**Cold areas** (below)
Indicated on these two maps are areas where the average daily maximum temperature is below 32°F throughout the months of January (**C**) and July (**D**).

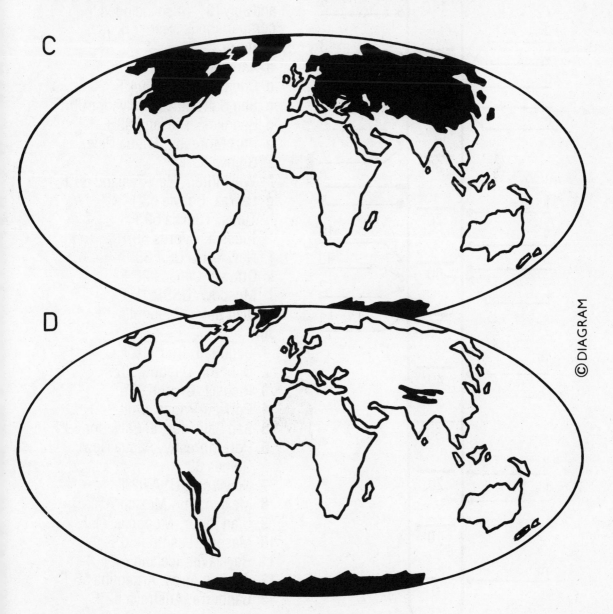

C

D

©DIAGRAM

# Temperature (2)

A

B

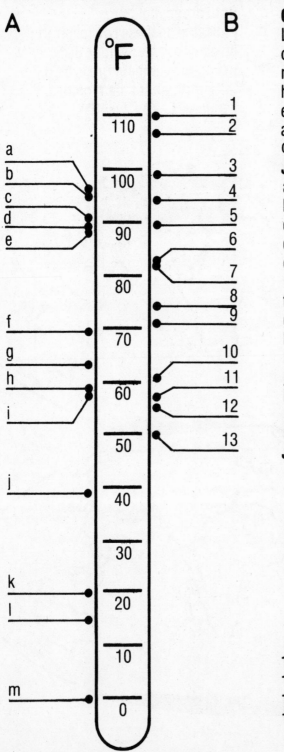

**City temperatures** (left)
Listed below and indicated on the diagram are average recorded daily maximum temperatures in the hottest and coldest capital cities in each continent during January (**A**) and July (**B**). (Also included for comparison is New York.)

## January
**a** Asunción, Paraguay 95°F
**b** Conakry, Guinea 94°F
**c** San Salvador, El Salvador 90°F
**d** Bangkok, Thailand 89°F
**e** Port Moresby, Papua New Guinea 89°F
**f** Wellington, New Zealand 69°F
**g** La Paz, Bolivia 63°F
**h** Tunis, Tunisia 59°F
**i** Nicosia, Cyprus 59°F
**j** New York, USA 38°F
**k** Ottowa, Canada 20°F
**l** Moscow, USSR 16°F
**m** Ulan Bator, Mongolia 0°F

## July
**1** Baghdad, Iraq 110°F
**2** Djibouti, Djibouti 107°F
**3** Nicosia, Cyprus 98°F
**4** Port-au-Prince, Haiti 94°F
**5** San Salvador, El Salvador 89°F
**6** Port Moresby, Papua New Guinea 83°F
**7** New York, USA 82°F
**8** Mexico City, Mexico 74°F
**9** Ulan Bator, Mongolia 71°F
**10** Maseru, Lesotho 60°F
**11** Reykjavik, Iceland 57°F
**12** Buenos Aires, Argentina 56°F
**13** Canberra, Australia 52°F

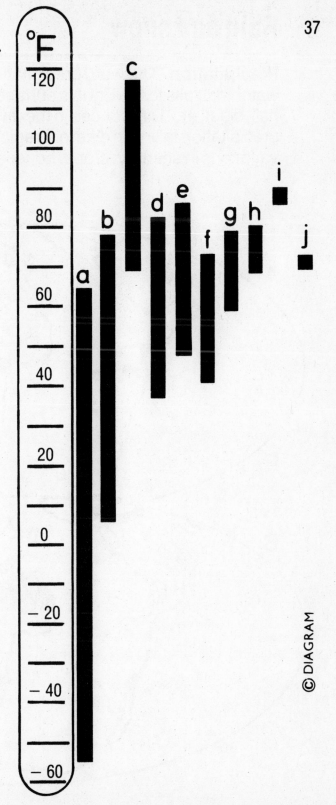

**Temperature ranges** (right)
This diagram shows temperature ranges in cities around the world. The top of each bar shows the average highest daily temperature for the hottest month. The bottom of each bar shows the same for the coldest month. Our list gives the differences.

**a** Verkhoyansk, USSR 119°F
**b** Winnipeg, Canada 71°F
**c** Ain Salah, Algeria 48°F
**d** New York USA 44°F
**e** Tokyo, Japan 39°F
**f** London, United Kingdom 31°F
**g** Sydney, Australia 20°F
**h** Cape Town, South Africa 12°F
**i** Singapore 4°F
**j** Quito, Equador 3°F

**Records for heat**
The highest shade temperature on record is 136.4°F, at Al'Aziziyah, Libya, on September 13th, 1922. The place with the highest temperatures all the year round is Dallol, Ethiopia, where the annual average is 93.9°F.

**Records for coldness**
The coldest screen temperature ever recorded on Earth is −126.9°F, at Vostok, Antarctica on August 24th, 1960.
The place with the coldest year-round temperatures is Polus Nedostupnosti (the Pole of Cold), Antarctica, averaging −72°F.

# Rain and snow

**Precipitation** The word precipitation is used to describe all the water that falls to the Earth's surface in the form of rain, snow, hail, sleet, etc. Differences in the amount and type of precipitation falling in different regions cause enormous variations in scenery, crops, houses and life styles.

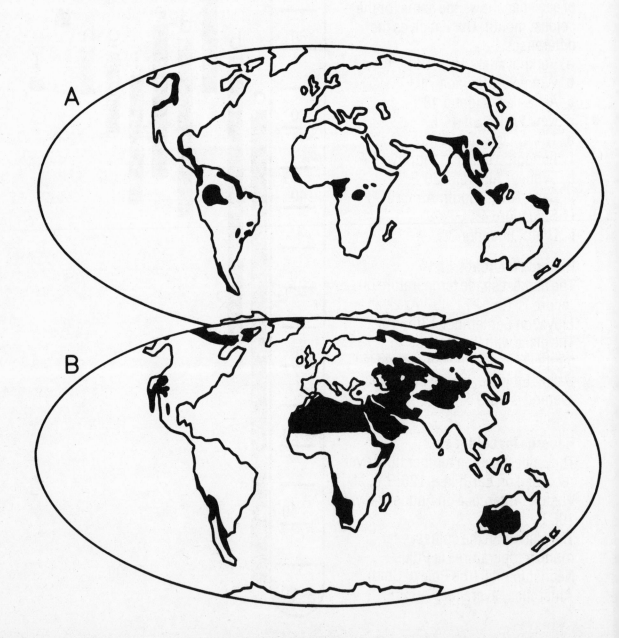

## Wettest and driest (left)

Indicated in black on these two maps are the world's wettest and driest areas. Black areas on map **A** all receive on average more than 80in of precipitation each year.

Black areas on map **B** all have an average annual precipitation of less than 12in. Average yearly rainfall in the US ranges from 451in (Mt Wai'ale'ale, Hawaii) to 2in (Death Valley, California).

## Records for wetness

The place with the highest average precipitation per year is Mt Wai-'ale'ale, Hawaii (451in).

The rainfall record for any year was at Cherrapunji, India, where 1,043in fell in 1860-61.

Cherrapunji also holds the rainfall record for any 1 month, receiving 366in in July 1861.

The rainfall record for 24 hours is 73.7in, which fell at Cilaos, Reunion Island in the Indian Ocean on March 15th–16th, 1952.

The rainfall record for 1 minute is 1.23in, at Unionville, Maryland, on July 4th, 1956.

## Record for dryness

The world's driest place is in the Atacama Desert, Chile. No rain at all was recorded for about 400 years up until 1971. A little rain has fallen since then but the yearly average remains nil.

## City comparisons (below)

This diagram compares the annual average precipitation in some of the world's capital cities.

Conakry, the capital of Guinea on the west coast of Africa, has on average more rain per year than any other capital city in the world.

Cairo, the capital of Egypt, has the lowest yearly rainfall average of all the world's capitals.

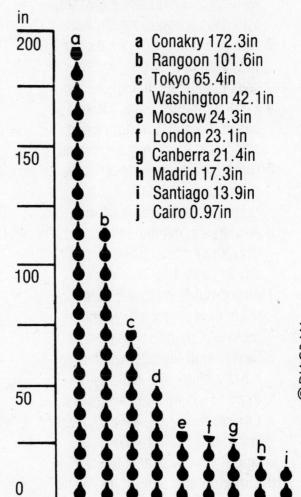

in

| | |
|---|---|
| **a** | Conakry 172.3in |
| **b** | Rangoon 101.6in |
| **c** | Tokyo 65.4in |
| **d** | Washington 42.1in |
| **e** | Moscow 24.3in |
| **f** | London 23.1in |
| **g** | Canberra 21.4in |
| **h** | Madrid 17.3in |
| **i** | Santiago 13.9in |
| **j** | Cairo 0.97in |

© DIAGRAM

# Clouds

**Clouds and the water cycle** Clouds form when damp air condenses around specks of matter in the atmosphere to form visible water droplets or ice crystals. By depositing rain, snow, etc, clouds return evaporated water to the Earth's surface.

**Main types of clouds** (far right)
1 Stratus: low, gray cloud layer or ragged patches, may produce drizzle or snow grains.
2 Cumulus: low, detached clouds, with dark, level bases and white tufted tops, may bring showers.
3 Stratocumulus: low, whitish or gray with dark parts, in wave-like layer or patches, usually no rain.
4 Cumulonimbus: usually low-based, tall and towering, white and black, bring thunderstorms.
5 Nimbostratus: middle-altitude, dark, dense cloud layer, often ragged beneath, rain or snow.
6 Altostratus: middle-altitude, grayish or bluish cloud sheets, thin in parts, rain-bearing.
7 Altocumulus: middle-altitude, white or gray, rolls or rounded masses, "mackerel" sky.
8 Cirrus: high-altitude, white or mostly white, silk-like sheen, thin and wispy, often in streaks.
9 Cirrostratus: high, whitish, like a veil, may be strand-like or smooth, may cover entire sky.
10 Cirrocumulus: high, thick, white patches of cloud, made up of small ripples, grains, etc.

**Heights of clouds**
Here we list typical heights for the 10 main types of clouds. In each case measurement is to the base.
1 Stratus, below 1,500ft
2 Cumulus 1,500-6,500ft
3 Stratocumulus 1,500-6,500ft
4 Cumulonimbus 1,500-6,500ft
5 Nimbostratus 3,000-10,000ft
6 Altostratus 6,500-23,000ft
7 Altocumulus 6,500-23,000ft
8 Cirrus 16,500-45,000ft
9 Cirrostratus 16,500-45,000ft
10 Cirrocumulus 16,500-45,000ft

**Content of clouds**
Different types of clouds are composed of water droplets, ice crystals or a mixture of these.
1 Stratus, water
2 Cumulus, water
3 Stratocumulus, water
4 Cumulonimbus, mixed
5 Nimbostratus, water
6 Altostratus, usually mixed, occasionally ice only
7 Altocumulus, water
8 Cirrus, ice
9 Cirrostratus, ice
10 Cirrocumulus, usually ice, occasionally mixed

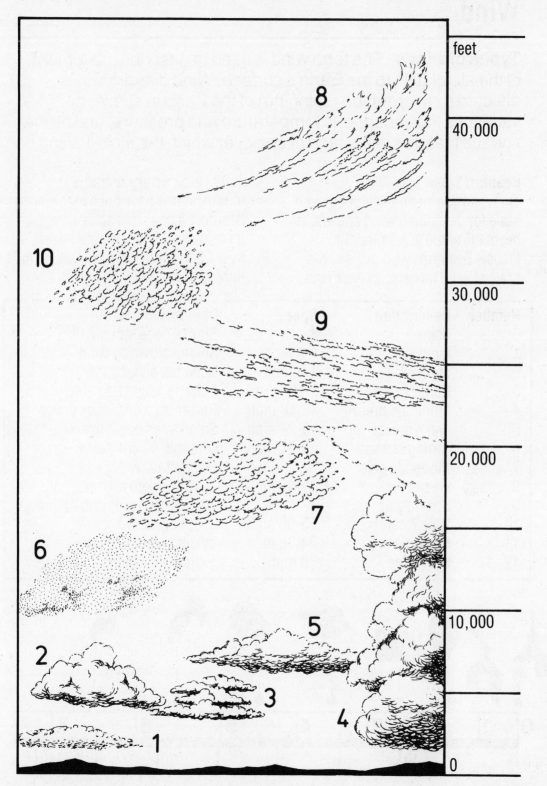

feet

40,000

30,000

20,000

10,000

0

# Wind

**Types of winds** The term wind is used to describe movement of the air relative to the Earth's surface. Wind direction is affected by the rotation (spinning) of the Earth in space, by variations in atmospheric temperature and pressure, and by the surface features of the land or sea over which the air is flowing.

**Beaufort Scale** (below)
This is an internationally recognized scale for describing wind speeds. It bears the name of Admiral Sir Francis Beaufort, who devised his scale of wind force numbers in the early 19th century. Various modifications have been made since Beaufort's day. This scale uses the term hurricane for all wind speeds over 75 mph, not only for winds in hurricane storms (see right).

| Number | Description | Speed | Characteristics |
|---|---|---|---|
| 0 | Calm | Below 1 mph | Smoke goes straight up |
| 1 | Light air | 1-3 mph | Smoke blown by wind |
| 2 | Light breeze | 4-7 mph | Wind felt on face |
| 3 | Gentle breeze | 8-12 mph | Extends a light flag |
| 4 | Moderate breeze | 13-18 mph | Raises dust and loose paper |
| 5 | Fresh breeze | 19-24 mph | Small trees begin to sway |
| 6 | Strong breeze | 25-31 mph | Umbrellas hard to use |
| 7 | Moderate gale | 32-38 mph | Difficult to walk |
| 8 | Fresh gale | 39-46 mph | Twigs broken off trees |
| 9 | Strong gale | 47-54 mph | Damage to roofs and chimneys |
| 10 | Whole gale | 55-63 mph | Trees uprooted |
| 11 | Storm | 64-75 mph | Widespread damage |
| 12–17 | Hurricane | 76 mph | Extremely violent |

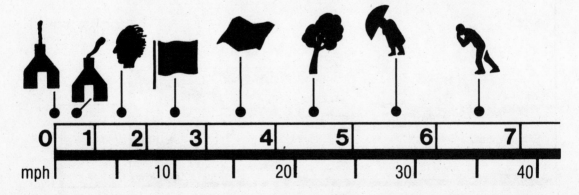

## Hurricanes (below)

This map shows those parts of the world where hurricanes occur. A hurricane is a very severe kind of storm characterized by powerful spiral ing winds and very heavy rainfall. Other names for a hurricane are tropical cyclone, typhoon and willy-willy. In 1970 a storm of this kind killed an estimated one million people in Bangladesh.

## Wind records

A wind speed of 231 mph was recorded on Mt Washington, New Hampshire in 1934. This is the fastest sustained surface wind speed ever recorded on the Earth. Faster surface speeds have been reached only briefly.
The world's windiest place is Commonwealth Bay, George V Coast, Antarctica, where several 200 mph winds occur each year.

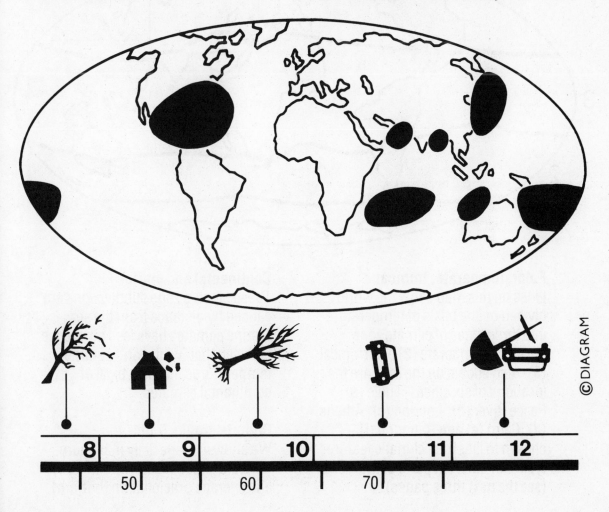

| 8 | 9 | 10 | 11 | 12 |

50    60    70

**Climate and weather**  Climate is the term used to describe the general character of a place's weather during the course of a year. The term weather relates to daily changes in atmospheric conditions and includes temperature, sunshine, precipitation (rain, snow, etc), humidity, fog, cloud and wind.

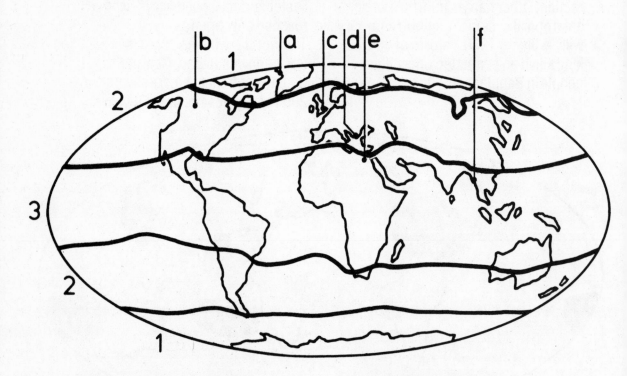

**Polar, temperate, tropical**
Lines on this map show the world divided on the basis of temperature into three types of climate zone: polar (**1**), temperate (**2**) and tropical (**3**). Also shown on the map are the locations of six cities – Thule (**a**), Peace River (**b**), London (**c**), Athens (**d**), Cairo (**e**) and Rangoon (**f**) – chosen to illustrate climatic features typical of different parts of the world (see the next three pages).

**Continental and marine**
These climate zone subdivisions are caused by distance from the sea. Marine climates have less difference between their winter and summer temperatures than is typical of continental climates.

**Climate graphs** (right)
We show average daily maximum temperatures for each month (top) and average precipitation (bottom).

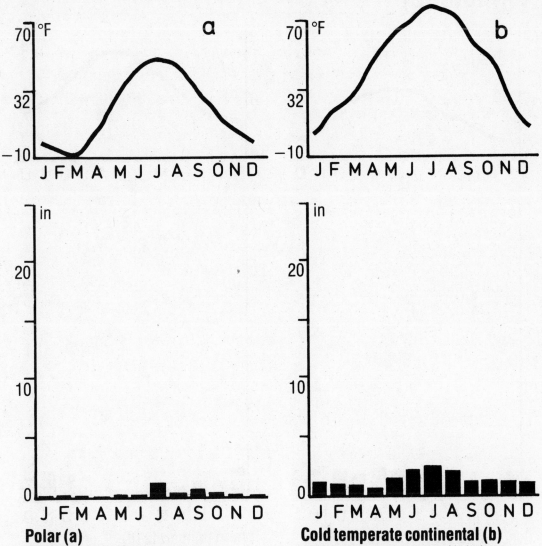

**Polar (a)**

A polar climate has cool or cold
summers and very cold winters.
Precipitation (rain or snow
depending on the time of year)
varies considerably from place
to place, but is typically low.
Example: Thule, Greenland
Latitude: 77° 29′N
Hottest month: 50.7°F
Coldest month: 2.12°F
Annual precipitation: 3.7in

**Cold temperate continental (b)**

Averaged over the year, this is not
as cold as a polar climate. Winters
are very cold but summers are hot.
Precipitation occurs all year, but
is highest in summer when
thunderstorms are common.
Example: Peace River, Canada
Latitude: 56° 14′N
Hottest month: 75.6°F
Coldest month: 9.68°F
Annual precipitation: 14.8in

©DIAGRAM

**Climate (2)**

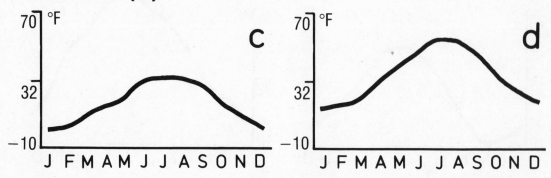

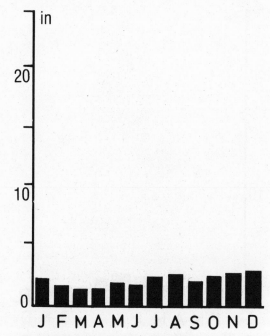

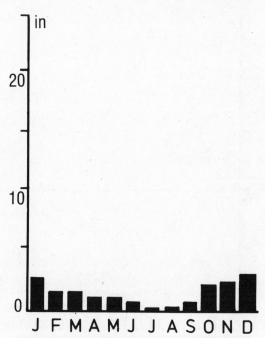

**Cool temperate marine (c)**
This type of climate is neither very cold nor very hot. Winters are usually fairly mild and summers generally warm rather than hot. Precipitation (usually rain) is fairly evenly spread throughout the year.
Example: London, United Kingdom
Latitude: 51° 30'N
Hottest month: 71.2°F
Coldest month: 43.3°F
Annual precipitation: 23.4in

**Warm temperate (d)**
Here we look at the warm temperate climate of southern Europe (also called Mediterranean climate). Its characteristic features are warm, wet winters and hot, dry summers.
Example: Athens, Greece
Latitude: 37° 58'N
Hottest month: 91.8°F
Coldest month: 55.2°F
Annual precipitation: 15.8in

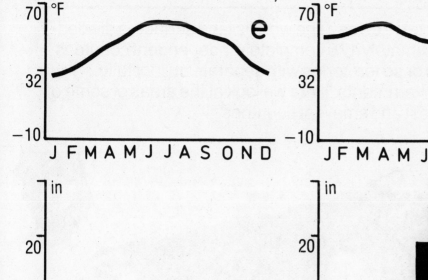

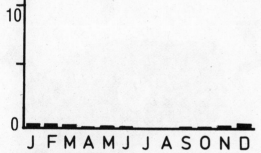

**Tropical: desert (e)**
Tropical climates are hotter than
temperate ones. Seasonal
variations in temperature increase
with distance from the Equator. All
desert climates have very little
rainfall.
Example: Cairo, Egypt
Latitude: 30° 08′N
Hottest month: 95.5°F
Coldest month: 66.9°F
Annual precipitation: 1.0in

**Tropical: monsoon (f)**
Near the Equator, temperatures are
very hot all year.
Monsoon climates take their name
from monsoon winds which bring
wet summers and dry winters to
parts of southeast Asia.
Example: Rangoon, Burma
Latitude: 16° 46′N
Hottest month: 96.9°F
Coldest month: 84.9°F
Annual precipitation: 103.2in

©DIAGRAM

# National areas (1)

**Countries and territories** The world's land surface is divided between approximately 170 completely independent countries and a further 50 or so territories with separate but not fully independent governments. Here we look at the areas of some of the world's largest and smallest countries.

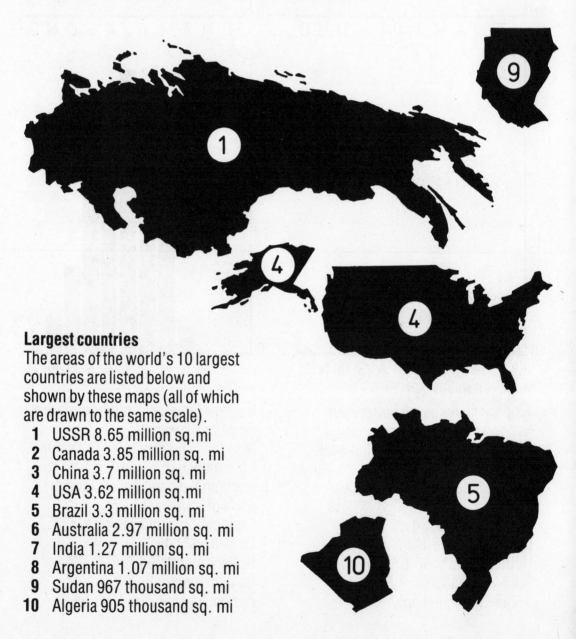

**Largest countries**
The areas of the world's 10 largest countries are listed below and shown by these maps (all of which are drawn to the same scale).
1 USSR 8.65 million sq.mi
2 Canada 3.85 million sq. mi
3 China 3.7 million sq. mi
4 USA 3.62 million sq.mi
5 Brazil 3.3 million sq. mi
6 Australia 2.97 million sq. mi
7 India 1.27 million sq. mi
8 Argentina 1.07 million sq. mi
9 Sudan 967 thousand sq. mi
10 Algeria 905 thousand sq. mi

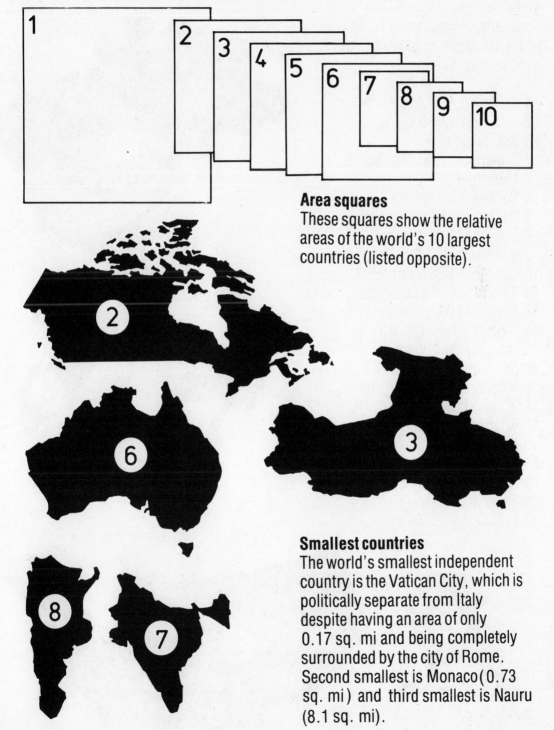

## Area squares
These squares show the relative areas of the world's 10 largest countries (listed opposite).

## Smallest countries
The world's smallest independent country is the Vatican City, which is politically separate from Italy despite having an area of only 0.17 sq. mi and being completely surrounded by the city of Rome. Second smallest is Monaco (0.73 sq. mi) and third smallest is Nauru (8.1 sq. mi).

©DIAGRAM

# National areas (2)

## The Americas

These maps show the relative areas of the 10 largest countries in the American continents

**1** Canada 3,850,000 sq.mi
**2** USA 3,623,000 sq.mi
**3** Brazil 3,286,000 sq.mi
**4** Argentina 1,065,000 sq.mi
**5** Mexico 762,000 sq.mi
**6** Peru 496,000 sq.mi
**7** Colombia 445,000 sq.mi
**8** Bolivia 424,000 sq.mi
**9** Venezuela 352,000 sq.mi
**10** Chile 292,000 sq.mi
**11** Paraguay 157,000 sq.mi
**12** Ecuador 109,000 sq.mi
**13** Guyana 83,000 sq.mi
**14** Uruguay 68,000 sq.mi
**15** Surinam 63,000 sq.mi
**16** Nicaragua 57,000 sq.mi
**17** Honduras 43,000 sq.mi
**18** Guatemala 42,000 sq.mi
**19** French Guiana 32,000 sq.mi
**20** Panama 30,000 sq.mi
**21** Costa Rica 20,000 sq.mi
**22** Belize 9,000 sq.mi
**23** El Salvador 8,000 sq.mi

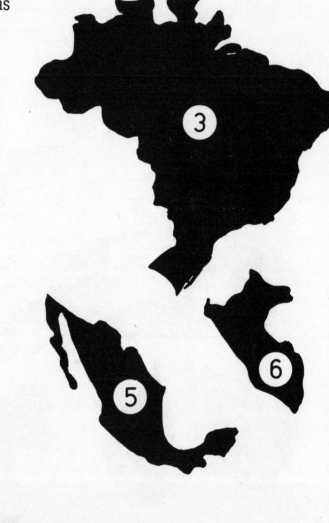

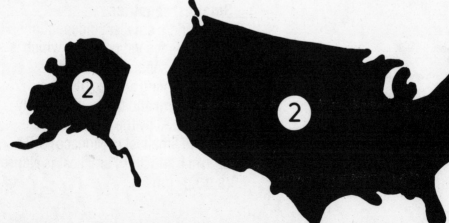

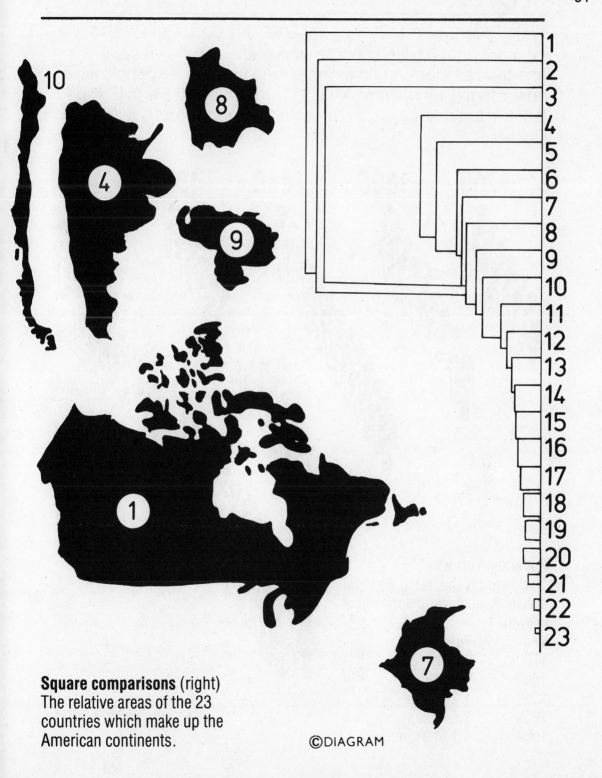

**Square comparisons** (right)
The relative areas of the 23
countries which make up the
American continents.

©DIAGRAM

# Population (1)

**World population**  By the year 2000 there are expected to be more than 6 billion people worldwide – approximately one-third as many again as there are today. Of the people alive now, roughly 64% live in Asia, 11% in Africa, 10.5% in Europe, 8.5% in Latin America, 5.5% in North America and 0.5% in Oceania.

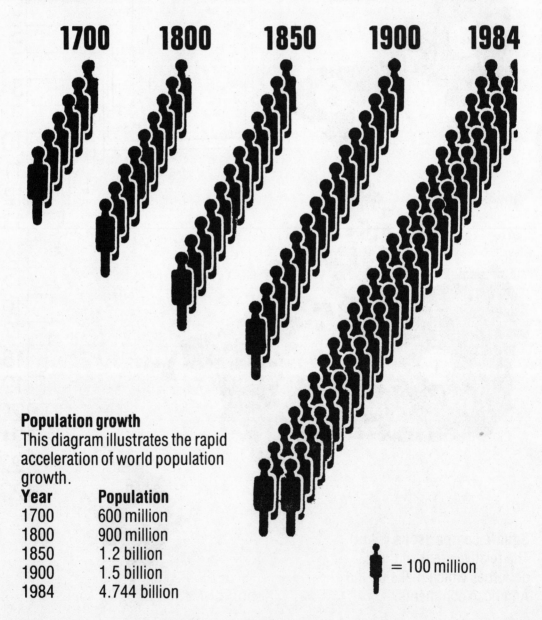

1700     1800     1850     1900     1984

**Population growth**
This diagram illustrates the rapid acceleration of world population growth.

| Year | Population |
|------|-----------|
| 1700 | 600 million |
| 1800 | 900 million |
| 1850 | 1.2 billion |
| 1900 | 1.5 billion |
| 1984 | 4.744 billion |

♀ = 100 million

## Population distribution
Shown on the diagram below and listed right are 1984 population estimates for different regions. (Asia includes the USSR.)

a Asia 3.041 billion
b Africa 530 million
c Europe 490 million
d Latin America 400 million
e North America 258 million
f Oceania 25 million

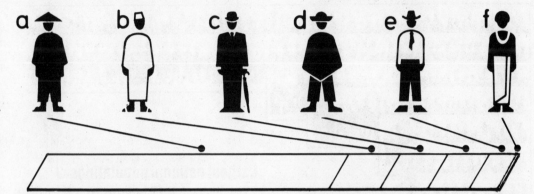

## Annual rates of increase
Populations are estimated now to be increasing at these rates.
World 1.7%
Africa 3.0%
Latin America 2.4%
Asia (including USSR) 1.7%
Oceania 1.4%
North America 1.0%
Europe 0.3%

## Population densities (below)
Our diagram shows the most (A) and fewest (B) people per sq. mi.
World 12.8 per sq. mi
Europe (not including USSR) 39.2 per sq. mi (A)
Asia (with all USSR) 24 per sq. mi
Latin America 7.6 per sq. mi
Africa per 7.2 per sq. mi
North America 4.8 per sq. mi
Oceania 1.2 per sq. mi (B)

 =1

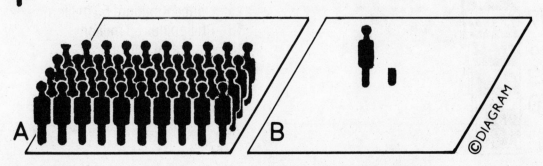

# Population (2)

**National populations** Of all the people alive today, nearly one-quarter live in China. Approximately one-half of the world's population live in five countries – China, India, the USSR, the USA and Indonesia. Roughly three-quarters of the world's population live in the 20 countries listed below.

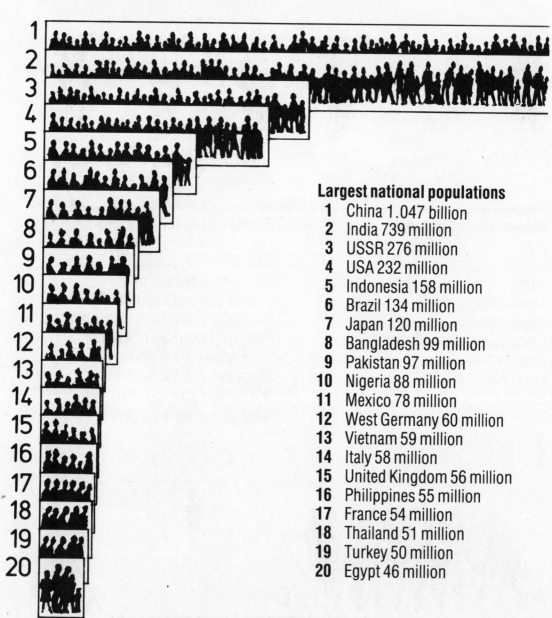

**Largest national populations**

1 China 1.047 billion
2 India 739 million
3 USSR 276 million
4 USA 232 million
5 Indonesia 158 million
6 Brazil 134 million
7 Japan 120 million
8 Bangladesh 99 million
9 Pakistan 97 million
10 Nigeria 88 million
11 Mexico 78 million
12 West Germany 60 million
13 Vietnam 59 million
14 Italy 58 million
15 United Kingdom 56 million
16 Philippines 55 million
17 France 54 million
18 Thailand 51 million
19 Turkey 50 million
20 Egypt 46 million

## Smallest national population

The independent country with the fewest people is the Vatican City, which has a population of only about 800 inhabitants.

## Greatest population density

The independent country with the greatest population density is Monaco, which has an estimated 5,514 persons per sq. mi.

## Population densities

Listed right (in population size order) are the population densities of the 10 countries with the largest populations. The diagram below compares the lowest (**A**) and highest (**B**) densities in this list. In the USA, more than half the population is concentrated in less than one-tenth of the land area.

**1** China 43.6 per sq. mi
**2** India 90 per sq. mi
**3** USSR 4.8 per sq. mi (**A**)
**4** USA 10 per sq. mi
**5** Indonesia 33.2 per sq. mi
**6** Brazil 6.4 per sq. mi
**7** Japan 129.2 per sq. mi
**8** Bangladesh 275.2 per sq. mi (**B**)
**9** Pakistan 48 per sq. mi
**10** Nigeria 38 per sq. mi

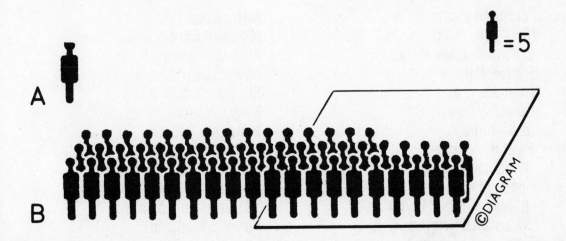

= 5

A

B

©DIAGRAM

# Cities

**City dwellers** In 1900 roughly one in twenty of the world's population lived in cities with more than 100,000 inhabitants. Today this figure is approximately one in four. More than 170 cities or conurbations (cities with their surrounding populated areas) now have more than one million inhabitants.

## Capital cities
Listed on this page are the names of some of the world's major capitals. For each continent we give the capital cities of the countries with the largest national populations.

## American capitals
(Countries in alphabetical order)
Argentina: Buenos Aires
Brazil: Rio de Janeiro
Canada: Ottawa
Chile: Santiago
Colombia: Bogotá
Cuba: Havana
Mexico: Mexico City
Peru: Lima
USA: Washington D.C.
Venezuela: Caracas

## European capitals
(Countries in alphabetical order)
Czechoslovakia: Prague
France: Paris
Germany (East): Berlin (East)
Germany (West): Bonn
Italy: Rome
Poland: Warsaw
Romania: Bucharest
Spain: Madrid
United Kingdom: London
Yugoslavia: Belgrade

## Oceanian capitals
(These three countries have much the biggest populations and areas.)
Australia: Canberra
New Zealand: Wellington
Papua New Guinea: Port Moresby

## Asian capitals
(Countries in alphabetical order)
Bangladesh: Dacca
China: Peking
India: Delhi
Indonesia: Jakarta
Japan: Tokyo
Korea (South): Seoul
Pakistan: Islamabad
Philippines: Manila
Thailand: Bangkok
USSR: Moscow

## African capitals
(Countries in alphabetical order)
Algeria: Algiers
Egypt: Cairo
Ethiopia: Addis Ababa
Kenya: Nairobi
Morocco: Rabat
Nigeria: Lagos
South Africa: Cape Town
Sudan: Khartoum
Tanzania: Dar es Salaam
Uganda: Kampala

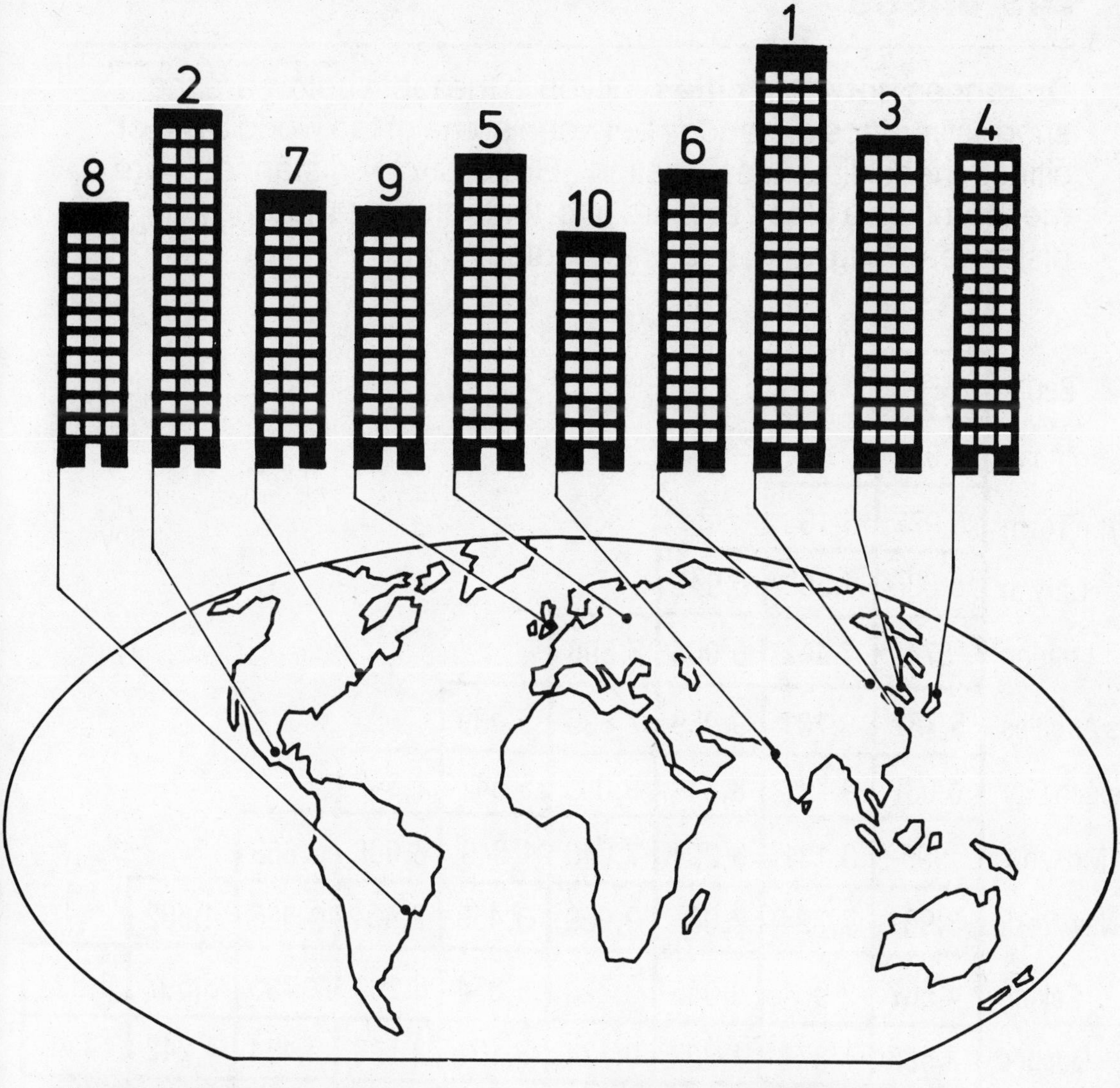

**World's largest cities** (above)
Here we show the locations and comparative sizes of the world's 10 largest cities (listed right). Other books may give different figures. This is because some city boundaries are difficult to define. Where possible, we list figures for the "city proper" without its surrounding areas.

**Millions of people**
1  Shanghai 10.8 million
2  Mexico City 9.2 million
3  Seoul 8.4 million
4  Tokyo 8.3 million
5  Moscow 8.0 million
6  Peking 7.6 million
7  New York 7.1 million
8  Sao Paulo 7.0 million
9  London 6.8 million
10 Bombay 6.0 million

©DIAGRAM

# Distances

**Distances between cities**  Given in the table below are the shortest surface distances between some of the world's major cities. These distances – called "Great Circle" distances – are measured on a globe and are shorter than actual journey distances using land, sea or air routes.

Distances in miles

| | Berlin | Bombay | Cape Town | Darwin | London | Los Angeles | Mexico City | Moscow | New York |
|---|---|---|---|---|---|---|---|---|---|
| Berlin | — | | | | | | | | |
| Bombay | 3,910 | | | | | | | | |
| Cape Town | 5,977 | 5,134 | | | | | | | |
| Darwin | 8,036 | 4,503 | 6,947 | | | | | | |
| London | 574 | 4,462 | 6,005 | 8,598 | | | | | |
| Los Angeles | 5,782 | 8,701 | 9,969 | 7,835 | 5,439 | | | | |
| Mexico City | 6,037 | 9,722 | 8,511 | 9,081 | 5,541 | 1,542 | | | |
| Moscow | 996 | 3,131 | 6,294 | 7,046 | 1,549 | 6,068 | 6,688 | | |
| New York | 3,961 | 7,794 | 7,081 | 9,959 | 3,459 | 2,451 | 2,085 | 4,662 | |
| Peking | 4,567 | 2,964 | 8,045 | 3,728 | 5,054 | 6,250 | 7,733 | 3,597 | 6,823 |
| Quebec | 3,583 | 7,371 | 7,857 | 9,724 | 3,101 | 2,579 | 2,454 | 4,242 | 439 |
| Rio de Janeiro | 6,114 | 8,257 | 3,769 | 9,960 | 5,772 | 6,296 | 4,770 | 7,179 | 4,820 |
| Rome | 734 | 3,843 | 5,249 | 8,190 | 887 | 6,326 | 6,353 | 1,474 | 4,273 |
| Tokyo | 5,538 | 4,188 | 9,071 | 3,367 | 5,938 | 5,470 | 7,035 | 4,650 | 6,735 |
| Wellington | 11,265 | 7,677 | 7,019 | 3,310 | 11,682 | 6,714 | 6,899 | 10,279 | 8,946 |

**Distances from New York** (right)
This diagram shows the shortest
distances between New York and
10 other cities around the world.

- **a** Darwin, Australia 9959 mi
- **b** Wellington, New Zealand 8946 mi
- **c** Cape Town, South Africa 7801 mi
- **d** Bombay, India 7794 mi
- **e** Peking, China 6823 mi
- **f** Tokyo, Japan 6735 mi
- **g** Rio de Janeiro, Brazil 4820 mi
- **h** Moscow, USSR 4662 mi
- **i** London, United Kingdom 3459 mi
- **j** Los Angeles, USA 2451 mi

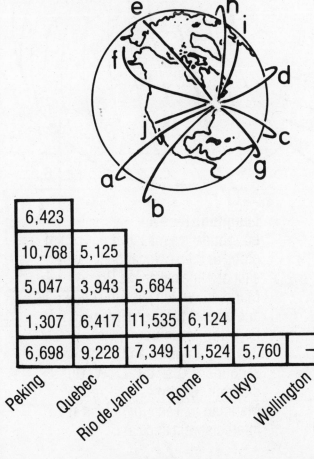

| | | | | | |
|---|---|---|---|---|---|
| 6,423 | | | | | |
| 10,768 | 5,125 | | | | |
| 5,047 | 3,943 | 5,684 | | | |
| 1,307 | 6,417 | 11,535 | 6,124 | | |
| 6,698 | 9,228 | 7,349 | 11,524 | 5,760 | — |
| Peking | Quebec | Rio de Janeiro | Rome | Tokyo | Wellington |

# Latitude and longitude

**The geographic grid** In order to describe the exact location of places on the Earth's surface it is usual to give references based upon the internationally accepted geographic grid system made up of lines of latitude (also called parallels) and lines of longitude (also called meridians).

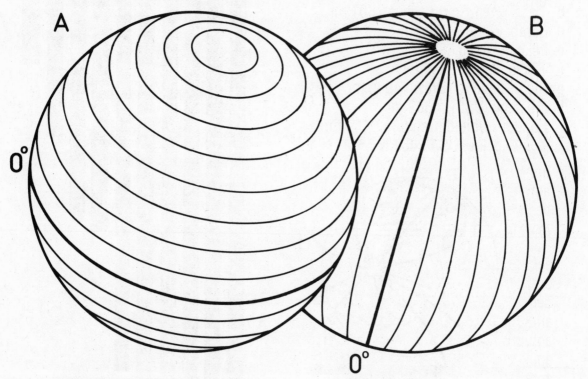

**Latitude** (above)
Latitude is a measurement on a globe or map of location north or south of the Equator. It is measured in degrees, minutes and sometimes seconds and is usually written with abbreviations, e.g. 53° 52′ 01″N. Our diagram (**A**) shows the Equator (0°) and parallels at 10° intervals north and south. The North Pole is at 90°N and the South Pole at 90°S.

**Longitude** (above)
Longitude is a measurement on a globe or map of location west or east of a line called the Prime Meridian, which joins the two Poles and passes through Greenwich, England. Measurement is in degrees, minutes and sometimes seconds, e.g. 2° 09′ 23″W. Our diagram (**B**) shows the Prime Meridian (0°) and meridians at 10° intervals west and east.

## Some important lines (right)

Shown on this diagram and listed here with their latitudes are some important lines of latitude. The Tropics mark the limits of places where the Sun is always vertically overhead.

1 Arctic Circle 66½°N
2 Tropic of Cancer 23½°N
3 Equator 0°
4 Tropic of Capricorn 23½°S
5 Antarctic Circle 66½°S

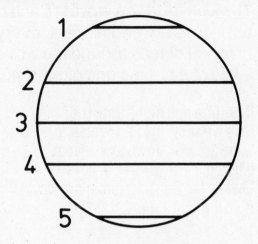

## City locations (right)

Listed below are the latitudes and longitudes of some major cities. The diagram shows the positions of two cities with similar latitudes (**a,b**) and two with similar longitudes (**c,d**).

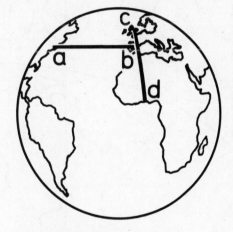

Accra 5° 32′N, 0° 12′W (**d**)
Bombay 18° 55′N, 73° 0′E
Buenos Aires 34° 50′S, 58° 37′W
Cairo 30° 08′N, 31° 14′E
Canberra 35° 15′S, 149° 10′E
Cape Town 33° 59′S, 18° 30′E
Caracas 10° 25′N, 66° 50′W
Helsinki 60° 13′N, 24° 55′E
London 51° 30′N, 0° 5′W (**c**)
Madrid 40° 27′N, 3° 42′W (**b**)
Mexico City 19° 25′N, 99° 5′W
Moscow 55° 50′N, 37° 40′E
New York 40° 45′N, 74° 0′W (**a**)
Quito 0° 20′S, 78° 45′W
Tehran 35° 37′N, 51° 22′E
Tokyo 35° 48′N, 139° 45′E
Vancouver 49° 14′N, 122° 50′W
Wellington 41° 15′S, 176° 46′E

©DIAGRAM

## Continental limits

This list shows approximate latitudes for the northernmost and southernmost points and approximate longitudes for the westernmost and easternmost points.

N. America: 80°N–10°N; 170°W–15°W
Europe: 80°N–35°N; 25°W–60°E
Asia: 80°N–5°S; 60°E–170°W
S. America: 15°N–55°S; 85°W–35°W
Africa: 35°N–35°S; 25°W–50°E
Oceania: 20°N–50°S; 115°E–110°W

# Time

**Time around the world**   Each day on the Earth lasts 24 hours, but it does not begin or end everywhere together. At any moment, different places around the world are at different points in the cycle of day-time and night-time caused by the Earth's rotation.

**Day-time and night-time** (right) Here we show the Earth rotating eastward on its own axis so that different parts of its surface face toward the Sun (day-time) or away from it (night-time).

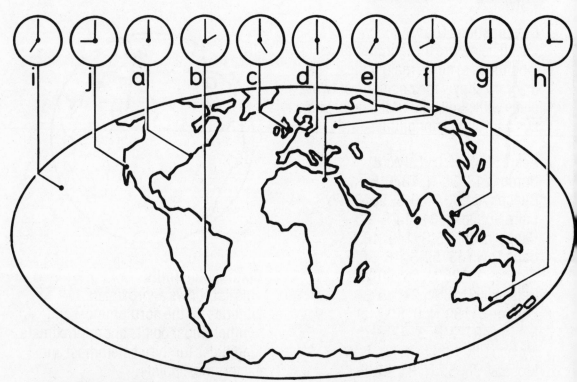

**12 o'clock in New York** (above) Clocks above this map show the time in different places when it is 12 o'clock in New York. (If it is noon in New York it is midnight in Bangkok, and vice versa).

| | | | |
|---|---|---|---|
| **a** | New York 12 | **f** | Moscow 8 |
| **b** | Montevideo 2 | **g** | Bangkok 12 |
| **c** | London 5 | **h** | Canberra 3 |
| **d** | Warsaw 6 | **i** | Honolulu 7 |
| **e** | Cairo 7 | **j** | Los Angeles 9 |

## Time by the Sun

Each day the Sun appears to move across the sky, rising in the East and setting in the West. (In fact the Sun stays still and the Earth is turning around.) If people used a time system based only on the position of the Sun in the sky, we would have to move our watches forward by 4 minutes for every degree of longitude that we traveled eastward.

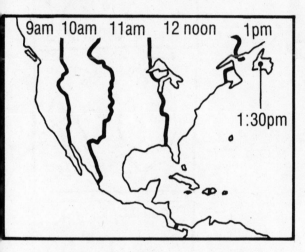

## Time zones (above)

Instead of everyone telling the time by the Sun, a system of time zones has been introduced. All the places in the same zone share the same time. Worldwide there are 24 zones, one for each hour of the day and night. Our map shows N. America's time zones, ranging from Newfoundland Standard Time (1½ hours ahead of Eastern Standard Time) westward to the Pacific.

## Times compared to GMT (below)

These lists show how standard (time zone) times in different cities around the world compare with Greenwich Mean Time (the standard time of the zone centered on Greenwich, England).

**Europe**
GMT London
GMT Reykjavik
+1 Madrid
+1 Rome
+1 Stockholm
+1 Warsaw
+2 Athens
+2 Helsinki
**Africa**
GMT Accra
+1 Lagos
+2 Cairo
+2 Pretoria
+3 Kampala
+3 Nairobi
**Asia**
+2 Tel Aviv
+3 Ankara
+3 Baghdad
+3½ Tehran
+4½ Kabul
+5 Islamabad
+5½ Delhi
+6 Dacca
+6½ Rangoon
+7 Jakarta
+8 Peking
+9 Seoul
+9 Tokyo

**USSR**
+3 Moscow
+6 Omsk
+8 Irkutsk
+13 Anadyr
**Oceania**
+8 Perth
+9½ Darwin
+10 Canberra
+12 Wellington
**North America**
−11 Nome
−10 Honolulu
−8 Los Angeles
−8 Vancouver
−7 Denver
−6 Chicago
−6 Mexico City
−5 New York
−5 Ottawa
−3½ St Johns
**South America**
−5 Lima
−4 Caracas
−4 Santiago
−3 Brasilia
−3 Buenos Aires

# Section 2

# The Living World

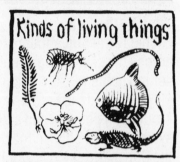
Kinds of living things

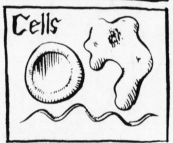
Extinctions

Cells

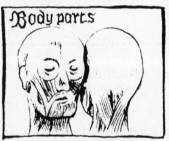
Body parts

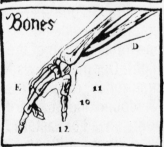
Bones

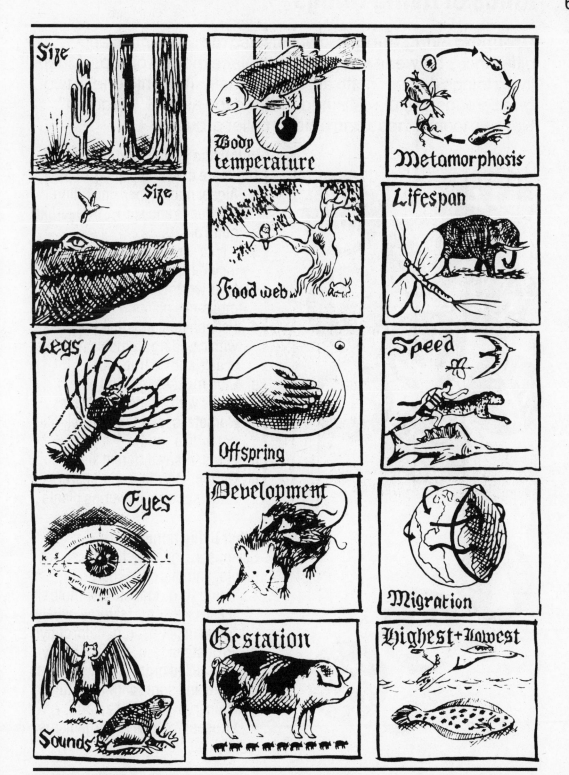

Size

Body temperature

Metamorphosis

Size

Food web

Lifespan

Legs

Offspring

Speed

Eyes

Development

Migration

Sounds

Gestation

Highest + Lowest

**Kinds of living things**

**Grouping living things** Scientists use the similarities and differences between living things to place them in groups. Most living things (but not quite all) can be easily fitted into one of two great groups: the plant "kingdom" and the animal "kingdom". Here we look at these and other smaller groups.

**Within the plant kingdom** (left)
These are the main plant groups.

**a** Algae: many types, including seaweeds and slimy, thread-like pond plants

**b** "True" mosses: most mosses, including bog or peat mosses

**c** Liverworts: small, creeping, moss-like plants

**d** Psilophytes: grass-like plants with creeping stems, leaves like scales and no true roots

**e** Club mosses (ground pines): herbs with conifer-like leaves

**f** Horsetails: plants with rush-like or tail-like shoots

**g** Ferns: many different kinds

**h** Gymnosperms: cone-bearers

**i** Angiosperms: flowering plants

**Other living things** (left)
Scientists argue whether these are plants, animals or neither.

**1** Fungi (e.g. toadstools, molds): these lack some features usually found in plants, e.g. chlorophyll

**2** Protistans (e.g. amebae): tiny one-celled organisms with some plant and some animal features

**3** Procaryotes (e.g. bacteria, viruses): one-celled organisms with no distinct nucleus

## Animals: invertebrates (right)

Some of the most important groups of invertebrates (animals without backbones) are listed here, with examples for each.

**a** Poriferans: sponge
**b** Coelenterates: jellyfish, coral, sea anemone
**c** Platyhelminths: flatworm, liverfluke, tapeworm
**d** Nematodes: roundworm
**e** Annelids: earthworm, leech
**f** Mollusks: snail, slug, clam, limpet, octopus
**g** Chilopods: centipede
**h** Diplopods: millipede
**i** Crustaceans: prawn, crab, barnacle, wood louse
**j** Insects: butterfly, wasp, ant, beetle, louse
**k** Arachnids: spider, harvestman, scorpion, mite
**l** Echinoderms: starfish, sea cucumber, sea urchin
**m** Urochordates: sea squirt

## Animals: vertebrates (right)

There are five main groups of vertebrates (backboned animals).

**1** Fishes: shark, trout, plaice, eel, seahorse
**2** Amphibians: frog, toad, newt, salamander
**3** Reptiles: lizard, snake, turtle, crocodile, tuatara
**4** Birds: crow, ostrich, parrot
**5** Mammals: man, dog, bat, whale, kangaroo, platypus

# Numbers of living things

**Living species** The Earth may hold five to ten million species or kinds of living things, but scientists have described fewer than two million. As shown below, 75% of these are animals, 18% are plants and 7% are simple organisms that lack some of the usual plant or animal characteristics.

**All known species** (below)
Here are known numbers of species for different groups.
1 Animals, over 1,200,000
2 Plants, about 300,000
3 Others, over 100,000

**Known animal species** (below)
Invertebrates (animals without a backbone) outnumber vertebrates.
a Insects 950,000
b Other invertebrates 227,000
c Vertebrates 45,000

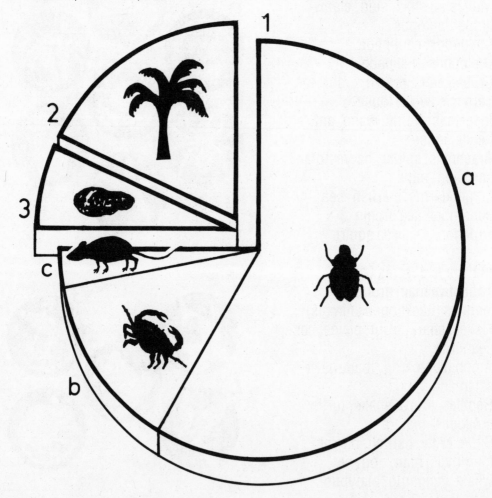

## Numbers of vertebrates (right)

This diagram shows (**a–e**) the known numbers of species in each group of backboned animals.

**a** Fishes 23,000
**b** Amphibians 3000
**c** Reptiles 6000
**d** Birds 8600
**e** Mammals 4200

Also shown here are the likely number of fish species yet to be discovered (**f**). Many of these fish swim in the immense depths of the oceans that cover more than two-thirds of the Earth's surface.

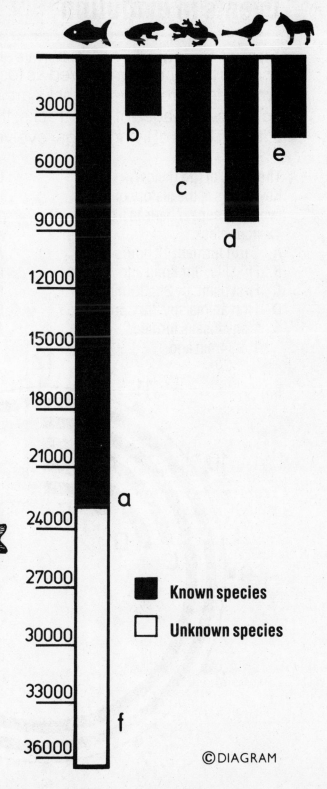

| Known species | Unknown species |

## Beasts by the billion (above)

The most numerous backboned land animal might be the red-billed quelea (**1**). Ten billion live in Africa. The most abundant backboned water animal may be the bristlemouth (**2**). This small deep-sea fish occurs worldwide.

©DIAGRAM

# Events in evolution

**First of their kind** For 1 billion years, newly dead plants and animals have been preserved as fossils in rocks. Fossils are embedded in rocks as the rocks are formed. Because scientists now know the ages of many rocks, they can work out when different kinds of living things evolved.

**The clock of life** (below)
Key events in the history of evolution appear here as if on a 12-hour clock.
A   Earth formed: 12 hours ago
B   First life: 9hr 8min ago
C   First plant: by 2hr 36min ago
D   First animal: by 2hr 36min ago
E   Many fossils formed:
      1hr 34min ago

**Time in years**
The events listed left in fact took place the following numbers of years ago.
A   4.6 billion years ago
B   3.5 billion years ago
C   by 1 billion years ago
D   by 1 billion years ago
E   600 million years ago

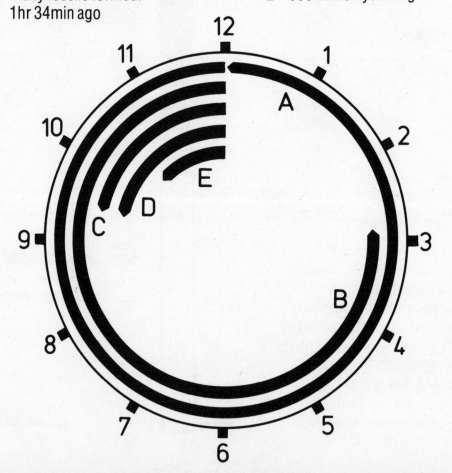

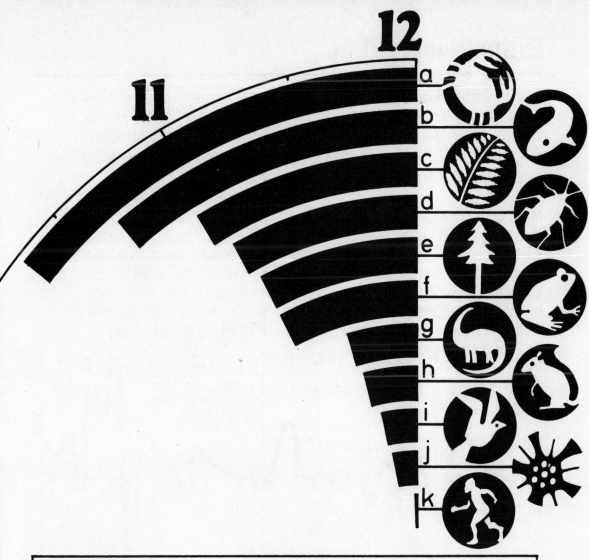

**11**

**12**

| First appearances | | On the clock | In years |
|---|---|---|---|
| **a** | Crustacean | 1hr 42min ago | 650 million years ago |
| **b** | Fish | 1hr 20min ago | 510 million years ago |
| **c** | Land plant | 1hr 3min ago | 400 million years ago |
| **d** | Insect | 58min ago | 370 million years ago |
| **e** | Seed plant | 55min ago | 350 million years ago |
| **f** | Amphibian | 55min ago | 350 million years ago |
| **g** | Dinosaur | 32min ago | 205 million years ago |
| **h** | Mammal | 30min ago | 190 million years ago |
| **i** | Bird | 24min ago | 150 million years ago |
| **j** | Flowering plant | 22min ago | 140 million years ago |
| **k** | Man | 37sec ago | 4 million years ago |

©DIAGRAM

# Extinction (1)

**Lost species** For every plant and animal species now alive 800 may have died out since life began about 3.5 billion years ago. Sometimes many kinds of animals became extinct together, perhaps killed by harsh changes in climate. The diagram below shows when most of these extinctions happened.

**Mass deaths** (below)
Dips in this line show times when the numbers of known kinds of backboned animals fell. The line spans five geological periods, running from 280 million to 2 million years ago.

**Geological periods** (below)
We list numbers of years ago.
**a** Permian 280–225 million
**b** Triassic 225–190 million
**c** Jurassic 190–135 million
**d** Cretaceous 135–65 million
**e** Tertiary 65–2 million

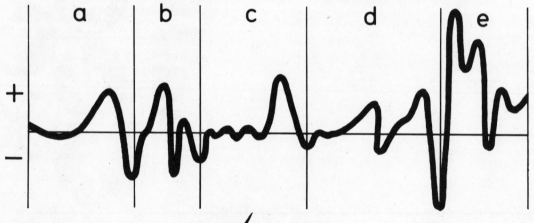

**Mystery deaths** (left)
Many groups of animals died out mysteriously at the end of the Cretaceous Period. Among them were these main groups.
**A** Saurischian dinosaurs
**B** Ornithischian dinosaurs
**C** Plesiosaurs (sea reptiles)
**D** Pterosaurs (flying reptiles)
**E** Ammonites (sea invertebrates)

**Mammal losses**
About 11,000 years ago many big mammals became extinct in North America. Stone Age hunters possibly wiped out these.
1 Mammoths
2 Giant ground sloths
3 Glyptodonts
4 Saber tooth cats
5 Dire wolves

©DIAGRAM

# Extinction (2)

**Vanishing species** One in five of all living species may be extinct by AD 2000. Those lost will be destroyed mostly by man. In the last 300 years people have helped wipe out nearly 300 species and subspecies of backboned animal. Shown below are the homes of most of these and how many each place lost.

**a** Hawaiian Islands 28
**b** Society Islands 7
**c** Galápagos Islands 4
**d** North America 45
**e** West Indies 54
**f** Europe 7

**g** Africa 9
**h** Mascarene Islands 28
**i** Asia 19
**j** Australia 11
**k** Howe Island 8
**l** New Zealand 23

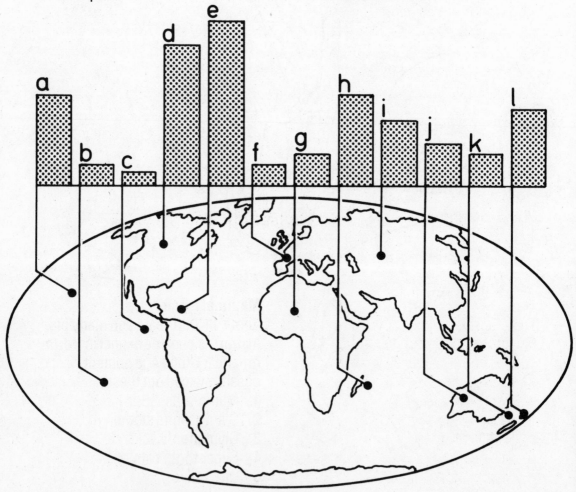

## Rare vertebrates (below)

Shown here are five rare species of backboned animal. Some have fewer than 100 individuals. All may very soon become extinct.

**1** Gila trout
**2** Houston toad
**3** Gharial
**4** Californian condor
**5** Javan rhinoceros

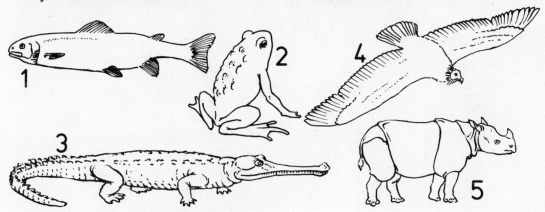

● = 25

## Threatened vertebrates (above)

This diagram shows estimated minimum numbers of vertebrate species and subspecies that are threatened with extinction.

**a** Fishes 190
**b** Amphibians 40
**c** Reptiles 150
**d** Birds 430
**e** Mammals 320

## Why species die out

This list shows the percentages of extinctions occurring for three common reasons. The total exceeds 100% because an extinction may have several causes.

1) Living area destroyed (67%)
2) Hunting and collecting (37%)
3) Competition from introduced animals (19%)

©DIAGRAM

# Size (1)

**Tallest and tiniest** Trees are the tallest living things and the tallest known, a *Eucalyptus regnans,* was 76 times taller than an average man. The tiniest living things include viruses, of which the smallest known is *necrosis virus*. Placed in a row, more than half a million of these would measure only 0.39in.

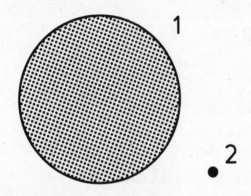

**Tallest plants** (right)
These plants all hold size records for their kind. (We have used two different scales so that the tops of the two tallest ones can be shown.) The tallest tree alive today is the Coast redwood (**h**) at 368.5ft. The tallest *Eucalyptus regnans* (**i**), at 438.3ft, was recorded in 1872.

**a**  Callie grass 18ft
**b**  Saguaro cactus 52.6ft
**c**  Tree fern 59.2ft
**d**  Giant horsetail (extinct) 100ft
**e**  Giant club moss (extinct) 100ft
**f**  Bamboo, a woody grass 122ft
**g**  Giant kelp, a seaweed 200ft
**h**  Coast redwood, a conifer, the tallest gymnosperm 368.5ft
**i**  Eucalyptus regnans, the tallest of all flowering plants 438.3ft

**Tiniest living things** (above)
The smallest known organisms capable of independent life are pleuro-pneumonia-like organisms of the microplasma (**1**). One of these has a maximum diameter of 0.0000117in. Viruses depend on other living cells. The smallest known is *necrosis virus* (**2**), which measures 0.00000066in across.

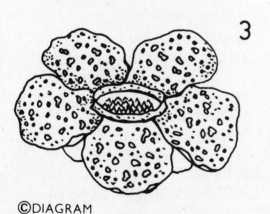

**Largest and smallest flowers**
Shown (**3**) is a stinking corpse lily, the largest known kind of flower, which sometimes measures 35in in diameter. The smallest known blooms are those of the artillery plant, which measures only 0.014in in diameter

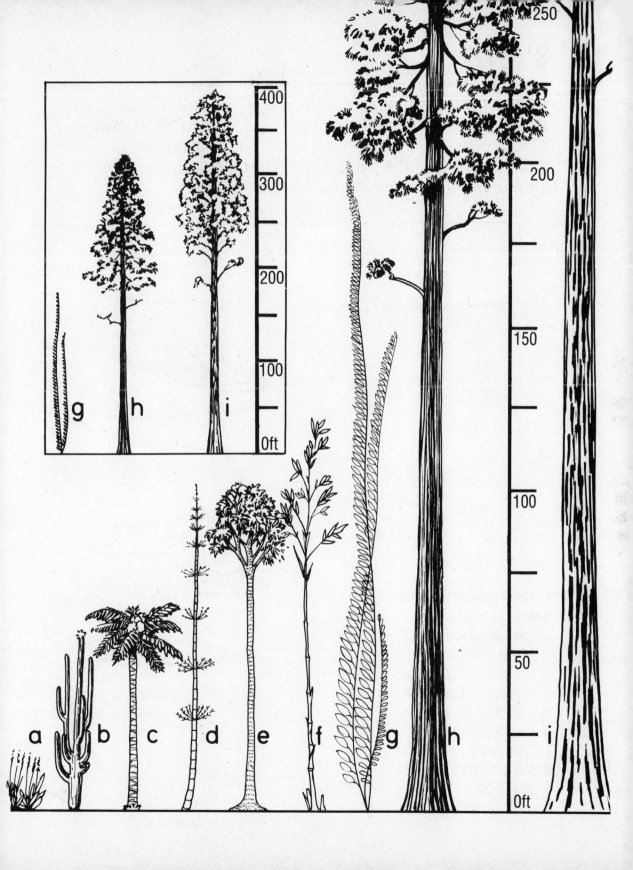

# Size (2)

**Largest and smallest animals** Shown on these two pages are the largest and smallest creatures belonging to different main groups of animals. The largest known kinds of reptile, amphibian and bird are all extinct. The other large and small creatures shown here are present-day animals.

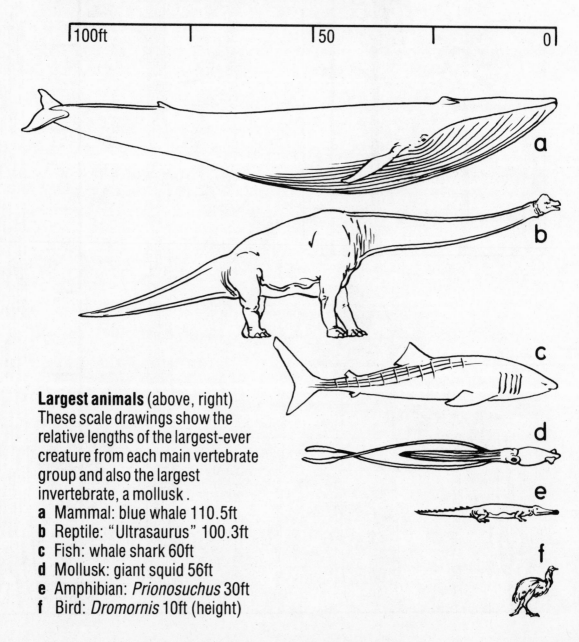

100ft — 50 — 0

**Largest animals** (above, right) These scale drawings show the relative lengths of the largest-ever creature from each main vertebrate group and also the largest invertebrate, a mollusk.
- **a** Mammal: blue whale 110.5ft
- **b** Reptile: "Ultrasaurus" 100.3ft
- **c** Fish: whale shark 60ft
- **d** Mollusk: giant squid 56ft
- **e** Amphibian: *Prionosuchus* 30ft
- **f** Bird: *Dromornis* 10ft (height)

## Animal heavyweights (below)

Shown in this diagram and listed right are the weights of the largest-ever mammal (**a**), reptile (**b**), fish (**c**), invertebrate (**d**), amphibian (**e**) and bird (**f**).

a Blue whale 186 tons
b "Ultrasaurus" 181 tons
c Whale shark 42 tons
d Giant squid 2 tons
e *Prionosuchus* 2 tons
f *Dromornis* 0.5 ton

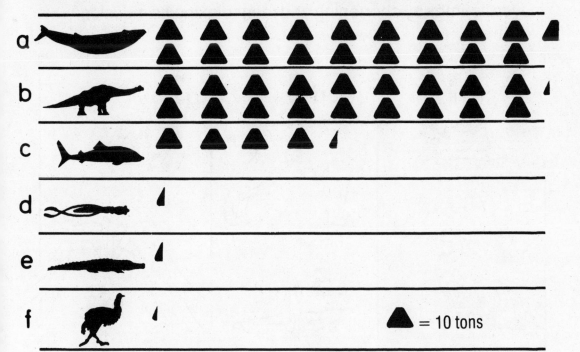

▲ = 10 tons

## Smallest vertebrates (right)

1 The smallest mammal is the bumblebee bat, wingspan 6.2in.
2 The smallest bird is the bee hummingbird, 2.2in long.
3 The smallest reptile is the *Sphaerodactylus* gecko, 1.4in. long.
4 The smallest amphibian is the *Sminthillus* frog, 0.4in long.
5 The smallest fish is the Marshall Islands goby, 0.55in long.

©DIAGRAM

# Limbs

**Levers and props** Most animals must move to find food or to avoid enemies. Many move with limbs acting as levers and props. (Props can be legs, arms, feet or fins.) Most creatures with six or more limbs are arthropods (insects and other small animals with jointed legs and no backbone). Others with many limbs include echinoderms like the starfish. Every creature moves its limbs by shortening and then relaxing its muscles.

## Number of limbs

Included here are examples of creatures with different numbers of legs – one each for all the numbers up to 10 and then some with even more. (Some creatures are magnified, while others are shown much smaller than true size.)

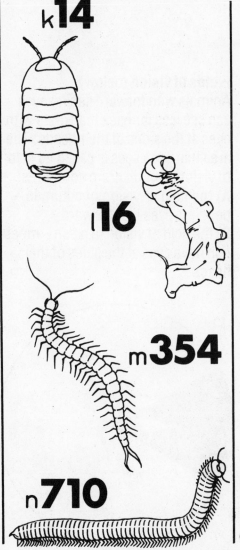

k **14**

l **16**

m **354**

n **710**

© DIAGRAM

**a** Snail. Snails and slugs slide along on a muscular foot.

**b** Heron. Birds and humans have two legs. Such animals are known as bipeds.

**c** Tripod fish. Two long fin rays and one long ray from its tail help it to rest on soft mud.

**d** Dog. Dogs and other four-legged animals are called quadrupeds or tetrapods.

**e** Starfish. Most starfish have five limbs called arms. Jutting from each arm are many tiny feet.

**f** Louse. Lice and other insects have six legs.

**g** Springtail. This has six true legs and also a forked springing organ at the rear which acts like a seventh leg.

**h** Harvestman. Like spiders and scorpions, this is an arachnid with eight legs.

**i** Sunstar. This example has nine legs, but others have up to 50. Sunstars are a type of starfish.

**j** Crab. Like lobsters and shrimp, this is a 10-legged crustacean.

**k** Wood louse. This is a type of crustacean with 14 legs.

**l** Caterpillar. A typical number of legs for a caterpillar is 16.

**m** Centipede. Although their name means 100 feet, centipedes have from 28 to 354 legs.

**n** Millipede. This means 1000 feet, but the record number of legs is 710.

# Eyes

**Seeing** The eyes of simple organisms can only tell light from darkness. Insects have more complicated eyes. A housefly's big compound eyes each have 4000 tiny lenses. Each lens forms a separate image. Insects' eyes are good at spotting movement. But backboned animals and mollusks such as the octopus have the best kinds of eyes for focusing on objects near and far.

**Keen sight** (above)
Birds of prey have the keenest sight of any animal. This diagram shows the results of a test conducted by a scientist who noticed that a buzzard could see a large insect from a long way away. He found that a buzzard could see an inch long green grasshopper from a distance of 300ft (**a**), but that a man could see it from no more than 100ft (**b**).

**Fields of vision** (below)
Animals with forward-facing eyes can see less far back than ones with eyes at the sides of their heads. The area that each sees is called its field of vision. Our diagram compares:
**A**) the field of vision of a human – people's eyes face forward;
**B**) the field of vision of a fish – most fish have eyes at the sides of their heads.

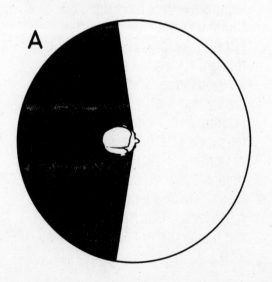

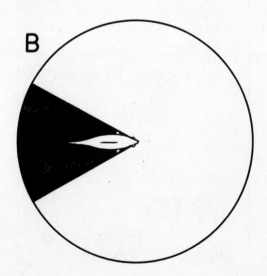

**Number of eyes** (below)
Included here are examples of animals with different numbers of eyes. Invertebrates show much more variety than vertebrates.
**a** Euglena (a tiny organism that lives in water), one eye spot
**b** Human being, two eyes
**c** Four-eyed fish, four eyes (really two, each split in half to see above and below water)
**d** Honeybee, five eyes (three simple and two compound)
**e** Wolf spider, eight eyes

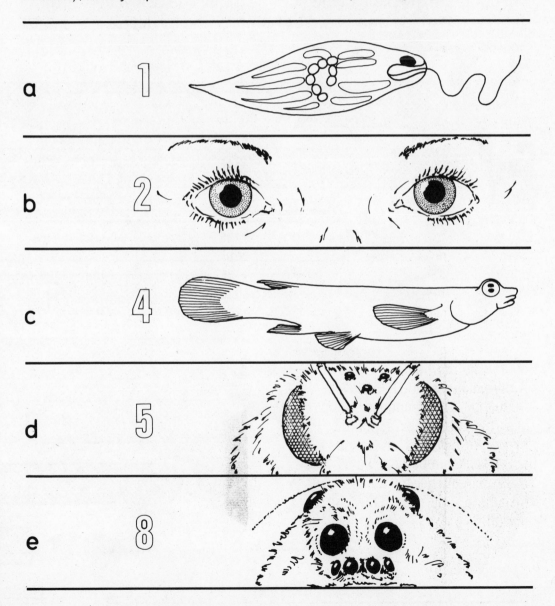

a 1

b 2

c 4

d 5

e 8

©DIAGRAM

# Ears and voices

**Sounds for survival** Most backboned animals and some others can make and hear sounds that signal danger or help them find a mate. Backboned animals make sounds by breathing out in special ways. Insects and some fishes scrape or vibrate part of the body. Backboned animals hear with ears in the head but insects' "ears" are on their bodies or antennae (feelers). Here we compare the pitch of the sounds (how high or low they are) that can be made and heard by humans and by different animals.

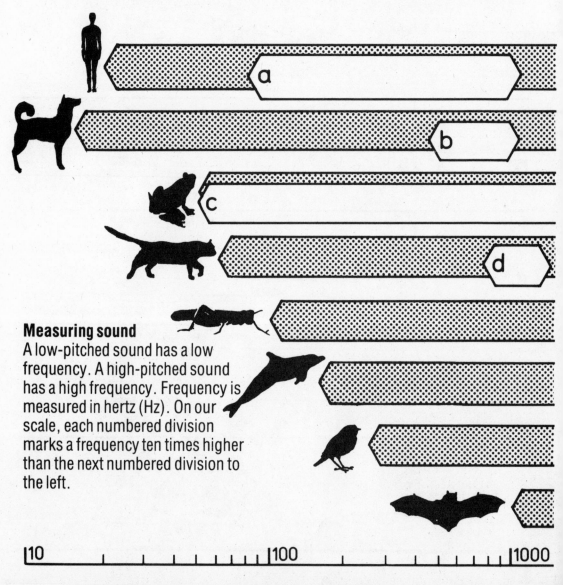

**Measuring sound**
A low-pitched sound has a low frequency. A high-pitched sound has a high frequency. Frequency is measured in hertz (Hz). On our scale, each numbered division marks a frequency ten times higher than the next numbered division to the left.

10    100    1000

| Animal | Sounds heard | Sounds made |
|--------|--------------|-------------|
| a  Man | 20–20,000Hz | 80–1100Hz |
| b  Dog | 15–50,000Hz | 452–1080Hz |
| c  Frog | 50–10,000Hz | 50–8000Hz |
| d  Cat | 60–65,000Hz | 760–1520Hz |
| e  Grasshopper | 100–15,000Hz | 7000–100,000Hz |
| f  Dolphin | 150–150,000Hz | 7000–120,000Hz |
| g  Robin (European) | 250–21,000Hz | 2000–13,000Hz |
| h  Bat | 1000–120,000Hz | 10,000–120,000Hz |

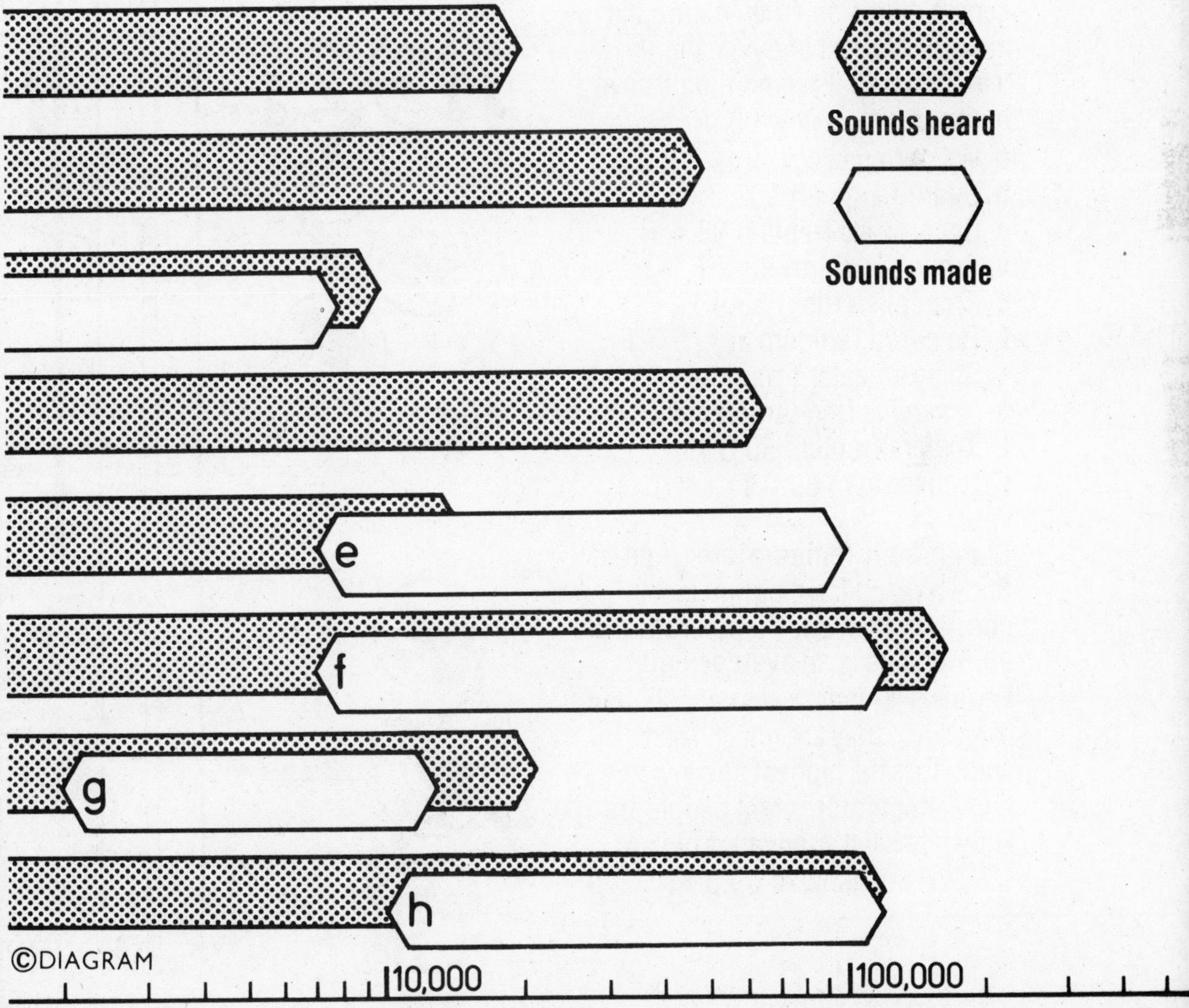

Sounds heard

Sounds made

©DIAGRAM

10,000    100,000

# Body temperatures

**Warmth for life** All animals need heat to keep their bodies alive, but not all living things need the same temperature. A body temperature that is too high for one animal can be too low for another. Too high a temperature can kill by "cooking". Too low a temperature can kill by causing cells to freeze and burst.

**Body temperatures** (right)
This diagram shows some of the highest and lowest normal or ideal body temperatures found in each group of backboned animal. In general, birds and then mammals have the highest body temperatures. Few mammals have temperatures below 95 °F

**a** Western pewee (bird) 112.6°F
**b** Goat (mammal) 103.8°F
**c** Spiny lizard (reptile) 98.4°F
**d** Arctic gull (bird) 93.2°F
**e** Archer fish (fish) 82.4°F
**f** Rain frog (amphibian) 79.7°F
**g** Spiny anteater (mammal) 73.9°F
**h** *Ascaphus* frog (amphibian) 50.1°F
**i** Tuatara (reptile) 50.0°F
**j** Icefish (fish) 30.2°F

**Human body temperature** (right)
Shown (**k**) on the diagram is the normal human body temperature of 98.6°F. This is an average figure. People's temperatures vary slightly even when they are not ill. Also shown are the highest and lowest body temperatures that people are known to have survived: a high of 111.9°F and a low of 60.8°F.

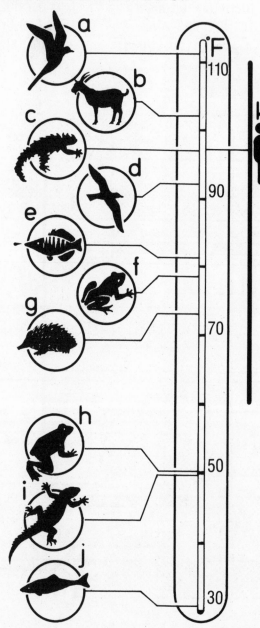

## Warm-blooded and cold-blooded

Warm-blooded animals: these have a built-in "thermostat" that helps keep body temperature at a certain level. Mammals and birds are warm-blooded. Cold-blooded animals: these animals lack internal temperature controls. Body temperatures rise and fall with changes in air or water temperatures around them. Reptiles, amphibians and fish are cold-blooded.

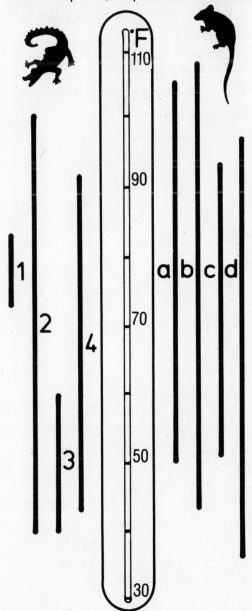

**Temperature ranges** (left)
Some animals can survive much greater variations in body temperature than others. Bars on the left of this diagram show variations in body temperature survived by four cold-blooded animals.

**1** Crocodile 73.4°F to 84.2°F
**2** Garter snake 39.6°F to 102°F
**3** *Ascaphus* frog 39.9°F to 60.3°F
**4** Catfish 42.8°F to 93.2°F

**Hibernating** (left)
Bars on the diagram's right show the lowering of body temperature in four mammals hibernating in cold weather. Letting body temperature fall saves energy and so prevents starvation when plant foods are scarce in winter.

**a** Marmot 107°F to 50°F
**b** Common hamster 110°F to 43°F
**c** Opossum 95°F to 50.5°F
**d** Dormouse 98.6°F to 35.6°F

©DIAGRAM

# Food and feeding

**How animals get food** All animals get their food directly or indirectly from plants. Some animals feed directly on plants. Some eat other animals that have eaten plants. Some eat animals that have eaten other animals that have eaten plants!

### Food for plants
Plants make their own food (starch) from carbon dioxide in the air and from water taken in by their roots. This food-making process, called photosynthesis, occurs only in daylight.

### Types of feeders
A herbivore is an animal that eats only plants.
A carnivore is an animal that eats only other animals.
An omnivore is an animal that eats both plants and animals.

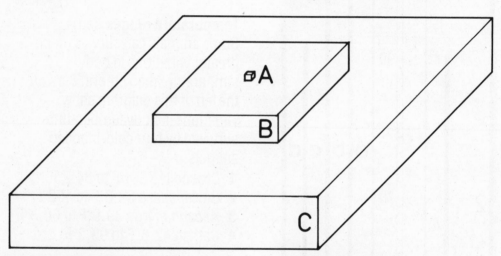

### A food pyramid (above)
This diagram compares the weights of animals and plants that can live on 250 acres of East African grassland. Carnivores need a much bigger weight of herbivores on which to feed. The herbivores in turn need a very much bigger weight of plants.
A Carnivores 330lb
B Herbivores 946,000lb
C Plants 11,561,000lb

### A food web (right)
Shown here is a food web linking eaters and eaten among the plants and animals in a N. American wood.
a Green tortrix
b Oak leaf
c Caterpillar
d Fly
e Screech owl
f Chickadee
g Deer mouse
h Seeds
i Red-backed vole
j Grass
k Rabbit
l Weasel

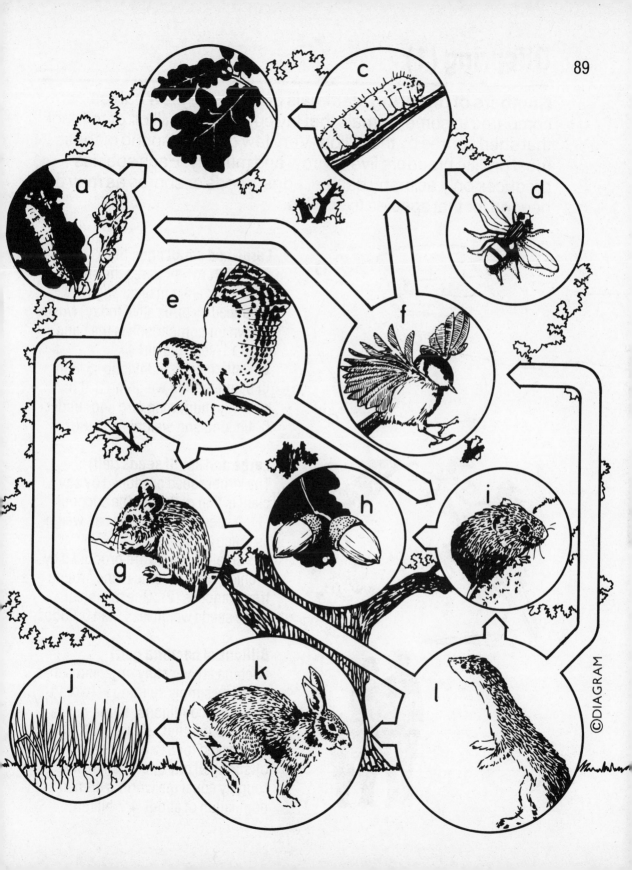

# Offspring (1)

**Numbers of offspring** Mammals produce very few babies compared to some animals that lay eggs by the million or to fungi that shed spores by the billion. Very few of the offspring of these most prolific breeders live to grow and multiply. Each species produces only as many babies, eggs, seeds or spores as may be needed for that species to survive.

**Large and small eggs** (left)
Our diagram compares the sizes of the largest and smallest eggs produced by birds alive today. (Also shown for comparison is the hand of an 11-year-old girl.)
**a** Ostrich egg, 7.8in long, 5.8in in diameter and weighing 3.9lb.
**b** Vervain humming bird egg, under 0.4in long and weighing 12.8oz.

**Large and small seeds** (left)
The largest seed produced by any plant is that of the double coconut (**1**). A seed from this tree can weigh as much as 40lb.
The smallest seeds are produced by orchids whose stems twine around tree branches (**2**). One million of these seeds weigh less than 0.035oz.

**Billions of bacteria** (left)
Bacteria are very tiny organisms that breed by simply splitting in two. In favorable conditions, some divide every 15 minutes. If this continued unchecked for 8¼ hours, the offspring of one bacterium would roughly equal the world's human population of about 4.7 billion.

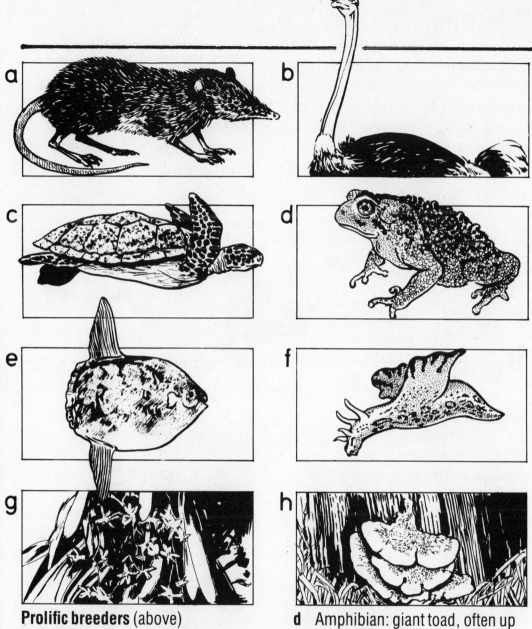

**Prolific breeders** (above)
The animals, plant and fungus shown here are among the record-holders for producing large numbers of offspring – at one time unless specified otherwise.

**a** Mammal: tenrec, 32 babies
**b** Bird: ostrich, 15 eggs
**c** Reptile: green turtle, 184 eggs
**d** Amphibian: giant toad, often up to 35,000 eggs
**e** Fish: sunfish, 300 million eggs
**f** Invertebrate: sea hare, 478 million eggs in four months
**g** Plant: orchid, 4.5 million seeds in each seed capsule
**h** Fungus: bracket fungus, 30 billion spores a day for six months

©DIAGRAM

# Offspring (2)

**The time it takes** Fertilized eggs or seeds develop into new animals or plants. Fertilization occurs when a sperm from a male animal or pollen from a male plant unites with an egg or seed from a female. Here we look at the lengths of time needed for different animals to hatch or be born and for different plants to produce seedlings after fertilization has taken place.

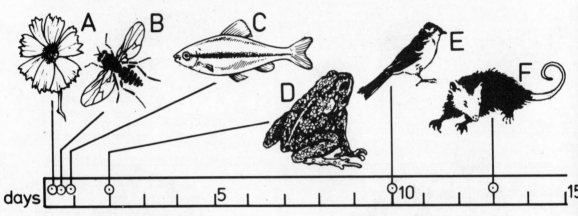

**Quick developers** (above)
This diagram shows some very short periods of incubation, gestation and germination.

**A**  Plant: tickweed, under 1 day
**B**  Insect: fruit fly, under 1 day
**C**  Fish: cherry barb 1 day
**D**  Amphibian: giant toad 2 days
**E**  Bird: some finches 10 days
**F**  Mammal: opossum 13 days
**G**  Reptile: skink 27 days

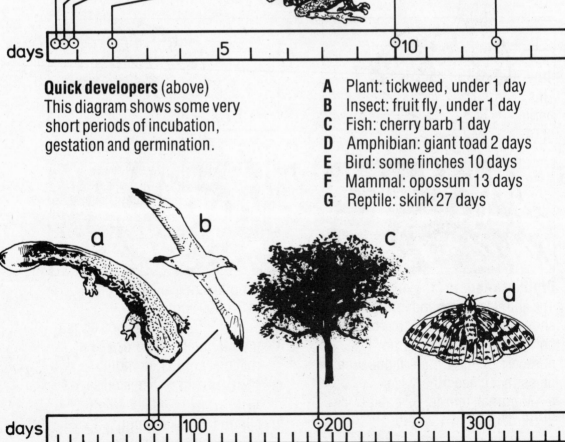

## Some terms defined

Incubation period: this is the time between fertilization and the hatching of an egg.

Gestation period: this is the time between fertilization and the birth of a baby.

Germination period: this is the time between fertilization and the sprouting of a seed.

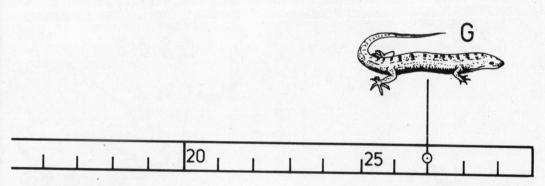

## Slow developers (below)

This diagram shows some long periods of incubation, gestation and germination.

a Amphibian: hellbender 76 days
b Bird: royal albatross 81 days
c Plant: black walnut 200 days
d Insect: a butterfly 270 days
e Reptile: tuatara 425 days
f Fish: dogfish 600 days
g Mammal: elephant 730 days

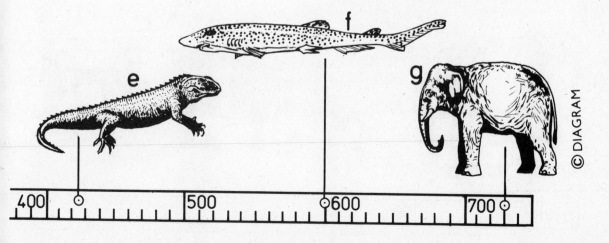

© DIAGRAM

# Offspring (3)

**Pets and farm animals** Shown below and listed right are typical gestation periods and litter sizes of some common pets and farm animals. Both gestation periods and litter sizes vary a great deal. Gestation in horses varies from 264 to 420 days. Examples of record litters are 34 mice, 26 hamsters and 23 dogs.

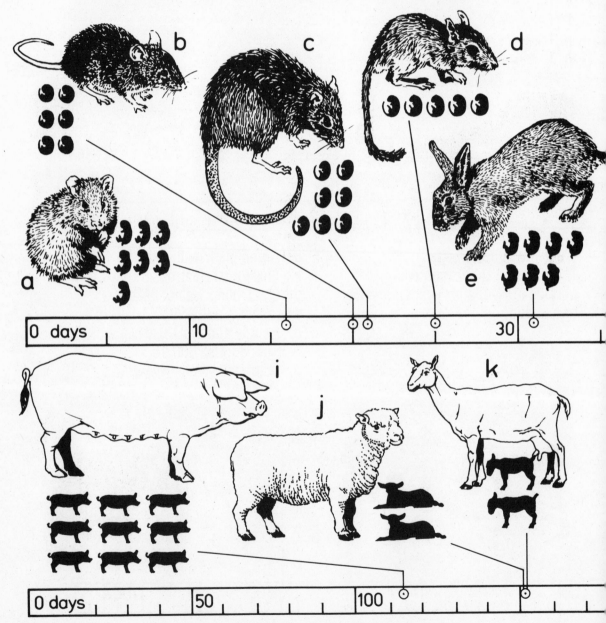

| | Pets | Gestation | Litter | | Farm animals | Gestation | Litter |
|---|---|---|---|---|---|---|---|
| a | Hamster | 16 days | 7 | i | Pig | 114 days | 9 |
| b | Mouse | 20 days | 6 | j | Sheep | 151 days | 2 |
| c | Rat | 21 days | 7 | k | Goat | 151 days | 2 |
| d | Gerbil | 25 days | 5 | l | Cow | 284 days | 1 |
| e | Rabbit | 31 days | 7 | m | Horse | 336 days | 1 |
| f | Cat | 63 days | 4 | | | | |
| g | Dog | 63 days | 7 | | | | |
| h | Guinea pig | 68 days | 3 | | | | |

f

g

h

©DIAGRAM

40    50    60

m

l

200    250    300

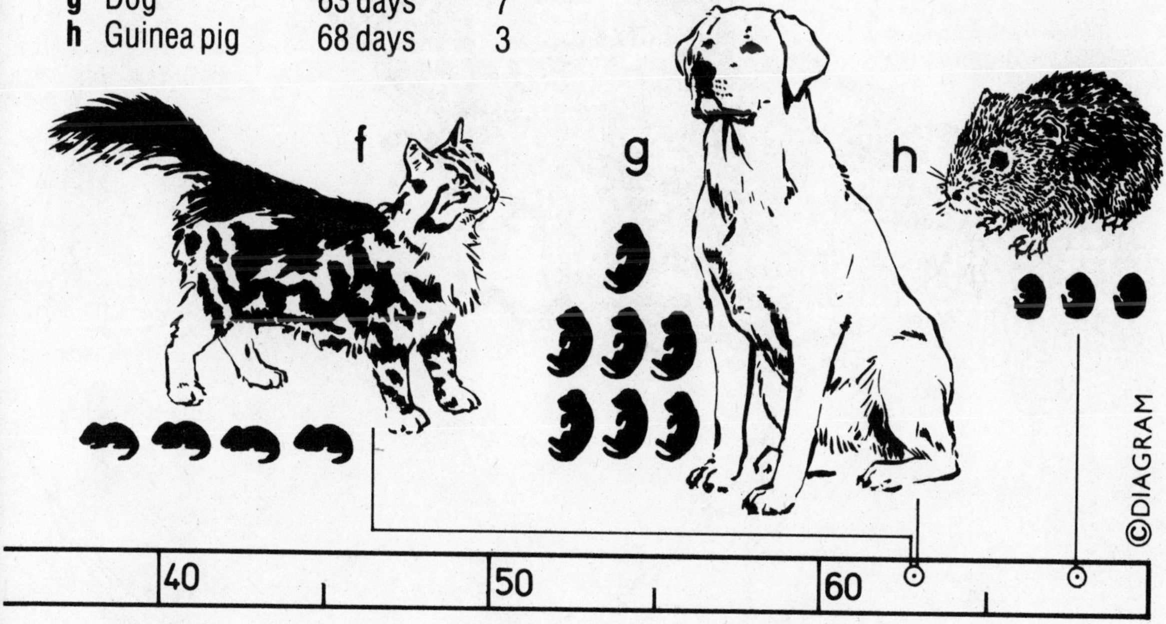

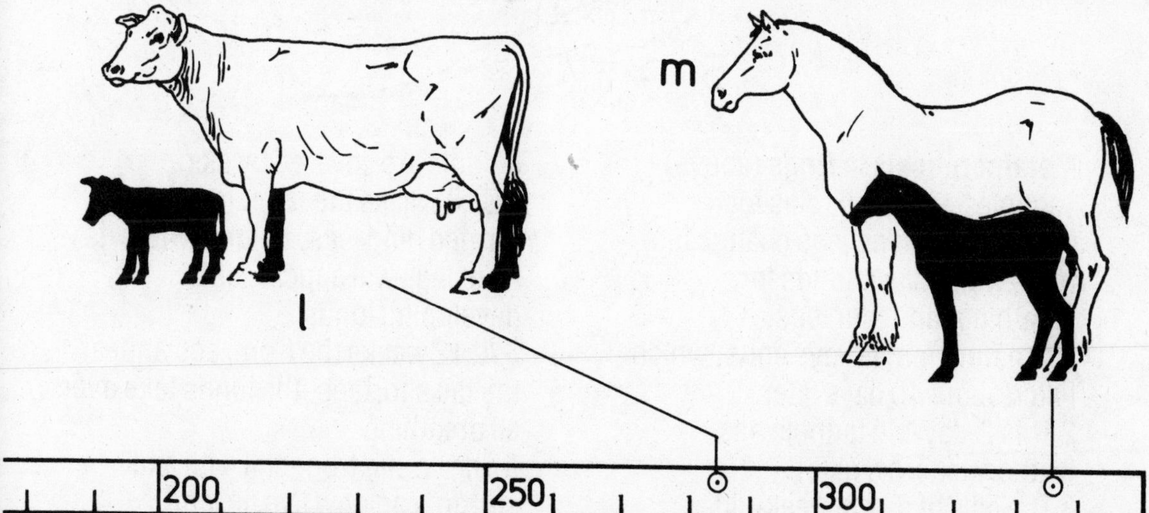

# Metamorphosis

**Changing bodies** Some creatures pass through several quite different stages before reaching their adult form. Among the animals that undergo major body change – known as metamorphosis – are amphibians such as frogs, insects such as lice and butterflies, and many sea worms and shellfish.

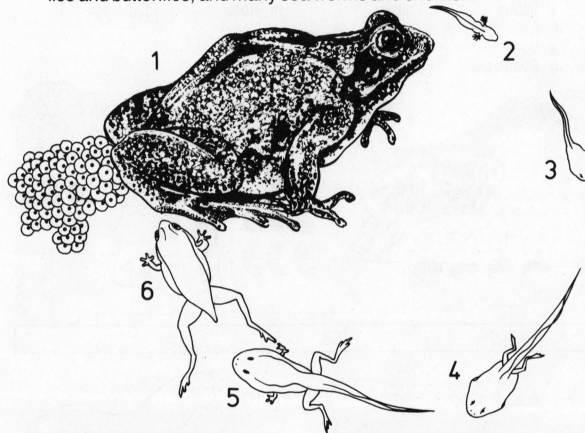

**Metamorphosis in frogs** (above) Tadpoles with a tail, gills for breathing, and no legs change into frogs with no tail, lungs for breathing, and four legs.

**1** A mature female lays eggs, which hatch about 10 days later.

**2** This 2-day-old tadpole has feathery external gills.

**3** The gills of this 3-week-old tadpole are covered by skin.

**4** By 8 weeks the tadpole has fully formed hind legs, bulges where its front legs will appear, and developing lungs.

**5** At 12 weeks the front legs appear, the tail shortens, the lungs take over all breathing.

**6** The young frog, still with a tail stump, can now live on land.

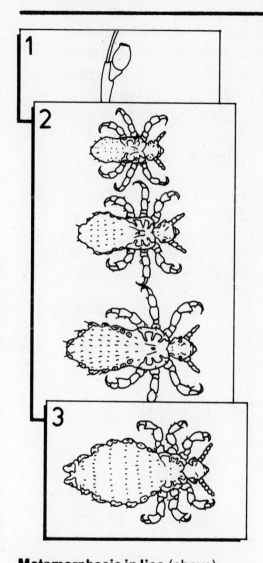

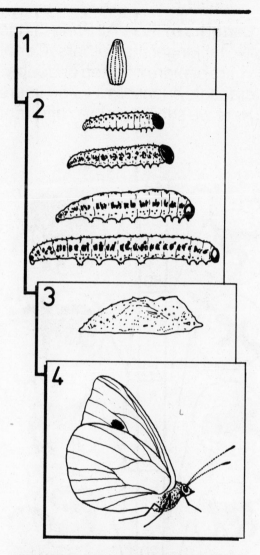

**Metamorphosis in lice** (above)
The louse is an example of an insect
that undergoes "gradual" or
"incomplete" metamorphosis. This
means it has three distinct stages in
its life cycle: egg (**1**), nymph (**2**) and
imago (adult) (**3**). Lice nymphs
molt three times and gradually
become more like an adult as they
grow.

**Butterfly metamorphosis** (above)
The butterfly is an insect in which
metamorphosis is "complete". This
means it has four stages: egg (**1**),
larva (caterpillar) (**2**), pupa
(chrysalis) (**3**) and imago (adult)
(**4**). Most types of caterpillar molt
four or five times as they grow.
Adult characteristics are not
acquired until the pupal stage.

© DIAGRAM

# Life spans

**Lengths of lives** All living things die eventually, but some kinds live far longer than others. Certain bacteria may survive a million years or more if frozen or deeply buried under salt. One group of creosote bushes is 11,700 years old. Animals live less long. Here we show how long different animals survive.

## Typical life spans

This diagram shows how long some different kinds of animals are likely to live. Tortoises (see opposite) and humans (see opposite) may be the only well-known types of animals that commonly live for more than 60 years.

**a**  Mayfly ("adult" stage) 1 day
**b**  Mouse 2–3 years
**c**  Trout 5–10 years
**d**  Sheep 10–15 years
**e**  Cat 13–17 years
**f**  Rattlesnake 18 years
**g**  Lion 25 years
**h**  Horse 30 years
**i**  Albatross 33 years
**j**  Hippopotamus 40 years
**k**  Ostrich 50 years
**l**  African elephant 60 years

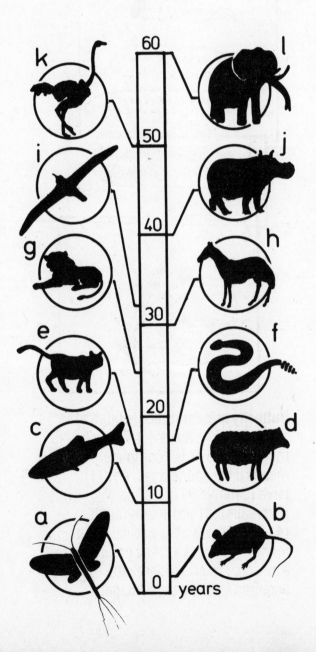

## Long-lived vertebrates

Shown (**1**) to the left of this time scale are record known survival times for different main groups of backboned animals.

**A** Amphibians: Japanese giant salamander 55 years

**B** Birds: Andean condor 70+ years

**C** Fishes: Lake sturgeon 82 years

**D** Mammals: Human 118 + years

**E** Reptiles: Tortoise 152+ years

## Long-lived invertebrates

Shown (**2**) to the right of this time scale are record known longest lives for different kinds of animals without backbones.

**a** Coelenterates: jellyfish 1 year

**b** Chilopods: centipede 10 years

**c** Segmented worms: leech 20 years

**d** Arachnids: spider 28 years

**e** Echinoderms: basketstar 30 years

**f** Insects: beetle 30+ years

**g** Crustaceans: lobster 50+ years

**h** Tapeworms: *Echinococcus* 56 years

**i** Mollusks: clam 150+ years

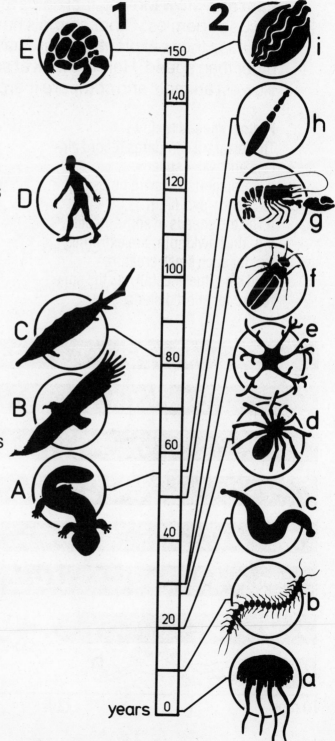

# Speeds

**Fast and slow** Moving fast helps many animals catch prey or escape enemies. Other animals have less need to hurry because they eat plant food and have some means of defense other than speed. Here we look at some of nature's fastest and slowest animals and compare them with man.

**Fastest speeds** (below)
This diagram compares record air, land and water speeds.
**a** The spine-tailed swift holds the record for level flight.
**b** The top speeds of some insects, e.g. the hawkmoth, are extremely fast for such small creatures.
**c** On land, the cheetah has the speed record for short distances.

**d** Fastest for longer distances is the pronghorn antelope.
**e** Included for comparison is man's record speed in a sprint.
**f** The sailfish is believed to be the fastest creature in water.
**g** The leatherback turtle can swim surprisingly quickly.
**h** This fastest human swimming speed was reached only briefly.

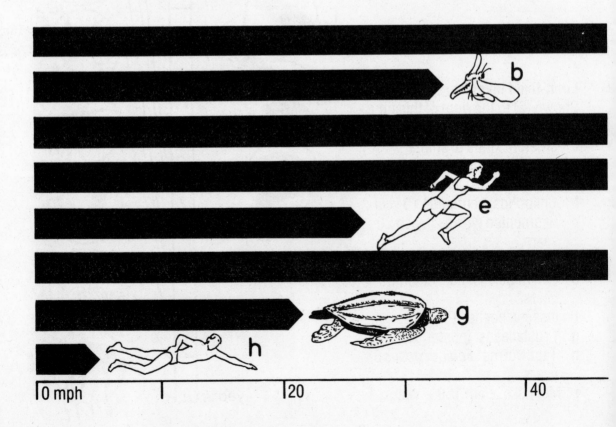

| 0 mph | 20 | 40 |

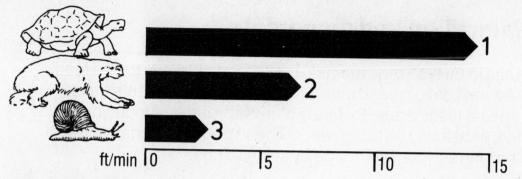

## Slow movers (above)

Some animals move only slowly and often cover only short distances at a time.

**1** A giant tortoise in tests went no faster than 15 ft/min.

**2** A three-toed sloth's average ground speed is only 6.9 ft/min.

**3** A common garden snail can manage only 2.7 ft/min.

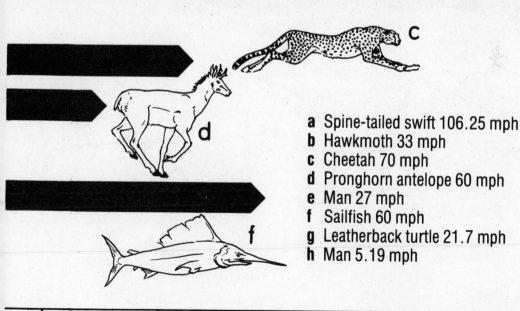

**a** Spine-tailed swift 106.25 mph
**b** Hawkmoth 33 mph
**c** Cheetah 70 mph
**d** Pronghorn antelope 60 mph
**e** Man 27 mph
**f** Sailfish 60 mph
**g** Leatherback turtle 21.7 mph
**h** Man 5.19 mph

©DIAGRAM

60   80

# Migration and dispersal

**Long journeys** Some animals make long journeys to find food, escape cold or reach breeding grounds. Even plants travel – or at least their seeds do. Many plants spread by producing seeds that float away on air or water. These pages describe some of the longest journeys made by living things.

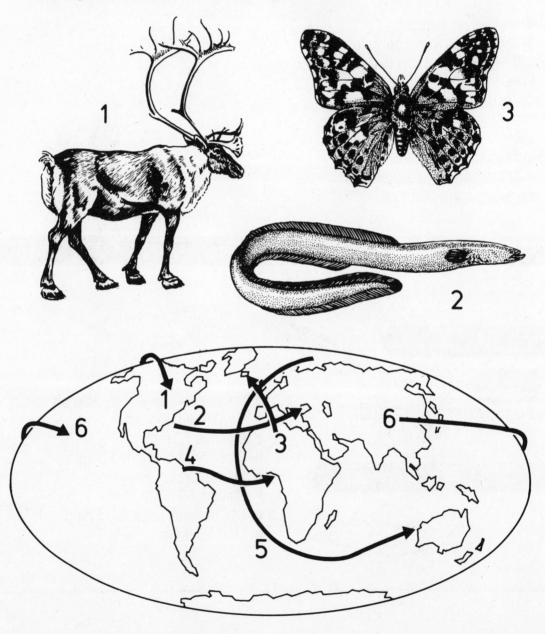

© DIAGRAM

**Record routes** (left)
This map shows some record one-way journeys. Caribou regularly migrate this far – and go back again. All the other journeys shown are unusually long.
**1** Mammals: caribou migrate south from Arctic North America.
**2** Fish: eels swim from the Sargasso Sea to the Black Sea.
**3** Insects: painted lady butterflies fly from North Africa to Iceland.
**4** Reptiles: a green turtle swam from South America to Africa.
**5** Birds: an Arctic tern flew from Arctic Russia to Australia.
**6** Plants: a seed from a plant in the daisy family was blown from Asia to Hawaii.

**Record distances**
Listed here are the distances traveled in some record journeys survived by animals and plants. Only the distances for caribou and whales are typical. All others are for exceptional journeys.
Land mammal: caribou 700 mi
Sea mammal: gray whale 5,600 mi
Flying mammal: bat 1,500 mi
Bird: Arctic tern 14,000 mi
Reptile: green turtle 3,700 mi
Amphibian: toad 2 mi
Fish: eel 5,200 mi
Insects: butterfly 4,000 mi
Plant: windblown seeds of a plant in the daisy family 4,000 mi
Plant: seaborne seeds of some coconut palms 3,000 mi

# Life levels

**The biosphere** Living things survive only where there is enough air, water, food and warmth. Earth's oceans, land surface and lower atmosphere are home to living things and are known as the biosphere, from the Greek word *bios* meaning life. Only the land surface and the top 500 ft of oceans are densely populated.

**Highest to lowest** (below)
This diagram compares the highest and the lowest points where animals have been seen with the highest and the deepest known points on Earth.
1 Highest creature 27,077ft
2 Lowest creature −35,860ft
A Highest land, Mt Everest 29,002ft
B Sea level 0ft
C Greatest ocean depth, Marianas Trench 36,198ft

**Highest life** (right)
Here we show the highest levels at which six kinds of living things have been observed. The bird was flying. The others were on mountainsides.
a Bird: whooper swan 27,077ft
b Amphibian: toad 26,000ft
c Arthropod: spider 22,000ft
d Flowering plant: 20,130ft
e Mammal: yak 20,000ft
f Reptile: lizard 18,100ft

**Lowest life** (right)
These are the lowest levels at which the following living things have been observed.
g Reptile: marine iguana −33ft
h Bird: emperor penguin −872ft
i Plant: blue-green alga −1,300ft
j Mammal: sperm whale −7,400ft
k Arthropod: shrimp −35,800ft
l Fish: a flatfish −35,800ft

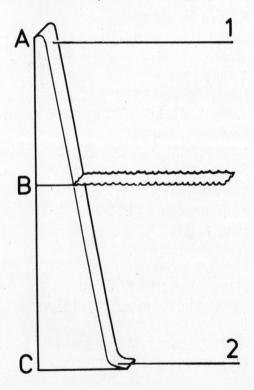

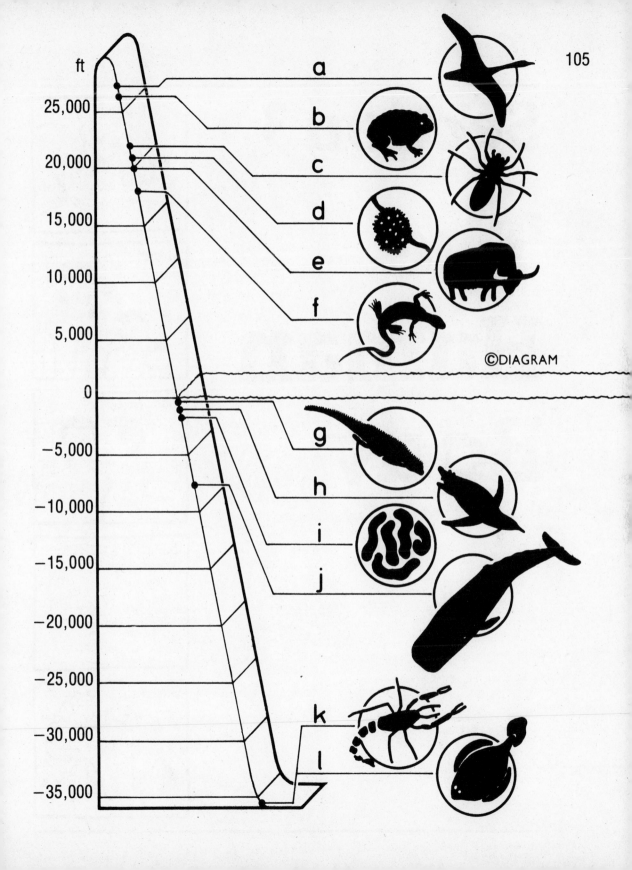

©DIAGRAM

# Section 3

# The Human Body

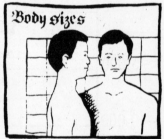

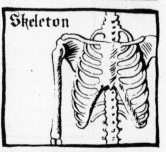

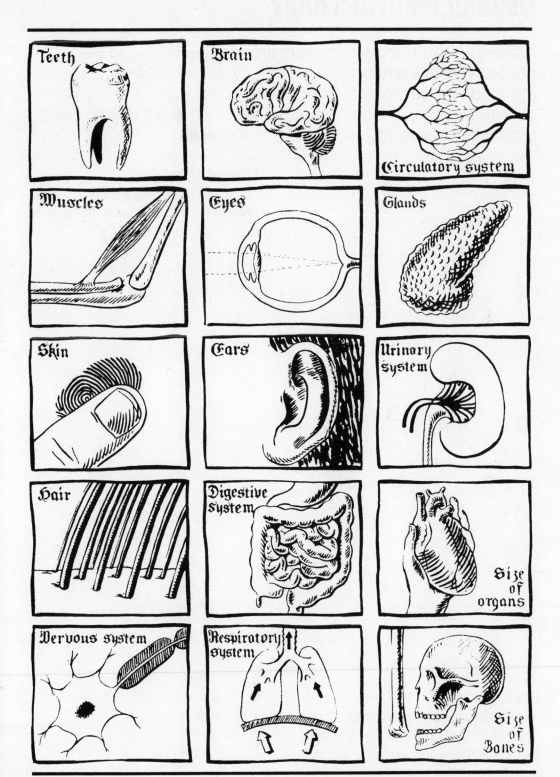

# Development of a baby

**A new human** The development process leading up to the birth of a baby begins when a sperm from the father fertilizes an egg produced by the mother. A human pregnancy typically lasts 266 days (38 weeks), but doctors usually count it as we do here, with fertilization in weeks 2-3 and birth at 40 weeks.

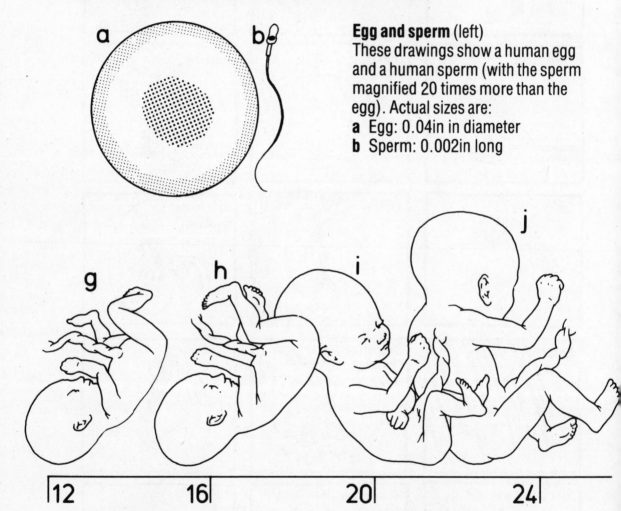

**Egg and sperm** (left)
These drawings show a human egg and a human sperm (with the sperm magnified 20 times more than the egg). Actual sizes are:
**a** Egg: 0.04in in diameter
**b** Sperm: 0.002in long

**Weeks 12 to 40**
These drawings (all to the same scale) show a baby's development up to the usual time of birth. Average lengths and weights are:

**g** 12 weeks: 3.6in; 0.5oz
**h** 16 weeks: 7.2in; 3.9oz
**i** 20 weeks: 10in; 11.9oz
**j** 24 weeks: 13.2in; 1lb 5oz

**Weeks 5 to 11** (right)
These drawings (not to scale) show some early stages in a baby's development. Actual sizes are:

**c** 5 weeks: 0.08in long
**d** 7 weeks: 0.5in long
**e** 9 weeks: 1.2in long
**f** 11 weeks: 2.2in long

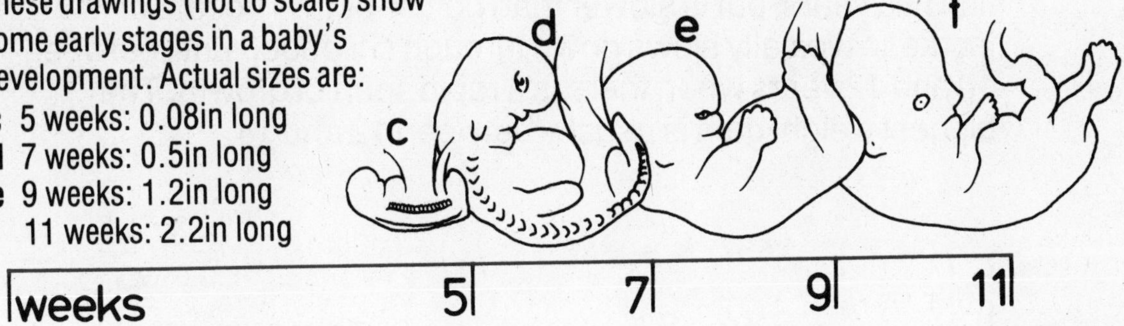

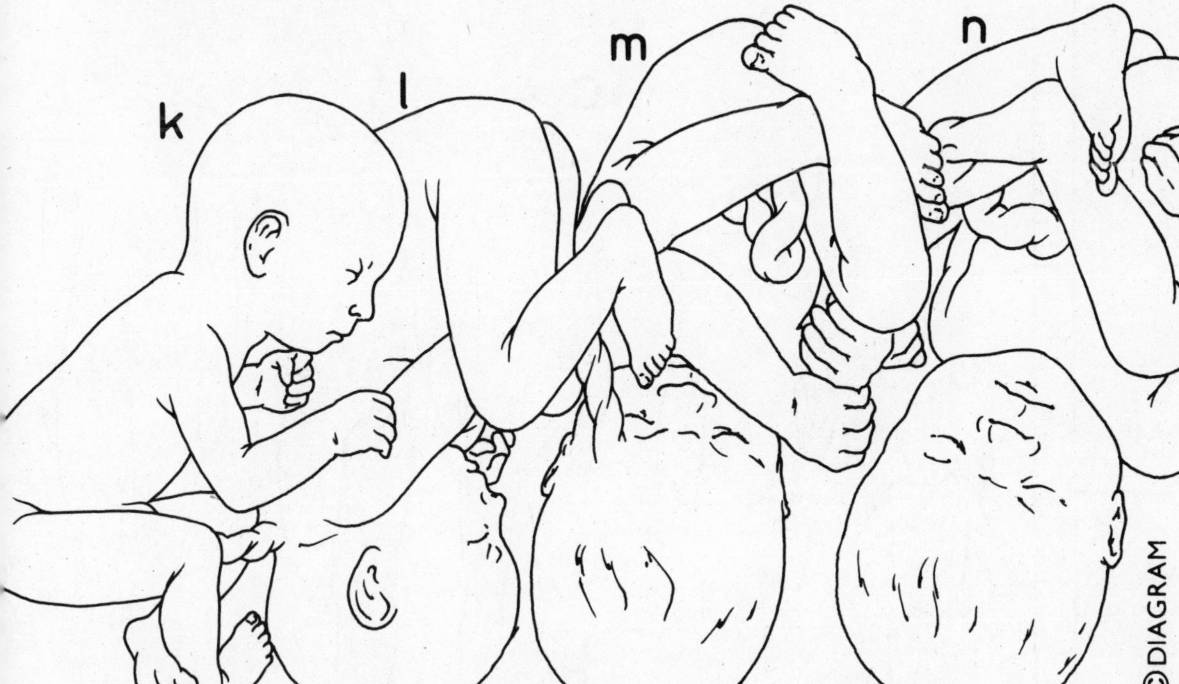

weeks    5    7    9    11

28    32    36    40

**k** 28 weeks; 15.2in; 2lb
**l** 32 weeks; 17.2in; 3lb 14oz
**m** 36 weeks; 18.4in; 5lb 3oz
**n** 40 weeks; 20.2in; 7lb 7oz

**Pre-birth growth rate**
In the last 12 weeks before birth at week 40, a baby's length typically increases by about 34% and its weight by about 250%.

©DIAGRAM

# Growth (1)

**Girls' growth patterns** Height increase in girls is very fast in the first two years, but is slower than before birth. The rate of increase typically slows down through childhood until between 10 and 12 years when there is a rapid spurt of growth. The biggest weight gain is usually between 12 and 14.

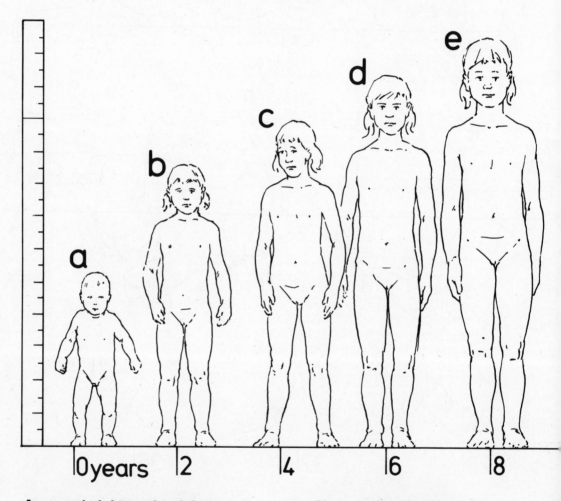

**Average heights and weights**
Here we give average heights and weights for girls of different ages. Wide variations in growth rates are usually quite normal.

a Birth: 1ft 8in; 7lb 7oz
b 2 years: 2ft 10in; 27lb
c 4 years: 3ft 4.5in; 35lb 12oz
d 6 years: 3ft 9in; 46lb 6oz
e 8 years: 4ft 3in; 58lb 1oz

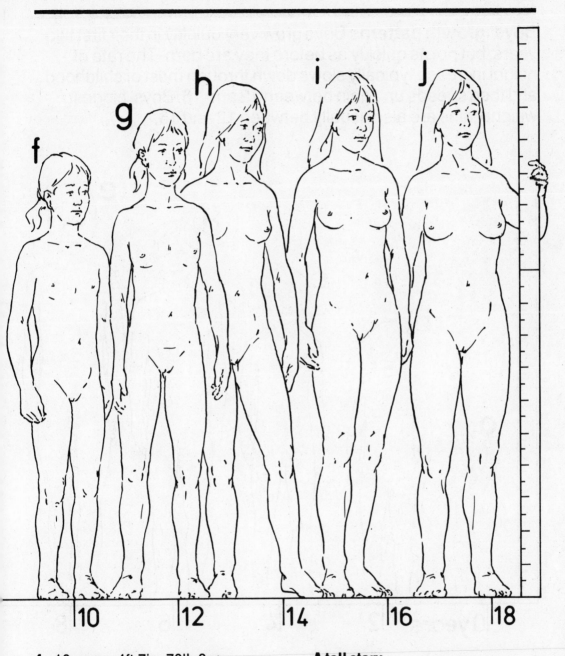

f    g    h    i    j

10    12    14    16    18

**f**   10 years: 4ft 7in; 70lb 3oz
**g**   12 years: 4ft 11in; 87lb 6oz
**h**   14 years: 5ft 4in; 108lb 3oz
**i**   16 years: 5ft 5in; 116lb 12oz
**j**   18 years: 5ft 5in; 116lb 14oz

**A tall story**
In the two years after birth a girl's height increases by 73%. If growth continued at this rate she would be 230ft tall at age 18!

©DIAGRAM

**Growth (2)**

**Boys' growth patterns** Boys grow very quickly in their first two years, but not as quickly as before they are born. The rate of height increase typically slows down through most of childhood and then speeds up again between 12 and 16. Boys' biggest weight gains are also usually between 12 and 16.

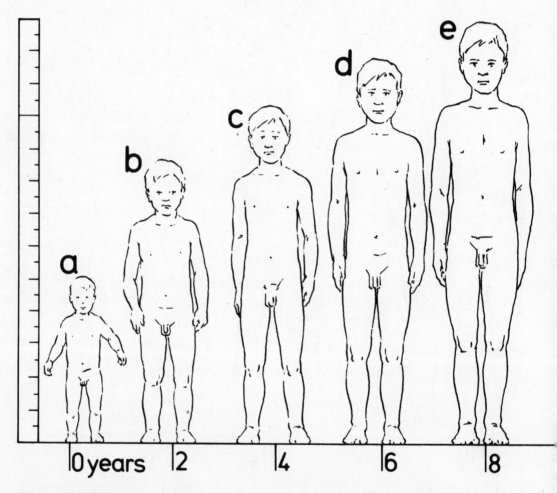

0 years    2    4    6    8

**Average heights and weights**
Here we give average heights and weights for boys of different ages. Wide variations in growth rates are usually quite normal.

**a** Birth: 1ft 8in; 7lb 7oz
**b** 2 years: 2ft 10.5in; 27lb 13oz
**c** 4 years: 3ft 4.5in; 36lb 6oz
**d** 6 years: 3ft 9in; 48lb 3oz
**e** 8 years: 4ft 3.5in; 60lb 1oz

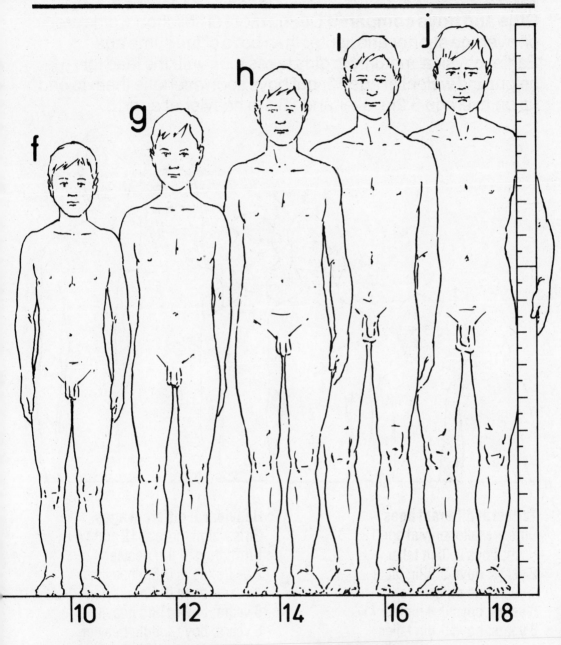

10    12    14    16    18

**f**  10 years: 4ft 7in; 71lb 13oz
**g**  12 years: 4ft 11in; 85lb 6oz
**h**  14 years: 5ft 2.5in; 107lb 6oz
**i**  16 years: 5ft 8in; 129lb 6oz
**j**  18 years: 5ft 9in; 142lb 14oz

**A weighty problem**
From birth to 2 years a boy's weight increases by 271%. If this rate of increase continued he would weigh over 990,000lb at age 18!

**Growth (3)**

**Girls and boys compared** During most of childhood, girls are on average shorter and lighter than boys of the same age. Earlier physical maturity in girls takes them into the lead for height and weight at age 12, but boys soon overtake them to end up on average 5.2in taller and 23.1lb heavier at age 18.

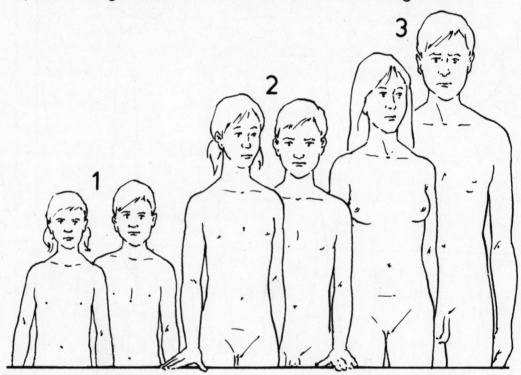

**Tallest at different ages**
Girls are taller only at age 12.
Birth: boys 0.08in taller
2 years: boys 0.32in taller
4 years: no difference
6 years: boys 0.8in taller (**1**)
8 years: boys 0.8in taller
10 years: boys 0.4in taller
12 years: girls 0.8in taller (**2**)
14 years: boys 1.2in taller
16 years: boys 4in taller
18 years: boys 5.2in taller (**3**)

**Heaviest at different ages**
Girls weigh more at 12 and 14.
Birth: boys 0.1lb heavier
2 years: boys 0.6lb heavier
4 years: boys 0.4lb heavier
6 years: boys 1.8lb heavier
8 years: boys 1.98lb heavier
10 years: boys 1.5lb heavier
12 years: girls 3lb heavier
14 years: girls 0.9lb heavier
16 years: boys 12.5lb heavier
18 years: boys 23.1lb heavier

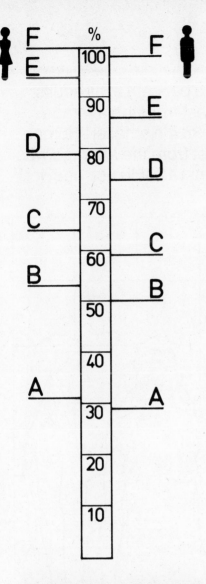

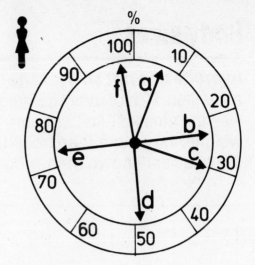

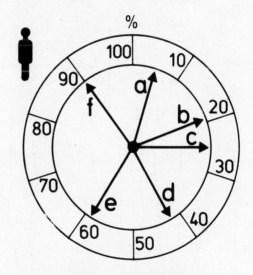

## Percentages of adult height
Shown above and listed below are
typical percentages of adult height
reached by girls and boys of
different ages.

| | Age | Girls | Boys |
|---|---|---|---|
| **A** | Birth | 31% | 29% |
| **B** | 2 years | 53% | 50% |
| **C** | 4 years | 64% | 59% |
| **D** | 8 years | 79% | 74% |
| **E** | 12 years | 94% | 86% |
| **F** | 16 years | 100% | 98% |

## Percentages of adult weight
These two diagrams and the list
below show percentages of adult
weight typically reached by children
of different ages.

| | Age | Girls | Boys |
|---|---|---|---|
| **a** | Birth | 6% | 5% |
| **b** | 2 years | 23% | 19% |
| **c** | 4 years | 30% | 25% |
| **d** | 8 years | 49% | 42% |
| **e** | 12 years | 73% | 59% |
| **f** | 16 years | 98% | 90% |

# Body sizes

**Average and not so average** Ninety-five per cent of all adults are within 10in of average height. Farthest from the average was the smallest-known man, who was 3ft 4in smaller. Human weights vary more than heights. Farthest from the average was the heaviest-known man, who was at least 1235lb 5oz heavier!

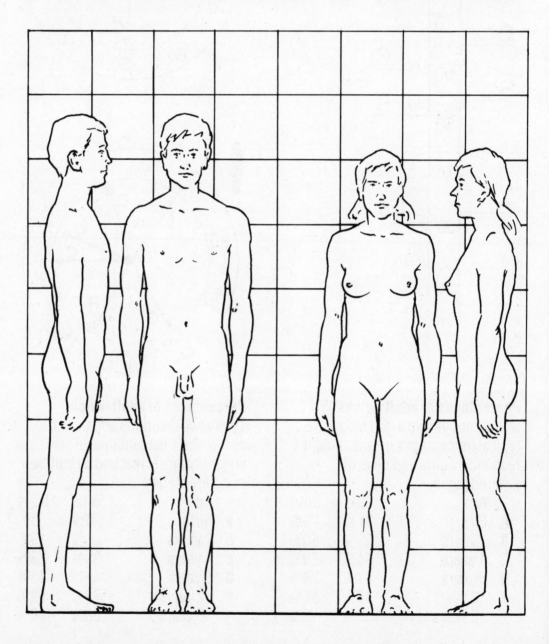

## Shapes and sizes (opposite page)

A man and a woman of average height and weight and with all other measurements of average size are here drawn in front of a grid showing 6in squares.

|           | Man     | Woman   |
|-----------|---------|---------|
| Height    | 5ft 9in | 5ft 3¾in |
| Weight    | 162lb   | 135lb   |
| Chest/bust | 38¾in  | 35½in   |
| Waist     | 31¾in   | 29¼in   |
| Hips      | 37¾in   | 38in    |

## Tall and short (right)

A man and woman of average height are here drawn to the same scale as the tallest-known man and woman and the shortest-known man and woman.

**a** Tallest man: 8ft 11in
**b** Tallest woman: 7ft 11in
**c** Average man: 5ft 9in
**d** Average woman: 5ft 3¾in
**e** Shortest man: 2ft 2½in
**f** Shortest woman: 1ft 11in

## Human heavyweights

The heaviest-known man was estimated by his doctor to have reached a weight in excess of 1,397lb – more than 8½ times the average man's 162lb.

The heaviest-known woman is believed to have weighed about 880lb – roughly 6½ times the average woman's weight of 135lb.

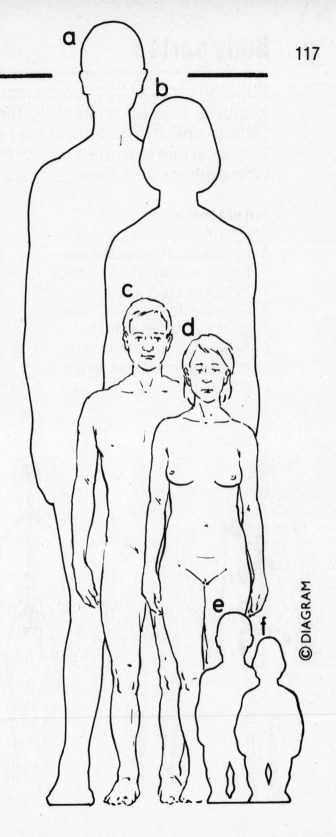

© DIAGRAM

# Body parts

**Building blocks** Chemical elements combine in living things to form cells, the basic units of life. Similar cells designed to perform similar tasks form tissues such as skin, muscle or bone. Tissues in turn form organs such as the brain, heart or lungs. Where organs work together these form body systems.

**Part of a human cell** (right)
Only the main features are shown.
A   Cytoplasm: a transparent jelly-like substance that is the basic living material of all cells
B   Cell membrane: a "skin" that gives each cell its shape
C   Nucleus: this is denser than the cytoplasm and acts as the cell's control center

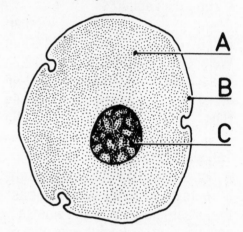

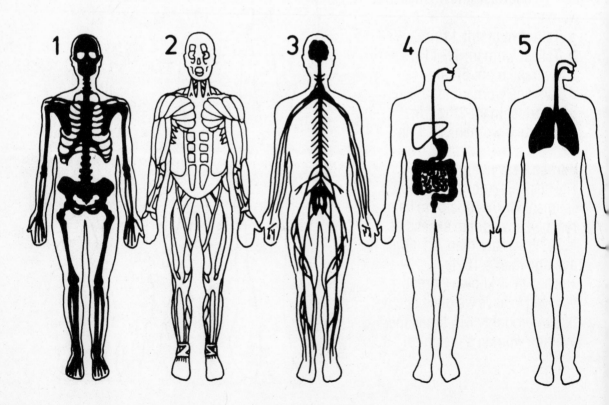

## Body systems (below)

These diagrams show the main body systems of humans. More facts and figures about these systems appear later in this book.

1 Skeletal system: this provides the body's framework of bones
2 Muscular system: this makes it possible for different parts of the body to move
3 Nervous system: consisting of brain, spinal cord and nerves, this transmits vital messages around the body
4 Digestive system: this processes food for the body's use and gets rid of solid waste
5 Respiratory system: this takes oxygen into the body and gets rid of waste carbon dioxide
6 Circulatory system: consisting of the heart, blood vessels and blood, this transports various substances around the body
7 Endocrine system: this consists of several different glands that regulate body functions
8 Urinary system: this gets rid of body wastes in the fluid called urine
9 Reproductive systems of the male (**a**) and female (**b**): these make babies possible

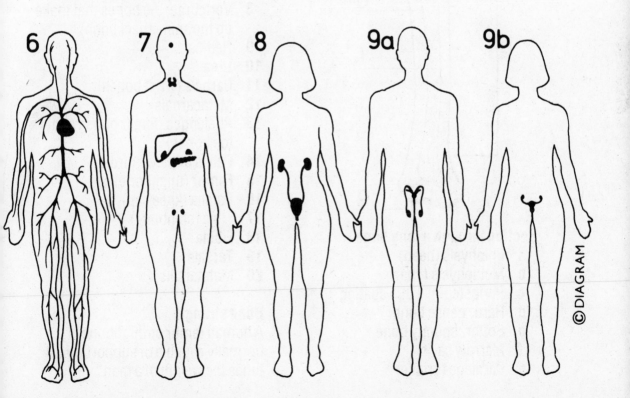

©DIAGRAM

# Skeleton (1)

**Human body frame** The functions of the skeleton are: to give the body its overall shape and so keep the body organs in their correct positions; to protect delicate organs such as the brain, heart and lungs; to move about when acted upon by muscles; to produce blood cells in the marrow of some bones.

## Types of bones

Bones are classified by shape into long bones (e.g. thighbone), short bones (e.g. in the wrist), flat bones (e.g. shoulder blade) and irregular bones (e.g. jawbone).

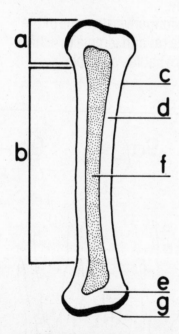

## Section through a long bone
**a** Epiphysis (head)
**b** Metaphysis (shaft)
**c** Periosteum: a thin coating
**d** Hard, dense bone
**e** Softer, spongy bone
**f** Marrow cavity
**g** Cartilage (gristle)

## Bones and their names

Identified right and listed below are some important human bones. Where a bone has a common name it is listed after the medical name.

1  Cranium (skull)
2  Mandible (jawbone)
3  Clavicle (collarbone)
4  Scapula (shoulder blade)
5  Sternum (breastbone)
6  Ribs
7  Humerus
8  Vertebrae: the bones that make up the spine (backbone)
9  Radius
10  Ulna
11  Carpals (wrist bones)
12  Metacarpals
13  Phalanges (finger bones and toe bones)
14  Pelvis or pelvic girdle
15  Femur (thighbone)
16  Patella (knee cap)
17  Tibia (shinbone)
18  Fibula
19  Tarsals
20  Metatarsals

## Bone strength

A human femur or thighbone is normally capable of supporting 30 times the weight of a man.

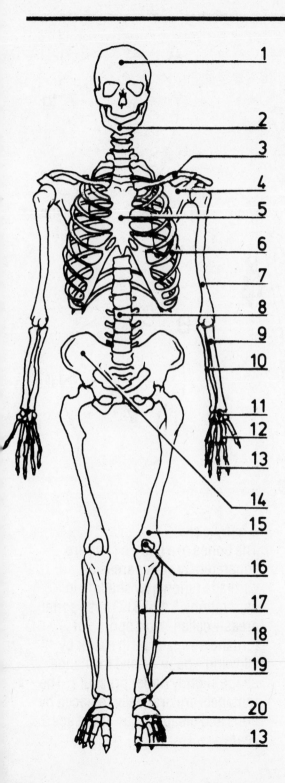

1
2
3
4
5
6
7
8
9
10
11
12
13
14
15
16
17
18
19
20
13

### Smallest bone

The smallest bone in the human body is the stapes or stirrup bone in the ear. This tiny bone is only 0.1–0.14 in long.

### Human backbone

This is made up of:
seven cervical (neck) vertebrae;
twelve thoracic (chest) vertebrae;
five lumbar vertebrae;
five sacral vertebrae, fused to make one bone called the sacrum;
four coccygeal vertebrae, fused to form the coccyx or tailbone.

### Human ribs

Most people have 12 pairs of ribs:
seven pairs of "true" ribs, attached to the spine and to the sternum;
five pairs of "false" ribs, which are not attached to the sternum.

### Funny bone

The "funny bone" is in fact only part of a bone. Its medical name is the olecranon process and it projects from the top of the ulna.

### Longest bone

The longest human bone is the femur, which is about 19.2in long in a man of average height (5ft 9in).

### Human feet

An adult has a total of 52 bones in the feet – just over a quarter of all the bones in the body.

©DIAGRAM

# Skeleton (2)

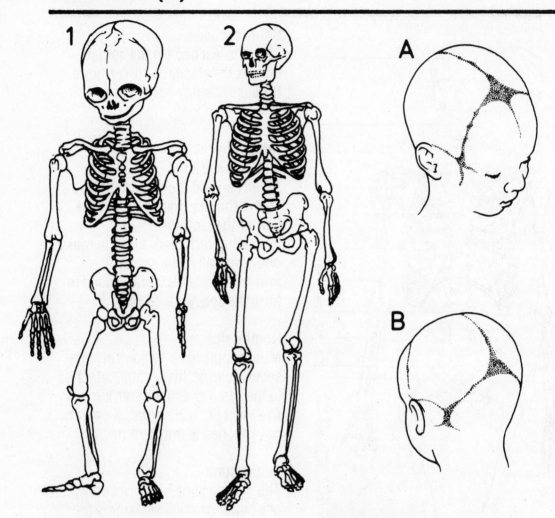

## A changing skeleton

Here we show the skeletons of a newborn baby boy (**1**) and of an adult man (**2**). Most adults have 206 bones, but a newborn baby has 330. As bones lengthen during childhood some of them join together to give fewer bones in total. Growth also changes body proportions. Compared to an adult, a baby has a large head, short neck, round chest and short limbs.

## A baby's skull

The bones of a baby's skull are separated by softer areas of cartilage (shown by shading in illustrations **A** and **B**). These softer areas – called ''soft spots'' or fontanels – make birth easier by allowing a baby's head to change shape slightly under pressure. The fontanels are gradually replaced by bone and disappear by about age 2 years.

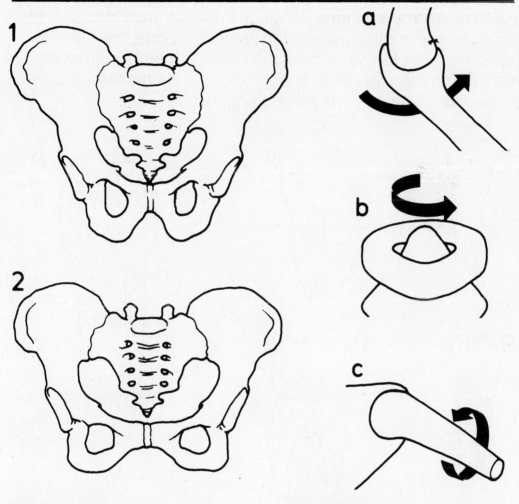

## Male or female

The best way of identifying the sex of a skeleton is from the pelvis. Here we show the pelvis of a man (**1**) and a woman (**2**). A woman's pelvis is wider than a man's and has a larger central hole (pelvic cavity). These differences help a woman carry an unborn baby and make it easier for the baby to pass through the pelvic cavity to be born.

## Types of joints

A joint is where two bones meet. Joints are either immovable (not allowing movement between bones, e.g. in the skull) or movable. Kinds of movable joints include:
**a** hinge, e.g. elbow and knee, moving backward and forward;
**b** pivot, e.g. in the neck, allowing the head to turn;
**c** ball and socket, e.g. shoulder, allowing most movement of all.

©DIAGRAM

**Teeth and body systems** Although the teeth grow from sockets in the jaw and contain tissue that resembles bone, they are not part of the skeleton. In terms of their development, teeth have more in common with skin than with bone. In terms of the work they do, teeth belong in the digestive system.

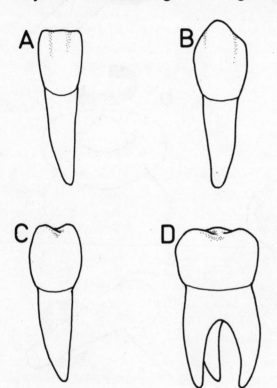

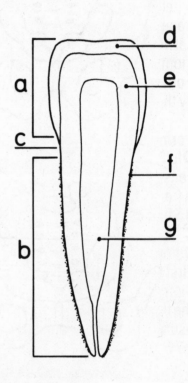

**Types of teeth**

Humans have four basic kinds of teeth designed to meet different eating requirements.

**A**  Incisors: chisel-shaped teeth for cutting food
**B**  Canines: pointed teeth for grasping and tearing food
**C**  Premolars: grooved teeth for slicing and grinding food
**D**  Molars: large, grooved teeth for grinding food

**Structure of a tooth**

**a**  Crown: jutting from the jaw
**b**  Root: embedded in the jaw
**c**  Neck: between crown and root
**d**  Enamel: covering the crown, the hardest body substance
**e**  Dentine: the main bulk of the tooth, similar to bone
**f**  Cementum: a hard, rough coating around the root
**g**  Pulp: soft tissue containing nerves and blood vessels

## Temporary teeth (1)

These are also called deciduous or milk teeth. A full set is made up of 20 teeth:

**A** eight incisors;
**B** four canines;
**D** eight molars.

Appearing in stages, usually between the ages of 6 and 30 months, these teeth are usually lost from age 7-12 years to be replaced by the permanent teeth.

## Permanent teeth (2)

A full set of permanent or adult teeth consists of 32 teeth:

**A** eight incisors;
**B** four canines;
**C** eight premolars;
**D** twelve molars.

First to appear are the first (front) molars, at age 6-7 years. Last are the third molars, or wisdom teeth, usually between the ages of 17 and 25 years.

## Tooth decay

A survey of American schoolchildren in 1980 revealed that, by the ninth year, each child had, on average, one tooth that was decayed, filled or extracted (taken out). Statistics show that the average number of decayed, filled or missing teeth is: for 5-year-olds, 0.07; for 10-year-olds, 1.69; and for 15-year-olds, 4.94.

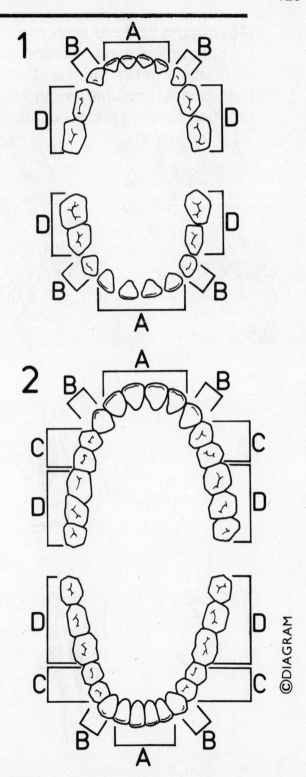

©DIAGRAM

**Muscles**

**Moving the body** All body movements are brought about by the contraction and relaxation of muscles. When a muscle contracts, it gets shorter and fatter. When it relaxes, it goes back to its longest possible length. Muscles attached to bones produce bending and straightening movements at the joints.

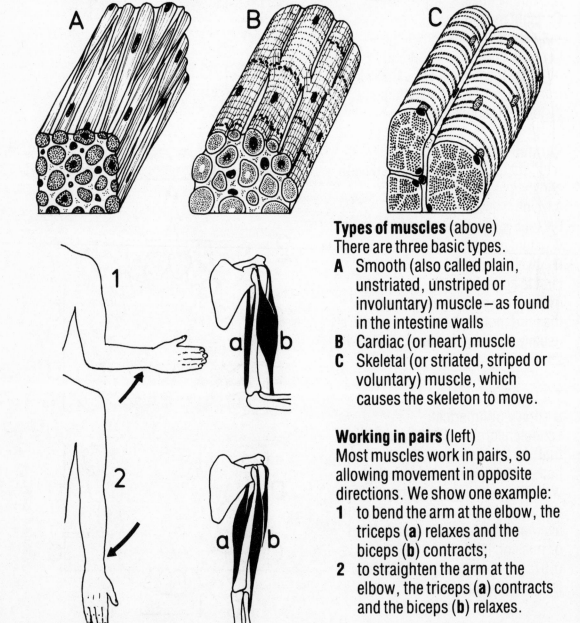

**Types of muscles** (above)
There are three basic types.

**A** Smooth (also called plain, unstriated, unstriped or involuntary) muscle – as found in the intestine walls

**B** Cardiac (or heart) muscle

**C** Skeletal (or striated, striped or voluntary) muscle, which causes the skeleton to move.

**Working in pairs** (left)
Most muscles work in pairs, so allowing movement in opposite directions. We show one example:

**1** to bend the arm at the elbow, the triceps (**a**) relaxes and the biceps (**b**) contracts;

**2** to straighten the arm at the elbow, the triceps (**a**) contracts and the biceps (**b**) relaxes.

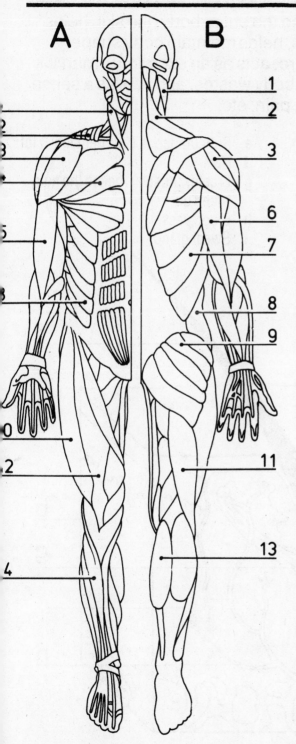

**A** **B**

## Some important muscles (left)

From the front (**A**) and back (**B**).

1 Sternomastoid
2 Trapezius
3 Deltoid
4 Pectoralis major
5 Biceps
6 Triceps
7 Latissimus dorsi
8 External oblique
9 Gluteus maximus
10 Vastus externus
11 Biceps femoris
12 Rectus femoris
13 Gastrocnemius
14 Tibialis anterior

## Number and weight

There are about 650 muscles in the human body. Muscles account for about 42% of a man's body weight and about 36% of a woman's.

## Peak strength

Human muscle strength typically increases up to about age 25 and then starts to decline.

## Largest muscle

The largest muscle in the human body is the gluteus maximus or buttock muscle.

## Smallest muscle

The smallest human muscle is the stapedius, which moves the stapes (a tiny bone in the ear). This muscle is less than 0.5in long.

© DIAGRAM

**Skin**

**Functions of the skin** Covering the entire body, the skin helps protect delicate internal organs, helps maintain body shape, helps regulate body temperature, acts as an excretory organ getting rid of excess water and body wastes, and acts as a sense organ responsive to heat, cold, pain, etc.

**Skin cross section** (below)
This diagram shows a typical piece of skin.

**a** Epidermis: outer skin layer, with dead cells on the outside and living ones below
**b** Dermis: inner skin layer
**c** Sebaceous (grease) gland
**d** Nerve

**e** Subcutaneous ("under skin") fat
**f** Hair
**g** Erector muscle: makes the hair stand up
**h** Blood vessel
**i** Sweat gland

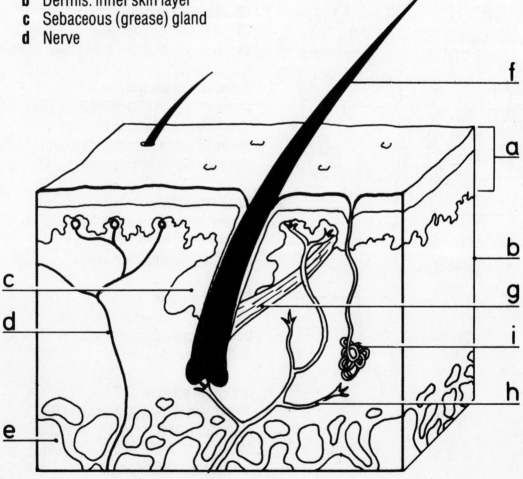

## Skin area (right)
An average man has roughly 19.4 square feet of skin (shown here by a rectangle drawn to the same scale as the man).
An average woman has roughly 17.2 square feet of skin (up to the dotted line in our diagram).

## Skin thickness
Skin varies in thickness from about 0.24in thick on the soles of the feet to only about 0.02in on the eyelids. Over most of the body it is 0.04–0.08in thick.

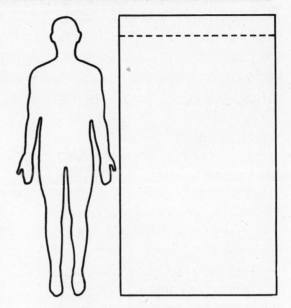

## Skin color
A person's skin takes its color partly from blood going through it and partly from various colored substances made by special skin cells. Most important of these substances is melanin, a brown pigment. How much melanin a person produces depends on heredity and on exposure to sunlight.

## Fingerprints (below)
No two people have an identical set of fingerprints. This makes it possible for the police to use them for identification purposes. Here we show five basic types of fingerprint pattern.

1 Low arch  4 Whorl (circle)
2 Tented arch  5 Mixed
3 Loop

©DIAGRAM

# Hair

**Functions of hair** Although hair is less important to humans than to most other mammals, it does play some part in keeping the body warm. This is especially true of the hairs on the head. A layer of stationary air becomes trapped between the hairs and provides the body with an insulating cover.

## Where hair grows

In humans, hair grows from all skin areas except from the lips, the soles of the feet and the palms of the hands. The densest areas of hair are the top and back of the head, the eyebrows and eyelashes, and certain areas of the body including the beard and moustache areas, the underarms and the pubic (lower trunk) areas which develop coarse hair as a child grows into an adult.

## Parts of a hair (right)

1 Shaft: hair above the skin
2 Root: hair embedded in skin
3 Follicle: a pit in the skin from which the hair grows
4 Papilla: the growth point
5 Medulla: hollow central core
6 Cortex: main part of the hair
7 Cuticle: a hard coating
8 Sebaceous (grease) gland
9 Erector muscle: raises the hair
10 Blood vessel
11 Nerve

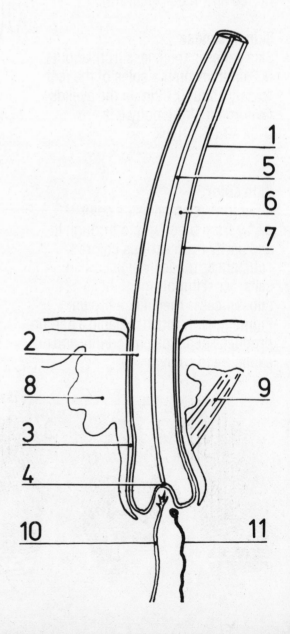

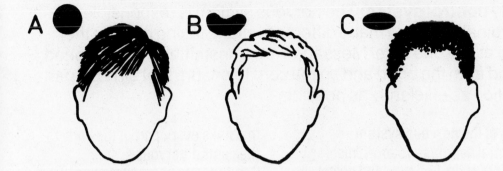

## Hairs on the head
Most people have 100,000-200,000 hairs on their scalps. The 100 or so scalp hairs lost each day are usually replaced by new ones. The growth rate for scalp hairs is about 0.4in a month, but not all of them are growing at any one time.

## Hair color
A person's hair takes its color from substances produced by special cells in the papillae. As many people get older these cells stop producing pigment. New hair growing from the follicles now appears transparent or white.

## Straight, wavy or curly (above)
Whether a person's hair is naturally straight, wavy or curly depends on the cross-sectional shape of the follicles.
**A** Round: naturally straight
**B** Kidney-shaped: naturally wavy
**C** Oval: naturally curly

## Balding (below)
Many men inherit a tendency to become bald in the following way.
**1** Loss of hair from temples
**2** Further hair loss from temples and loss from crown
**3** Complete loss of hair from crown and front of head

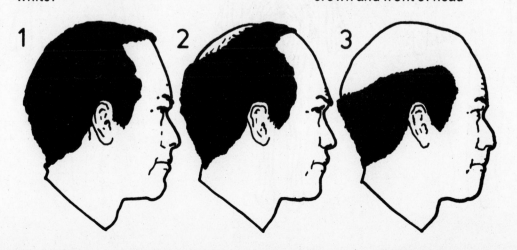

© DIAGRAM

**Nervous system**

**Body control system** The nervous system is responsible for coordinating all the many different actions taking place in the body at any one time. Messages are transmitted at great speed to and from the brain and spinal cord to ensure that all body parts function as efficiently as possible.

**Parts of the nervous system**
**A** Central nervous system. This consists of the brain (**a**) and spinal cord (**b**). It is the control center for all conscious and unconscious body actions.
**B** Peripheral nervous system. This is a complex network of nerves that links every part of the body to the central nervous system.
**C** Autonomic nervous system. This directs unconscious body actions such as heartbeat, breathing, digestion and blinking.

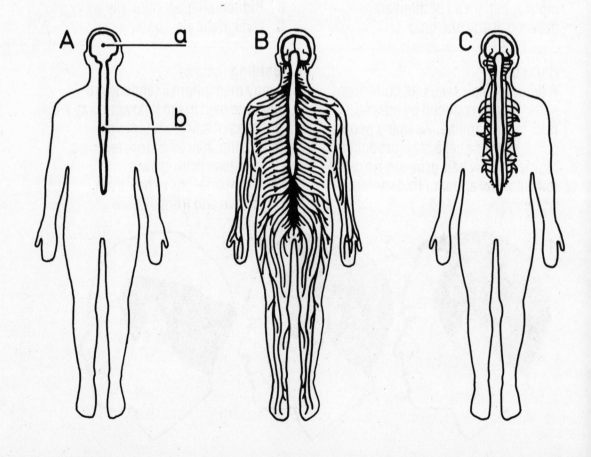

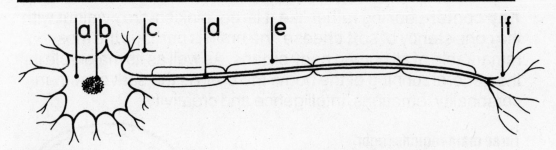

## Nerve cells

These vary in size and shape according to the job they do. Cells taking information to the central nervous system are called sensory neurons: cells taking information away from it are called motor neurons.

## Parts of a motor neuron (above)

**a** Cell body
**b** Nucleus
**c** Dendrites: these gather information into the cell
**d** Axon: this sends messages out
**e** Sheath: a fatty covering
**f** Terminal (end) processes

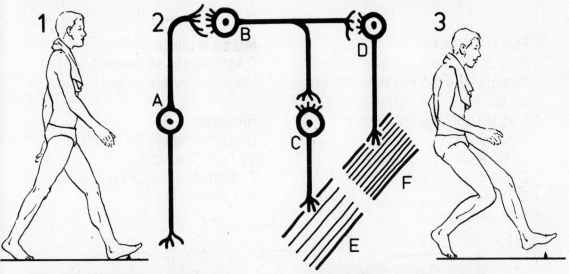

## Nerve cells in action (above)

As shown here, nerve cells work together to regulate body actions.
**1** The foot touches a sharp nail.
**2** Nerve cell **A** (a sensory neuron with dendrites in the skin of the foot) sends a warning signal to nerve cell **B** (situated in the central nervous system). Nerve cell **B** registers pain and instantly passes this information to nerve cells **C** and **D** (motor neurons ending in the leg muscles). Nerve cells **C** and **D** instruct leg muscles **E** and **F** to relax or contract.
**3** The foot is moved from the nail.

© DIAGRAM

# Brain

**Key center** Looking rather like a large, pinkish-gray walnut with the consistency of soft cheese, the brain is perhaps the most remarkable of all human body organs. As well as its major role in the general running of the body, the brain is the seat of human personality, emotions, intelligence and creativity.

**Three main regions** (right)
**A** Forebrain: where memory and intelligence are based
**B** Midbrain: which works mainly as a relay station for messages to and from the brain
**C** Hindbrain: which coordinates complex body movements, especially of arms and legs

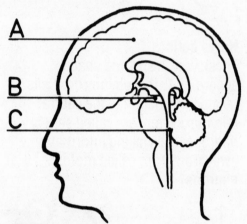

**Forebrain** (below)
Diagram **A** shows a human brain cut through the middle to show parts of the forebrain. The corpus callosum links the right and left cerebral hemispheres.
1 Cerebral hemisphere
2 Corpus callosum
3 Thalamus
4 Hypothalamus

**Midbrain** (below)
Diagram **B** shows the midbrain (the top part of the brainstem, **5**).

**Hindbrain**
Diagram **C** shows the hindbrain.
6 Pons (brainstem)
7 Medulla oblongata (brainstem)
8 Cerebellum

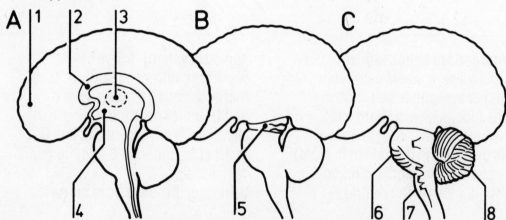

## Left and right halves
The left half of the brain controls the right side of the body. The right half of the brain controls the left side of the body.

## Average brain size (right)
Deep surface wrinkles give the human brain a large surface area compared to its volume of 85.4 cu.in. This diagram shows a human brain (from above) and two rectangles representing the brain's visible surface area (**A**) and its total surface area of 324 sq.in with all the wrinkles ironed out (**B**).

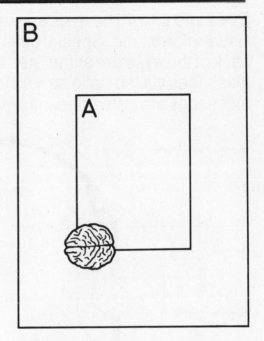

● = 0.5lb

a ●●
b ●●●●●
c ●●●●●●
d ●●●●●●

## Average brain weight (right)
A baby's brain nearly triples in weight in the first year. Men's brains are usually heavier than women's, but women's brains form a bigger percentage of body weight.
a  Newborn 12.25oz
b  12-month-old 2.2lb
c  Adult male 3lb (1.9%)
d  Adult female 2.8lb (2.1%)

## Brain work
Shown on this illustration of the left side of a human brain are areas involved with the following important functions.
1  Movement of body parts
2  Receiving body sensations
3  Speech
4  Hearing
5  Sight

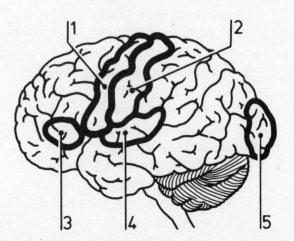

©DIAGRAM

# Eyes

**Eyes and sight** The eyes are sense organs designed to receive visual information. Special cells (called rods and cones) at the back of the eyes are stimulated by rays of light into sending messages via the optic nerves to the brain. In the brain these messages are converted into a visual picture.

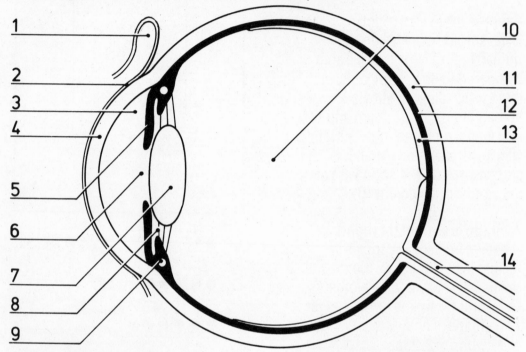

### Section through an eye

1 Lachrymal (tear) gland: this produces tears to wash the eye
2 Conjunctiva: a thin protective membrane (tissue layer)
3 Aqueous humor: watery liquid
4 Cornea: a transparent disc at the front of the eyeball
5 Iris: a colored disc that adjusts the size of the pupil
6 Pupil: a hole in the iris through which light passes
7 Lens: soft and transparent, this focuses images in the eye

8 Suspensory ligaments: these hold the lens in place
9 Ciliary muscles: these alter the shape of the lens
10 Vitreous humor: transparent jelly-like substance
11 Sclera: tough outer layer
12 Choroid layer: this very dark layer stops light being reflected around the eye
13 Retina: light-sensitive layer where images are received
14 Optic nerve: this sends visual information to the brain

**Front view of an eye** (right)
**a** Eyelid: protects the eye
**b** Lashes: also protect the eye
**c** Tear duct: drains away tears
**d** Pupil **e** Iris **f** White

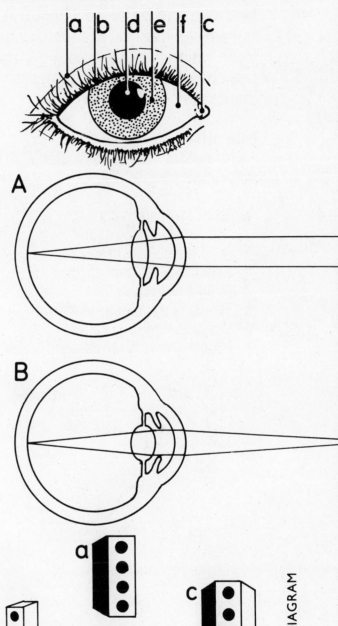

**Focusing** (right)
These diagrams show how the lens focuses far and near objects.
**A** Light rays from a distant object are almost parallel when they reach the eye. The lens needs to bend them only slightly to focus them on the retina.
**B** Rays from a near object are diverging (moving apart) when they reach the eye. The lens must bulge and so become stronger to bring them into focus.

**Composite view** (below)
As this diagram shows, the same object is seen slightly differently by the left eye (**a**) and the right eye (**b**). The brain combines these two images into a composite view (**c**).

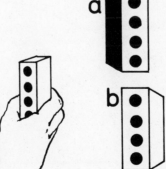

©DIAGRAM

# Ears

**Hearing and balance** The ears are sense organs responsible not only for hearing but also for helping us to keep our balance. Information about the sounds that enter the ears and about the position of our heads is sent along the auditory nerves to be interpreted by the brain.

## Parts of the ear
There are three main regions, each with various parts.

**1 Outer ear**
**a** Pinna (ear flap): a cartilage flap on the outside of the head that gathers in sounds
**b** Auditory canal (ear canal)

**2 Middle ear**
**c** Tympanic membrane (ear drum)
**d** Ossicles: three tiny bones
**e** Middle ear cavity: an air-filled hollow

**f** Eustachian tube: leading to the throat, this keeps air pressure inside the ear equal to air pressure outside

**3 Inner ear**
**g** Oval window
**h** Organs of balance (see facing page for details)
**i** Cochlea: a fluid-filled spiral
**j** Round window
**k** Auditory nerve: this sends information to the brain

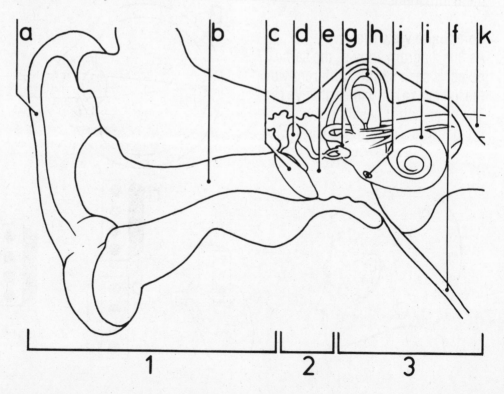

## Stages in hearing

**1** Sound waves that have been gathered by the ear flap pass through the ear canal.
**2** The sound waves make the ear drum vibrate.
**3** Vibrations from the ear drum are passed on and strengthened by the three ossicles:
   **a** the malleus (hammer);
   **b** the incus (anvil);
   **c** the stapes (stirrup).
**4** The oval window now vibrates.
**5** Vibrations pass into the fluid in the cochlea, where they are detected by special cells.
**6** Information is sent via the auditory nerve to the brain.

## Organs of balance

**A** Semicircular canals: swellings at their bases contain special cells that detect changes as the head is rotated.
**B** Utriculus: this has special cells that detect changes when the head is tilted.

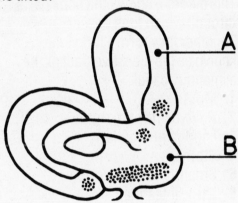

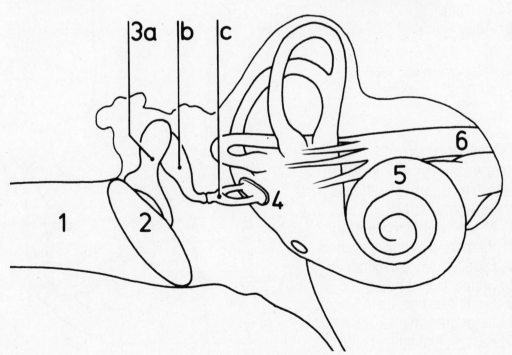

©DIAGRAM

# Digestive system (1)

**Digestion** This is the process by which food is broken down into simple substances that can be carried in the blood to feed every cell in the body. Cells need food to supply them with energy for doing work and to provide them with the substances they need for growth and repair.

## The digestive tract
This diagram shows the body parts through which food passes.
Together they form a long tube known as the digestive tract or the alimentary canal.
1  Mouth
2  Pharynx (throat)
3  Esophagus (gullet)
4  Stomach
5  Small intestine
6  Large intestine
7  Rectum
8  Anus

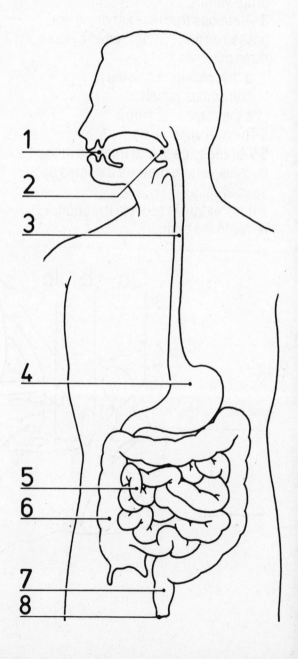

## The time it takes
Here we list typical times taken by food to pass through different parts of the digestive tract.
1  Mouth (voluntary control)
2  Pharynx: less than 1 second
3  Esophagus: 10 seconds
4  Stomach: 3–4 hours
5  Small intestine: up to 5 hours
6  Large intestine: 12–36 hours
7  Rectum (voluntary control)

## In the mouth (right, A)

**1** The front teeth bite and the back teeth chew the food.

**2** The fluid called saliva is produced by salivary glands in the floor of the mouth. Saliva moistens food and begins to break it down chemically.

**3** Taste buds send information to the brain.

**4** The tongue forms the food into a ball ready for swallowing.

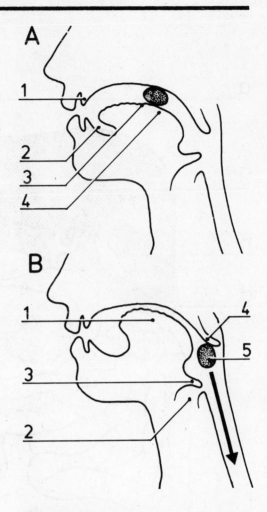

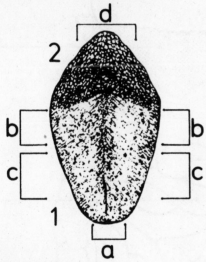

## Taste (above)

The sense of taste (helped by the sense of smell) enables us to identify suitable foods. Taste buds (most of them in the tongue) contain special nerve cells that send taste information to the brain. As shown here, different areas of the tongue respond to different kinds of tastes.

**1** Front    **a** Sweet    **c** Salt
**2** Back     **b** Sour     **d** Bitter

## Swallowing (above)

Diagram **B** shows how we swallow. (**A** is a mouth before swallowing.)

**1** The tongue moves up and back to push the food into the throat.

**2** The larynx rises.

**3** The epiglottis drops down and blocks off the trachea (wind pipe).

**4** The false palate (the soft part of the mouth's roof) moves back to block the airway to the nose.

**5** Food goes down the esophagus.

# Digestive system (2)

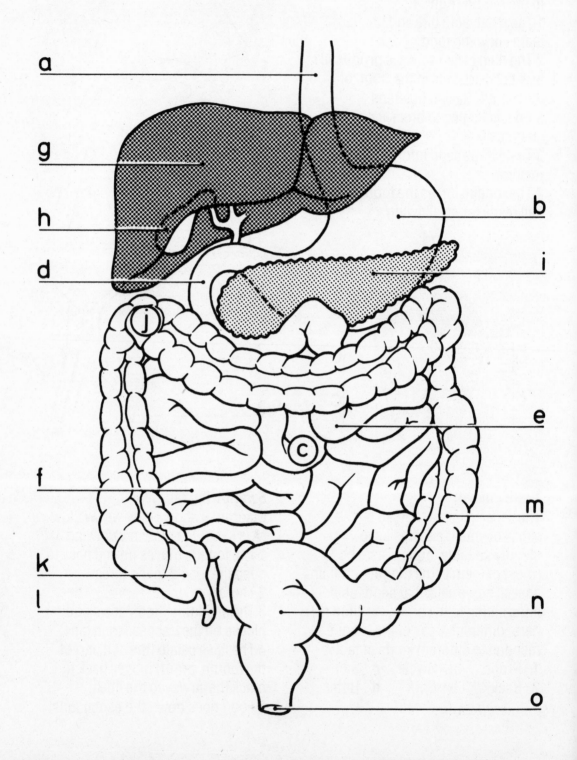

a

g

h

d

j

b

i

e

f

c

m

k

l

n

o

**The digestive system** (left)
Here we look in more detail at the main parts of the human digestive system. The digestive system consists of the digestive tract, together with various other body organs that produce juices used to break down food.

**a** Esophagus: this is a muscular tube about 10in long and 0.6–0.8in wide that takes food from the pharynx to the stomach.

**b** Stomach: this varies in size and shape depending on how much food is in it. More than 1 quart can be held comfortably. After being mixed with gastric juices containing hydrochloric acid, food is released a little at a time into the small intestine.

**c** Small intestine: this is a looped tube about 21ft long and up to about 1.4in wide. There are three sections: the duodenum (**d**), jejunum (**e**) and ileum (**f**).

**g** Liver: this produces an alkaline digestive juice called bile.

**h** Gall bladder: this stores bile.

**i** Pancreas: this produces juices used in digestion.

**j** Large intestine: this is about 6ft long and up to about 2.6in wide. It has three main sections: the cecum (**k**) – which includes the appendix (**l**) – the colon (**m**) and the rectum (**n**).

(**o**) Anus: this is the body opening from the rectum.

**Food requirements**
Humans need six types of foods.

**Carbohydrates** (sugars and starches): these are used mainly to provide the body with energy. High-carbohydrate foods include potatoes, rice, flour.

**Proteins:** these are used by the body to make new cells. Meat, eggs, beans and nuts are all rich in protein.

**Fats:** these are used to provide energy stores and to keep warm. Vegetable oils, butter and fried foods are all high in fat.

**Minerals and vitamins:** small amounts of these are needed for chemical reactions in the body. They are found in various foods.

**Water:** this is needed for chemical reactions, for transporting materials around the body and for removing waste products. Many different foods contain water.

**What is processed where**
This is a list of body parts mainly responsible for breaking down and absorbing different foods.
Carbohydrates: mouth, stomach and small intestine
Proteins: stomach and small intestine
Fats: small intestine
Minerals and vitamins: small and large intestine
Water: large intestine

# Respiratory system

**Respiration** Every cell in the body uses oxygen from the blood and gives off carbon dioxide in a chemical reaction that releases energy from food. Oxygen enters the body through the lungs, where it crosses into the blood. Waste carbon dioxide is carried by the blood back to the lungs to be breathed out.

**Parts of the system** (right)
Here we show the main parts of the human respiratory system.

1 Nasal (nose) cavity: where air is warmed and moistened
2 Mouth: an additional airway
3 Pharynx (throat)
4 Larynx (voice box): its vocal cords make sounds for speech
5 Trachea (wind pipe): a ridged tube about 9in long which takes air to and from the lungs
6 Lungs: two pink, spongy organs
7 Bronchi: two tubes leading one to each lung
8 Bronchioles: smaller branches leading off the bronchi

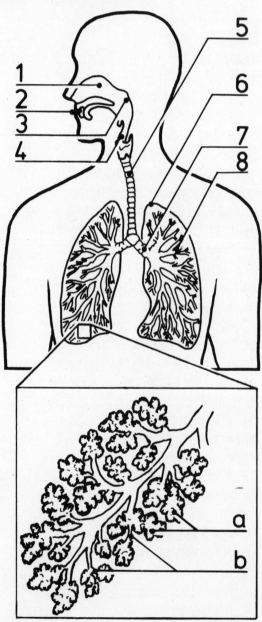

**Parts of a bronchiole** (right)
a Alveoli (air sacs): where gases are exchanged
b Alveolar ducts: tiny tubes leading to the alveoli

**Chest cavity**
The lungs lie in the pleural (chest) cavity. This is formed by the back and chest muscles, the ribs, and the diaphragm (a muscular sheet below the lungs).

## Lung capacity
A man's lungs hold about 6 quarts of air, and a woman's about 4.25 quarts. A person at rest takes in about 0.4 quarts in one breath.

## Breathing rate
A new baby takes about 40 breaths per minute. An adult takes about 13–17 when at rest and up to 80 when exercising vigorously.

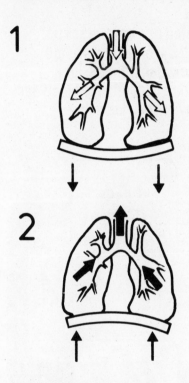

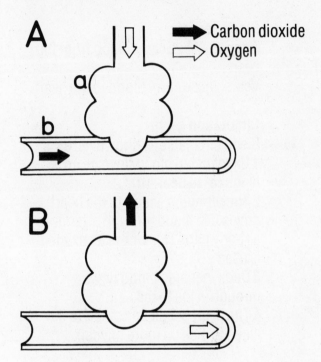

Carbon dioxide
Oxygen

## How we breathe (above)
**1** Breathing in: the diaphragm is pulled down, the ribs move outward, the chest cavity becomes larger, air pressure in the chest cavity is reduced and air enters the lungs.
**2** Breathing out: the diaphragm rises, the ribs move inward, the chest cavity becomes smaller, pressure in the cavity increases and air is forced out of the lungs.

## Exchange of gases (above)
The air we breathe out typically contains nearly 4% more carbon dioxide and nearly 4% less oxygen than the air we breathe in. This gas exchange occurs in the lungs.
**A** Oxygen enters air sacs (**a**) during breathing in; carbon dioxide is carried to the lungs in blood vessels (**b**).
**B** Oxygen has entered the blood; carbon dioxide is breathed out.

© DIAGRAM

# Circulatory system (1)

**Parts of the system** The human circulatory system consists of the blood, the blood vessels and the heart. The heart is a muscular organ weighing about 10oz. Its pumping action keeps the blood circulating through blood vessels everywhere in the body. Without a constant supply of blood, body cells soon die.

### Blood vessels
Arteries: these carry blood from the heart.
Veins: these carry blood to the heart.

### Circulation (right)
Blood circulates as shown here.
**1** Oxygenated blood flows from lungs (**a**) to heart (**b**).
**2** The pumping action of the heart drives this blood through arteries to all body parts (**c**), where its oxygen is used.
**3** Deoxygenated blood flows through veins to the heart.
**4** The heart sends this blood to the lungs to pick up more oxygen.

### Capillary network (below)
In body organs, blood from an artery (**A**) passes through a capillary network (**B**) – where it releases oxygen and food – and then leaves in a vein (**C**).

### Oxygenated and deoxygenated
Oxygenated blood: this is blood carrying oxygen from the lungs.
Deoxygenated blood: this blood has hardly any oxygen left in it.

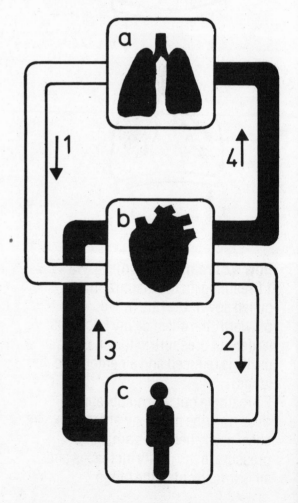

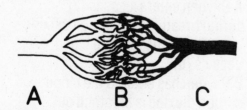

A    B    C

## Some important arteries (below)
1 Carotid artery: to head
2 Subclavian artery: to arm
3 Brachial artery: in arm
4 Pulmonary artery: to lung
5 Aorta (the largest artery): from heart to rest of body
6 Renal artery: to kidney
7 Hepatic artery: to liver
8 Gastric artery: to stomach
9 Iliac artery: to leg
10 Femoral artery: in leg

## Some important veins (below)
a Jugular vein: from head
b Subclavian vein: from arm
c Brachial vein: in arm
d Pulmonary vein: from lung
e Vena cava: from body to heart
f Renal vein: from kidney
g Hepatic vein: from liver
h Hepatic portal vein: from intestines to liver
i Iliac vein: from leg
j Femoral vein: in leg

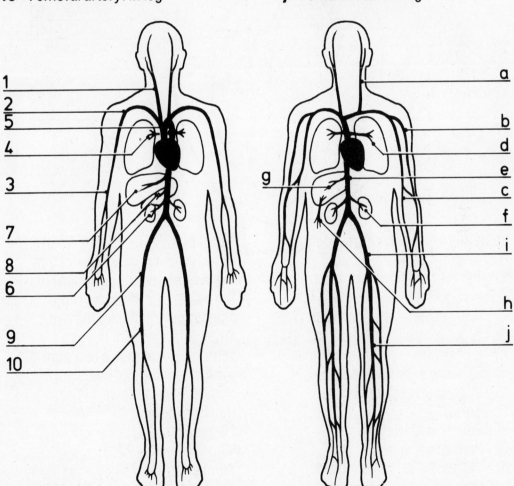

© DIAGRAM

# Circulatory system (2)

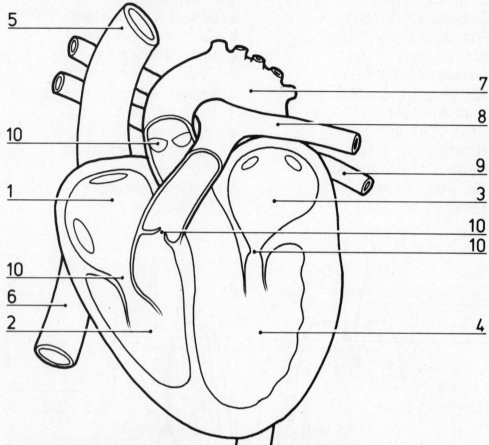

5

10

1

10

6

2

7

8

9

3

10

10

4

**Heart and blood vessels** (above)
This diagram shows a section
through the heart and the blood
vessels leading to and from it.

 1  Right atrium (upper chamber)
 2  Right ventricle (lower chamber)
 3  Left atrium   4  Left ventricle
 5  Superior (upper) vena cava
 6  Inferior (lower) vena cava
 7  Aorta
 8  Pulmonary artery
 9  Pulmonary vein
10  Valves: these prevent blood
     from flowing the wrong way.

**Heart beats**
Blood is sent around the body by
the beating (pumping action) of
the heart. Each beat has three
stages: contraction of the two
atria, contraction of the two
ventricles, and then a rest period.
Typical numbers of beats per
minute are as follows.
Newborn baby: 140
10-year-old: 90
Man at rest: 70–72
Woman at rest: 78–82
At vigorous exercise: 140–180

**Bloodflow through heart** (right)
**a** Deoxygenated blood enters right atrium by way of vena cava.
**b** Deoxygenated blood goes from right atrium to right ventricle.
**c** Deoxygenated blood goes to lungs via pulmonary artery.
**d** Oxygenated blood from lungs goes by way of pulmonary vein to left atrium.
**e** Oxygenated blood goes from left atrium to left ventricle.
**f** Oxygenated blood leaves heart via aorta to travel around body.

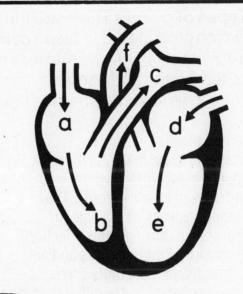

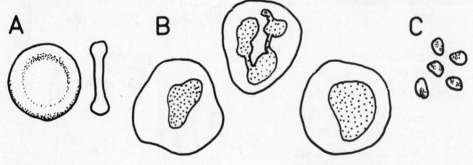

**The blood** (above)
Most healthy adults have about 5 quarts of blood. It consists of an almost colorless fluid, called plasma, and three types of cells.
**A**   Red corpuscles (blood cells): dented disks, diameter about 0.0003in, no nuclei
**B**   White corpuscles: spherical, 0.00036–0.0008in in diameter, with nuclei of different shapes
**C**   Platelets: colorless, oval or irregularly shaped, diameter about 0.000078in, no nuclei

**Functions of blood**
a) Red corpuscles carry oxygen to all parts of the body. (Blood carrying oxygen is red in color: deoxygenated blood is purplish.)
b) Plasma carries food products.
c) Plasma carries carbon dioxide and other waste products.
d) White corpuscles destroy disease organisms, e.g. bacteria.
e) Platelets form clots to stop bleeding after injury.
f) Blood helps maintain body temperature, by transporting heat.

©DIAGRAM

# Glands

**Types of glands** There are three main types: lymph glands (which produce white blood cells); exocrine glands (which make a variety of chemicals that leave the glands through tiny tubes called ducts); and endocrine or ductless glands (which make chemicals called hormones that regulate body activities).

### Lymph glands
These are found mainly in the neck, underarms and groin (where legs and trunk meet at the front). They produce leukocytes – a type of white blood cell that fights infection. Because they produce cells and not chemicals, they are more correctly known as lymph nodes rather than lymph glands.

### Exocrine glands (right)
These include the sebaceous and sweat glands in the skin, and various glands in the digestive, respiratory and reproductive systems, as well as those shown here: salivary glands (**a**); milk glands (**b**); liver (**c**); pancreas, which is both an exocrine and an endocrine gland (**d**); prostate (**e**).

### Liver: the largest gland
This has maximum dimensions of about 8.6in by 7.6in by 5.6in in an average adult. It produces a liquid called bile, which passes via a tube called the bile duct to the small intestine, where it is needed to digest fats. The liver also makes heparin, which stops the blood from clotting.

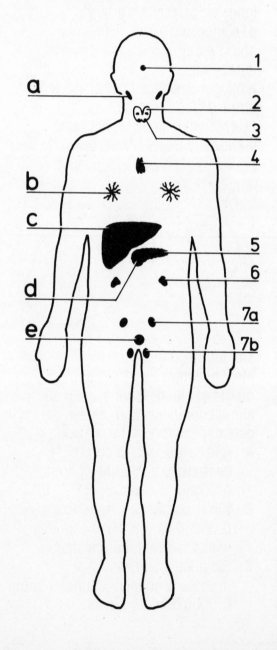

## The endocrine system

The glands belonging to this body system are located on the diagram (left) and shown (right).

**1 Pituitary gland:** the body's "master gland". Its hormones control many body activities. These include general body growth, the use of stored fat, the amount of water in urine, and the production of milk. Other pituitary hormones work indirectly, by stimulating the thyroid, adrenal and sex glands.

**2 Thyroid gland:** this produces a hormone that controls growth rate and the rate at which the body uses stored energy.

**3 Parathyroid glands:** four tiny glands embedded in the thyroid. Their hormones control the body's use of calcium and phosphorus.

**4 Thymus:** in young children this helps the body fight infection.

**5 Pancreas:** cells called Islets of Langerhans produce the hormone insulin, which controls sugar use.

**6 Adrenal glands:** one above each kidney. Their hormone adrenaline controls physical effort and prepares the body to face danger.

**7a Ovaries:** female sex glands. These produce hormones involved in sexual development and in the menstrual cycle (monthly periods).

**7b Testes or testicles:** male sex glands. These produce hormones for male sexual development.

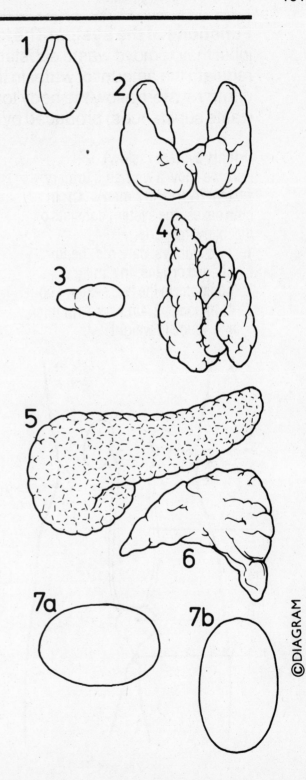

©DIAGRAM

# Urinary system

**Functions of the system** The kidneys perform two important jobs: they remove waste substances from the blood and they regulate the amount of water in the blood. The other parts of the urinary system allow the body to get rid of the urine (water plus waste substances) produced by the kidneys.

**Urinary system** (below)
Here we show a woman's urinary system (**A,B**) and a man's (**C**). In both sexes, the system consists of the following parts.

**1** Two kidneys: dark red, bean-shaped organs, in similar positions in the two sexes, about 4.4in long, 2.4in wide, 1in thick and 4.9oz in weight

**2** Two ureters: tubes about 1–1.2in long, carrying urine from the kidneys to the bladder

**3** Bladder: a hollow, muscular organ, forming a reservoir for about 17oz of urine

**4** Urethra: a tube about 8in long in men and 1.2–1.8in long in women, taking urine from the bladder to leave the body

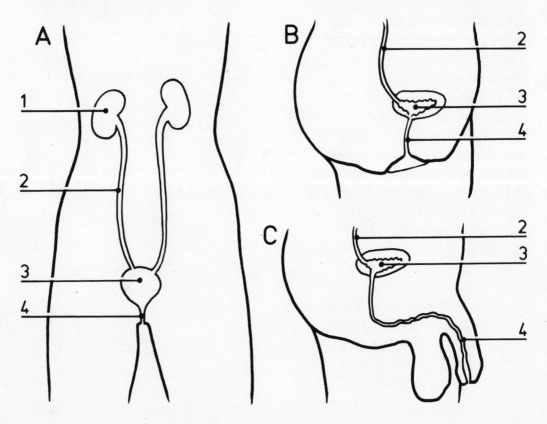

## Filtering the blood

A resting person's kidneys filter about 4oz of blood per minute. The entire blood supply is filtered about 30 times a day.

## Parts of a kidney (right)

**a** Capsule: protective skin
**b** Cortex: outer region, where blood enters filter units
**c** Medulla: its pyramid-shaped structures hold filter loops
**d** Renal pelvis: collects urine
**e** Renal artery: brings blood
**f** Renal vein: removes blood
**g** Ureter: drains off urine

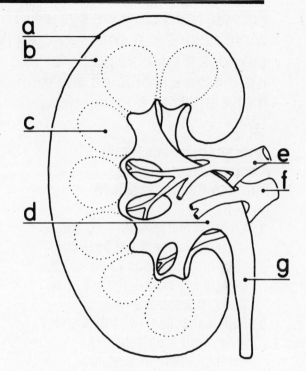

## Filter units (right)

Each kidney contains about one million tiny filter units (called nephrons or tubules).
**1** Blood vessels bring blood from the renal artery.
**2** Water, salts and urea (a waste product from the liver) enter the filter capsule (**a**) and tube (**b**).
**3** Blood vessels linking with the renal vein reabsorb salts and water needed by the body.
**4** Waste products and surplus water leave by a drainage duct.

## Amount of urine produced

This varies with how much water people drink or take in as food, and with how much they sweat. An average man in the US produces about 1.5 quarts of urine a day.

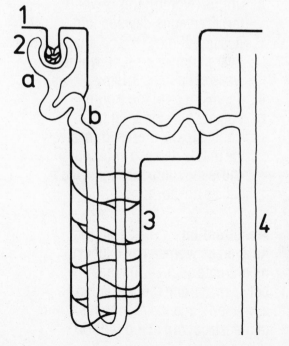

©DIAGRAM

# Reproductive system (1)

**Female reproductive system** This makes three most important contributions to human reproduction: it produces eggs, it provides a suitable place for eggs to be fertilized by sperm, and it provides a protected environment and life support system so that a fertilized egg can grow into a baby.

**Parts and functions** (right)
A woman's reproductive organs are here shown from the side (**A**) and front (**B**).

**a** Ovaries: two female sex glands about 1.6in by 0.8in by 0.4in; they produce eggs (ova) and the female sex hormones estrogen and progesterone

**b** Fallopian tubes: two tubes about 4.4in long; ripe eggs pass through them for possible fertilization by a man's sperm

**c** Uterus (womb): this is where fertilized eggs develop into babies; it is about the size and shape of a pear in non-pregnant women; its walls expand as a baby grows

**d** Cervix (neck of the womb)

**e** Vagina: a 4–5in long tube leading to the uterus; it receives the man's penis in intercourse and is the route through which babies are born

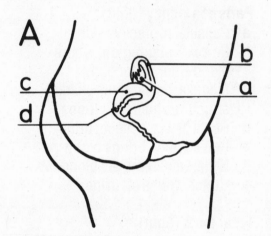

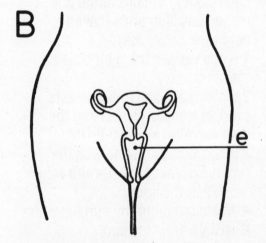

## Menstruation

An average woman can expect to menstruate about 450 times between starting menstruation at e.g. age 12 and the menopause (end of menstruation) at e.g. age 50.

## Number of eggs

A baby girl is born with her whole lifetime's supply of about two million tiny unripe eggs. Only about one egg in 2500 will ever ripen and leave an ovary.

**Girl into woman** (below)
Here we show typical stages as a girl grows into a woman. In both sexes, the process of becoming sexually mature is called puberty.
**1** Before puberty (about age 10): body shape is similar to a boy's, breasts still undeveloped.
**2** Early puberty (perhaps age 11): breasts developing, hips widening, body hair growing under arms and in pubic region (at base of trunk).

**3** Mid puberty (perhaps age 14): now much taller, with larger breasts and wider, fat-covered hips. Underarm and pubic hair is darker, thicker and curlier. Internal sex organs have been growing rapidly and menstruation has probably started.
**4** Late puberty (perhaps age 16): adult height has been reached, breasts and hips are larger, sex organs are mature, periods regular.

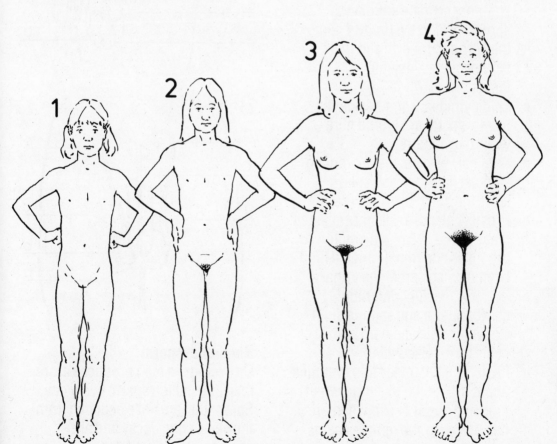

© DIAGRAM

# Reproductive system (2)

**Male reproductive system** A man's reproductive system produces the male sex cells (sperm) that must unite with a female sex cell (egg) if a new baby is to develop. A man's penis is designed for insertion into a woman's vagina so that fertilization of eggs by sperm can occur within the woman's body.

**Parts and functions** (right)
A man's major reproductive organs are here shown from the side (**A**) and front (**B**).

**a**  Scrotum: a skin pouch that holds the testes and keeps them cooler than the rest of the body

**b**  Testes (or testicles): two egg-shaped male sex glands about 1.6–2in by 1in by 1.2in; they produce sperm and male sex hormones including testosterone

**c**  Epididymides: lying beside the testes; sperm are stored here while they mature

**d**  Seminal vesicles: these produce seminal fluid in which sperm leave the body

**e**  Prostate gland: a chestnut-shaped gland about 1.2in in diameter; it produces additional seminal fluid

**f**  Urethra: also part of the urinary system, this 8in long tube carries sperm and seminal fluid (together called semen) to the penis tip for ejaculation

**g**  Penis: in adult males this averages about 3.2–4.4in in length when limp and about 5–7in when erect; it is placed in the female vagina during sexual intercourse

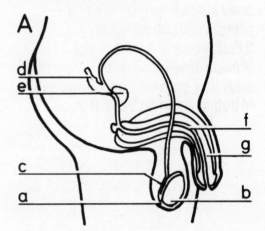

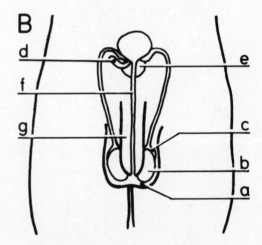

**Number of sperm**
On average, a man produces more than 500 million sperm every day. Sperm that are not ejaculated from the penis soon decay and are absorbed back into the body.

**Boy into man** (below)
Here we show typical stages as a boy grows into a man. In males and females, the process of becoming sexually mature is called puberty.

**1** Before puberty (about age 10): penis and scrotum are small, and there is no coarse body hair.

**2** Early puberty (perhaps age 12): penis, testes and scrotum are growing, hair appears in pubic region (at base of penis).

**3** Mid puberty (perhaps age 15): now much taller. Penis, testes and scrotum are growing. Penis erects spontaneously more often than before. Sperm are produced, and sometimes ejaculated during sleep. Body and facial hair is increasing. Voice is deepening.

**4** Late puberty (perhaps age 18): approaching adult height, sex organs now much larger, more body and facial hair, voice deeper.

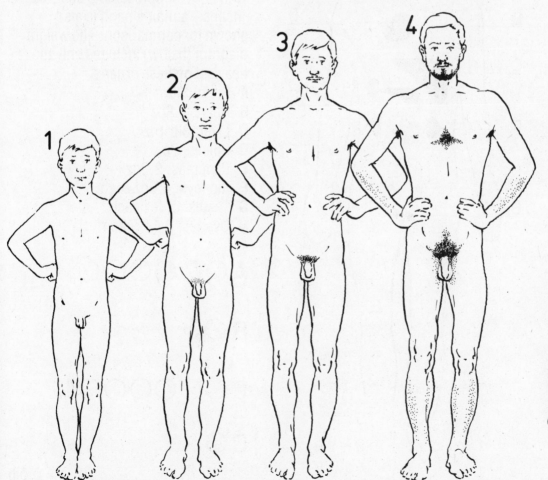

©DIAGRAM

# Size of organs

**Major organs compared** Here we show the relative positions, sizes and weights of some of the body's main organs. Male and female reproductive organs are both included. For all other organs, the sizes and weights given here are for a typical man; the organs are comparatively smaller in women and children.

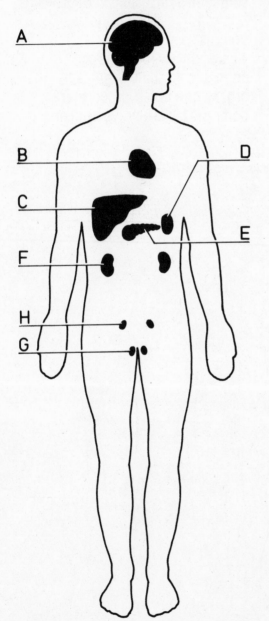

**Positions, sizes and weights**
This list names the organs shown on the location diagram (left) and included in the scale diagram (right). In this scale diagram each grid square represents 5 square inches – a man's hand is also shown for comparison. The weight diagram (below) includes only the heaviest of these organs.

**A** Brain: 3lb
**B** Heart: 9.8oz
**C** Liver: 3lb 1oz
**D** Spleen: 7oz
**E** Pancreas: 2.9oz
**F** Kidneys: 4.9oz each
**G** Testes: 0.4oz each
**H** Ovaries: 0.1oz each

A ○○○○○○

B ○◖

C ○○○○○○◗

D ○

○ = 0.5lb

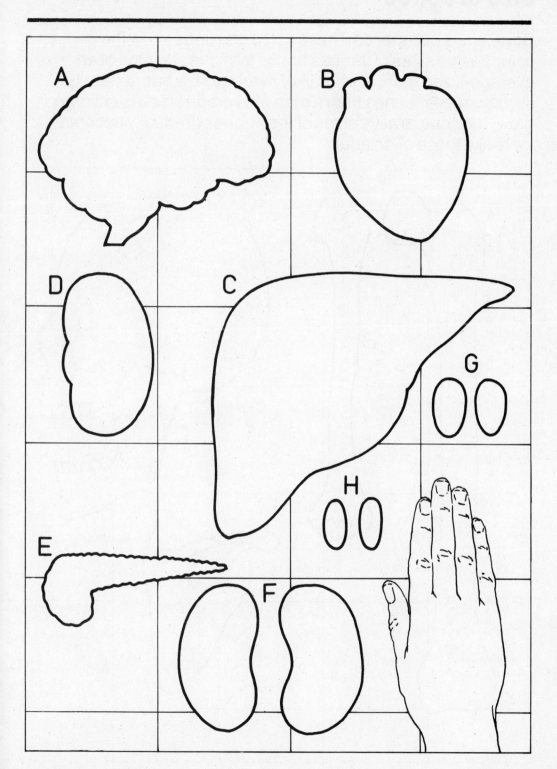

# Size of bones

**Bone sizes compared** These scale drawings show the comparative sizes of various bones from the skeleton of an average-sized man. A woman of average size has generally slightly smaller bones than a man of average size. As children grow, the comparative sizes of their bones gradually become more like those of an adult.

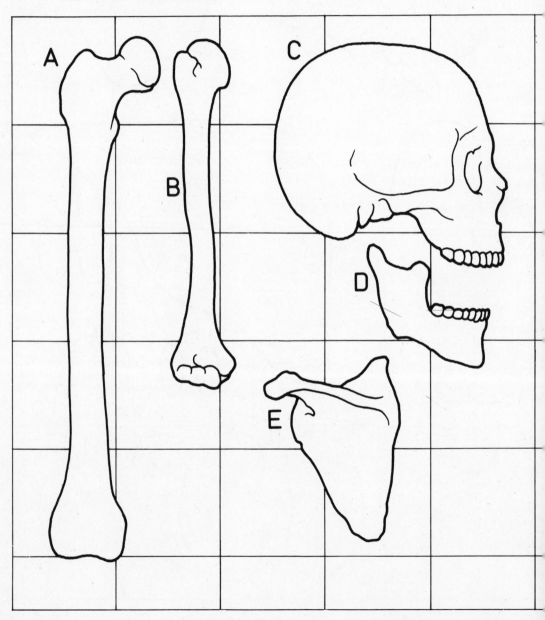

**Bones shown to scale**
Grid squares represent 4 sq. in.
A   Femur (thighbone)
B   Humerus (bone in upper arm)
C   Cranium (skull)
D   Mandible (jawbone)
E   Scapula (shoulder blade)
F   Bones of hand
G   Bones of foot
H   Ribs and sternum (breastbone)
I   Clavicle (collarbone)
J   Patella (knee cap)

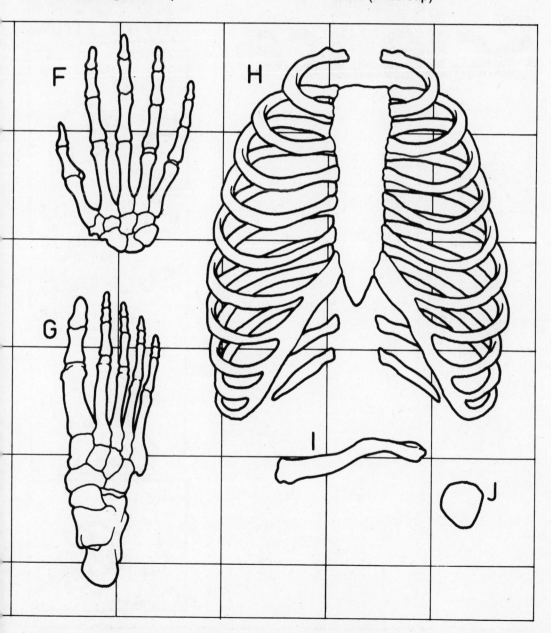

© DIAGRAM

# Section 4

# Science

Atoms & Upwa

particles

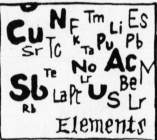

Elements

Elements

Crystals

Mass, Volume, de.

Cold

Air

Forces

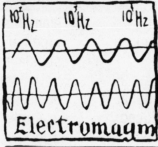

Electromagn

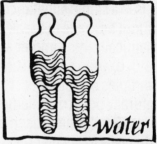

Water

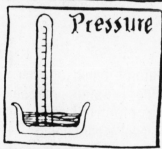

Pressure

Light

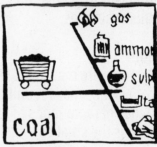

Coal

Energy

Sound

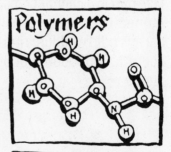

Polymers

Heat

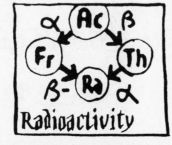

Radioactivity

Carbon

# Atoms and upwards

**Matter and substance** Everything in the universe is made up of matter. Matter can be packed close together, as in a solid, or it can be spread far apart, as in a gas. Matter of any one particular type is called a substance. For example, salt and sugar are both made of matter but they are different substances.

### Element
This is a single substance that cannot be made to break down chemically into simpler substances. Gold, oxygen and zinc are all examples of elements. There are 90 naturally occurring elements but at least 13 more have been produced artificially in nuclear reactors or other machines.

### Compound
This is made up of two or more elements which have been joined together to form a completely new substance. The new substance will have different characteristics from the elements that make it up. For example, water, which is a liquid, is a compound of hydrogen and oxygen, which are gases.

### Atom
Elements are made up of atoms. An atom is the smallest unit that keeps all the characteristics of an element and it is the smallest unit that can take part in a chemical reaction. Atoms are extremely small. A narrow gold wedding ring contains about 1000000000000000000000 atoms.

### Molecule
Two or more atoms joined together form a molecule. The atoms may be from the same or from different elements. Molecules containing atoms of two or more elements are the units that make up compounds. If a molecule is broken down, it splits into atoms of the elements of which it was made up.

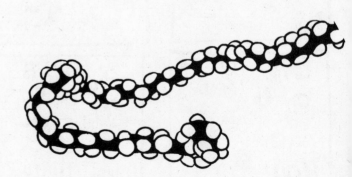

## How many atoms?

A molecule contains at least two atoms but can contain many more.

| | |
|---|---|
| Oxygen | 2 atoms |
| Water (**a**) | 3 atoms |
| Ammonia gas | 4 atoms |
| Methane gas | 5 atoms |
| Antifreeze<br>    (ethylene glycol) | 10 atoms |
| Aspirin (**b**) | 21 atoms |
| Lemon juice | 21 atoms |
| Glucose (sugar) (**c**) | 24 atoms |
| Animal fat | 173 atoms |
| Starch | 1500–150,000 atoms |
| Rubber (**d**) | 13,000–65,000 atoms |

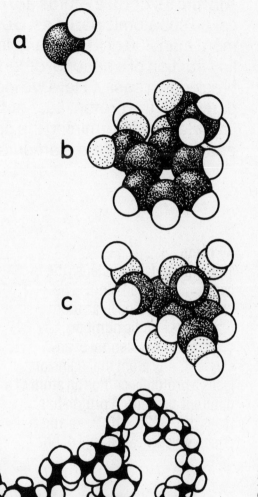

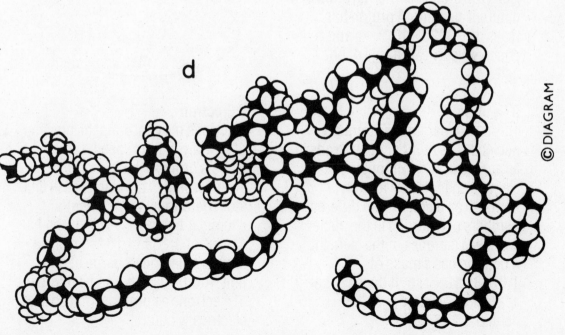

© DIAGRAM

# Splitting the atom

**Atomic structure** Atoms are made up of even smaller units called subatomic particles. So far scientists have discovered more than 200 of these particles, some of which last for only a tiny fraction of a second, others of which are stable and do not break down easily. Here we look at three of these stable particles – the proton, the neutron and the electron – which are important in determining the properties (i.e. the characteristics and behavior) of the elements.

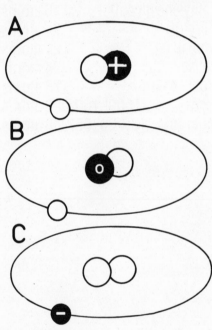

**A Proton**
This is part of the nucleus (the central core) of an atom. The number of protons in an atom (called the atomic number) determines the identity of an element. Any atom that gains or loses a proton becomes an atom of a different element. A proton has a mass of $1.6726 \times 10^{-27}$kg and a positive electrical charge of one unit.

**B Neutron**
This is also part of the atomic nucleus. The number of neutrons in an atom can vary without the element changing its identity. Forms of an element with different numbers of neutrons in the nucleus are called isotopes of the element. A neutron has a mass of $1.6748 \times 10^{-27}$kg. It does not carry an electrical charge, i.e. it is neutral.

**C Electron**
Electrons move around the nucleus of an atom at high speed, rather like planets orbiting the Sun. The arrangement of the electrons in an atom determines an element's chemical behavior. An electron has a mass of $9.1096 \times 10^{-31}$kg and a negative electrical charge of one unit. Atoms have the same number of electrons as protons, and so are electrically neutral.

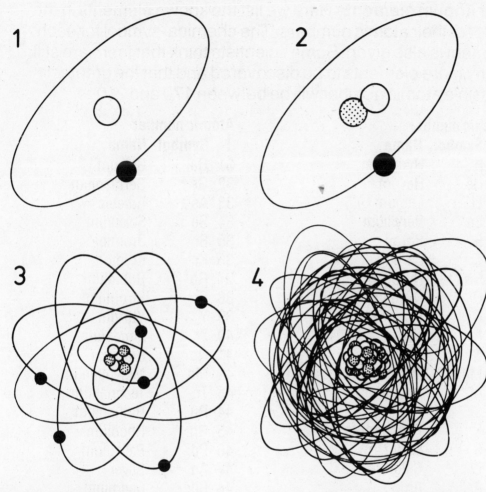

## How many particles?

**1** 99.9% of hydrogen atoms consist of one proton and one electron. They are the only atoms that do not have neutrons in the nucleus.

**2** The other 0.1% of hydrogen atoms are isotopes with neutrons in the nucleus. Most have one neutron, as shown here, but 1 in $10^{17}$ atoms of hydrogen have two neutrons.

**3** Carbon atoms have six protons and six electrons. 98.89% of all naturally occurring carbon atoms have six neutrons. The other naturally occurring isotope of carbon has seven neutrons.

**4** Uranium atoms have 92 protons and 92 electrons. 99.28% of all naturally occurring uranium atoms have 146 neutrons. The other naturally occurring isotopes of uranium have either 142 or 143 neutrons.

© DIAGRAM

# Elements (1)

**The known elements** Here we list the known elements in the order of their atomic numbers. The chemical symbol for each element is also given. Some scientists think that there are still many more elements to be discovered and that the greatest possible atomic number will be between 170 and 210.

| Atomic number | Symbol | Name | | Atomic number | Symbol | Name |
|---|---|---|---|---|---|---|
| 1 | H | Hydrogen | | 31 | Ga | Gallium |
| 2 | He | Helium | | 32 | Ge | Germanium |
| 3 | Li | Lithium | | 33 | As | Arsenic |
| 4 | Be | Beryllium | | 34 | Se | Selenium |
| 5 | B | Boron | | 35 | Br | Bromine |
| 6 | C | Carbon | | 36 | Kr | Krypton |
| 7 | N | Nitrogen | | 37 | Rb | Rubidium |
| 8 | O | Oxygen | | 38 | Sr | Strontium |
| 9 | F | Fluorine | | 39 | Y | Yttrium |
| 10 | Ne | Neon | | 40 | Zr | Zirconium |
| 11 | Na | Sodium | | 41 | Nb | Niobium |
| 12 | Mg | Magnesium | | 42 | Mo | Molybdenum |
| 13 | Al | Aluminum | | 43 | Tc | Technetium |
| 14 | Si | Silicon | | 44 | Ru | Ruthenium |
| 15 | P | Phosphorus | | 45 | Rh | Rhodium |
| 16 | S | Sulfur | | 46 | Pd | Palladium |
| 17 | Cl | Chlorine | | 47 | Ag | Silver |
| 18 | Ar | Argon | | 48 | Cd | Cadmium |
| 19 | K | Potassium | | 49 | In | Indium |
| 20 | Ca | Calcium | | 50 | Sn | Tin |
| 21 | Sc | Scandium | | 51 | Sb | Antimony |
| 22 | Ti | Titanium | | 52 | Te | Tellurium |
| 23 | V | Vanadium | | 53 | I | Iodine |
| 24 | Cr | Chromium | | 54 | Xe | Xenon |
| 25 | Mn | Manganese | | 55 | Cs | Cesium |
| 26 | Fe | Iron | | 56 | Ba | Barium |
| 27 | Co | Cobalt | | 57 | La | Lanthanum |
| 28 | Ni | Nickel | | 58 | Ce | Cerium |
| 29 | Cu | Copper | | 59 | Pr | Praseodymium |
| 30 | Zn | Zinc | | 60 | Nd | Neodymium |

## Atomic number

| | Symbol | Name |
|---|---|---|
| 61 | Pm | Prometheum |
| 62 | Sm | Samarium |
| 63 | Eu | Europium |
| 64 | Gd | Gadolinium |
| 65 | Tb | Terbium |
| 66 | Dy | Dysprosium |
| 67 | Ho | Holmium |
| 68 | Er | Erbium |
| 69 | Tm | Thulium |
| 70 | Yb | Ytterbium |
| 71 | Lu | Lutecium |
| 72 | Hf | Hafnium |
| 73 | Ta | Tantalum |
| 74 | W | Tungsten |
| 75 | Re | Rhenium |
| 76 | Os | Osmium |
| 77 | Ir | Iridium |
| 78 | Pt | Platinum |
| 79 | Au | Gold |
| 80 | Hg | Mercury |
| 81 | Tl | Thallium |
| 82 | Pb | Lead |
| 83 | Bi | Bismuth |
| 84 | Po | Polonium |
| 85 | At | Astatine |
| 86 | Rn | Radon |
| 87 | Fr | Francium |
| 88 | Ra | Radium |
| 89 | Ac | Actinium |
| 90 | Th | Thorium |
| 91 | Pa | Protactinium |
| 92 | U | Uranium |
| 93 | Np | Neptunium |
| 94 | Pu | Plutonium |
| 95 | Am | Americium |
| 96 | Cm | Curium |

## Atomic number

| | Symbol | Name |
|---|---|---|
| 97 | Bk | Berkelium |
| 98 | Cf | Californium |
| 99 | Es | Einsteinium |
| 100 | Fm | Fermium |
| 101 | Md | Mendelevium |
| 102 | No | Nobelium |
| 103 | Lr | Lawrencium |
| 104 | Unq | Unnilquadium |
| 105 | Unp | Unnilpentium |
| 106 | Unh | Unnilhexium |
| 107 | Uns | Unnilseptium |
| 108 | *not yet discovered* | |
| 109 | Une | Unnilennium |

### Chemical symbols

The letters forming the chemical symbol of an element are usually an abbreviation of the name of the element. W, the symbol for tungsten, is an abbreviation of its alternative name, wolfram. Some elements have symbols based on their Latin names, as listed below.

| Element | Symbol | Latin name |
|---|---|---|
| Sodium | Na | *Natrium* |
| Potassium | K | *Kalium* |
| Iron | Fe | *Ferrum* |
| Copper | Cu | *Cuprum* |
| Silver | Ag | *Argentum* |
| Tin | Sn | *Stannum* |
| Antimony | Sb | *Stibium* |
| Gold | Au | *Aurum* |
| Mercury | Hg | *Hydrargyrum* |
| Lead | Pb | *Plumbum* |

© DIAGRAM

# Elements (2)

## Discovery of the elements

No one is sure when the first elements were discovered but some have been known since ancient times. The numbers of elements discovered in different centuries are listed below.

| | |
|---|---|
| Before 1700 | 12 elements |
| 18th century | 22 elements |
| 19th century | 49 elements |
| 20th century | 25 elements |

## Recent discoveries

| Atomic number | Date of discovery |
|---|---|
| 100 | 1953 |
| 101 | 1955 |
| 102 | 1958 |
| 103 | 1961 |
| 104 | 1964 |
| 105 | 1970 |
| 106 | 1974 |
| 107 | 1976 |
| 108 | *not yet discovered* |
| 109 | 1982 |

**Abundance of elements** Some elements occur naturally in greater quantities than others, i.e. they are more abundant. Scientists have found that elements with low atomic numbers (less than 30) are more abundant than elements with higher atomic numbers. The abundance of elements on the Earth is different from their abundance in the Universe as a whole.

## Abundance in the Universe

Scientists estimate that about 99% of the matter in the Universe is made up of just two elements – hydrogen and helium. Hydrogen is far more abundant than helium: the Universe contains about 10,000 atoms of hydrogen for every 500 atoms of helium and every 1 atom of other elements. Of the other elements, those with even atomic numbers are more abundant than those with odd atomic numbers. The ten most abundant elements in the Universe are listed in order right.

1 Hydrogen
2 Helium
3 Oxygen
4 Carbon
5 Nitrogen
6 Silicon
7 Magnesium
8 Neon
9 Sulfur
10 Iron

## A Abundance in the Earth's crust

9 elements make up nearly 99% of the Earth's crust.

1 Oxygen 46.6%
2 Silicon 27.7%
3 Aluminum 8.1%
4 Iron 5.0%
5 Calcium 3.6%
6 Sodium 2.8%
7 Potassium 2.6%
8 Magnesium 2.1%
9 Titanium 0.44%

The rarest of the naturally occurring elements in the Earth's crust is astatine.

## B Abundance in living things

9 elements make up over 99% of all living things.

1 Oxygen 62%
2 Carbon 20%
3 Hydrogen 10%
4 Nitrogen 3%
5 Calcium 2.5%
6 Phosphorus 1.14%
7 Chlorine 0.16%
8 Sulfur 0.14%
9 Potassium 0.11%

## C Abundance in seawater

5 elements make up over 99% of the world's seawater.

1 Oxygen 85.7%
2 Hydrogen 10.7%
3 Chlorine 1.94%
4 Sodium 1.08%
5 Magnesium 0.13%

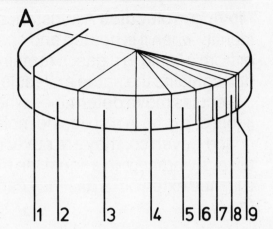

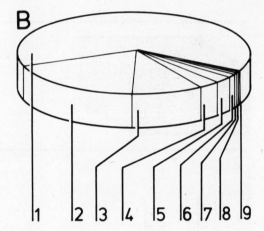

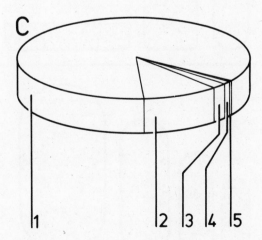

© DIAGRAM

# Solids, liquids, gases

**Moving molecules** A substance does not change its chemical identity when it is heated and changes from a solid to a liquid or from a liquid to a gas. It remains the same substance and contains the same molecules. The way in which these molecules move determines whether the substance is a solid, a liquid or a gas. In a solid, the molecules cannot move through space – even so, they are never completely still as they are always vibrating. In a liquid the molecules can move, but only to a limited extent. In a gas they can move around completely freely.

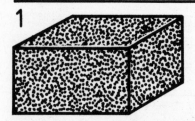

**Sizes and shapes**
**1** A solid takes up a definite amount of space. It will not alter its shape unless forced to do so.

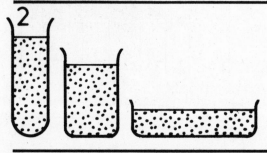

**2** A liquid also takes up a definite amount of space but can alter its shape easily. It will take the shape of any container into which it is poured.

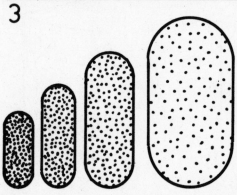

**3** A gas has no definite size and shape. Because the molecules in a gas can move freely, they will spread out to fill the whole of any container, however large. If a gas is not confined in a container it will simply continue to expand.

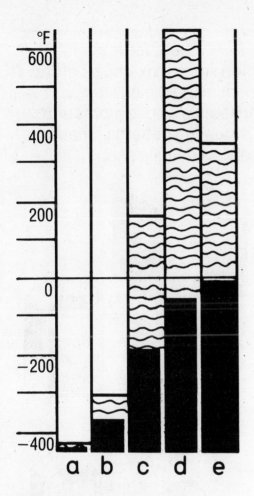

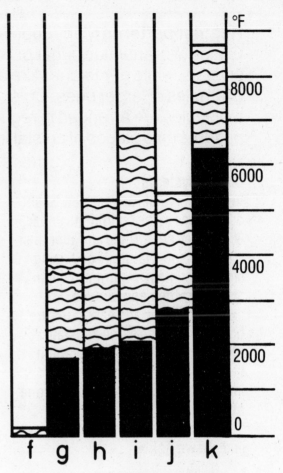

a b c d e        f g h i j k

## Solid to liquid to gas

A solid that is made hot enough will
melt and become a liquid, and a
liquid that is made hot enough will
vaporize and become a gas.
Similarly, a gas that is cooled
sufficiently will condense and
become a liquid, and a liquid that is
cooled sufficiently will freeze and
become a solid. Here we list the
temperatures at which these
changes take place for a selection of
different substances. They are
shown on the diagrams above.

|   |   | Solid to liquid | Liquid to gas |
|---|---|---|---|
| a | Hydrogen | −432°F | −423°F |
| b | Oxygen | −362.2°F | −297.4°F |
| c | Alcohol | −173.2°F | 172.4°F |
| d | Mercury | −38.2°F | 678.2°F |
| e | Antifreeze (ethylene glycol) | 8.6°F | 388.4°F |
| f | Water | 32°F | 212°F |
| g | Silver | 1763.6°F | 4010°F |
| h | Gold | 1947.2°F | 5252°F |
| i | Uranium | 2069.6°F | 6904.4°F |
| j | Iron | 2796.8°F | 5432°F |
| k | Carbon | 6422°F | 8717°F |

# Crystals

**Regular patterns** Many substances are able to form crystals. Grains of granulated sugar or common salt are examples of tiny crystals, while gemstones like diamonds and rubies are examples of larger ones. Crystals are solids whose atoms and molecules are arranged in regular, repeating patterns. These patterns give pieces of crystalline solids a definite shape.

## Crystal systems

Very few crystals are perfect. Slight differences in the conditions under which they are formed will alter their size or shape. Naturally occurring crystals contain impurities which also affect their appearance. For example, rubies and sapphires are both made of the same substance, but different impurities give them their different colors. However imperfect, all crystals belong to one of seven basic groups or "systems". These are listed below and shown right.

1 Cubic
2 Hexagonal
3 Trigonal
4 Tetragonal
5 Orthorhombic
6 Monoclinic
7 Triclinic

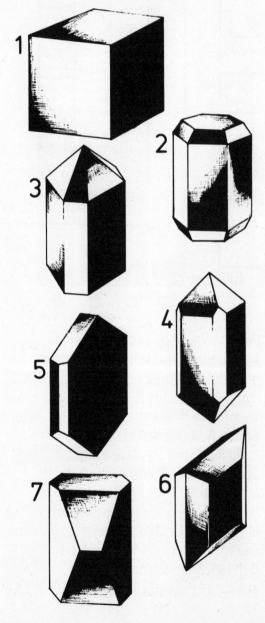

## Ice crystals (below)

Snowflakes are tiny ice crystals. Although no two are alike, their shape is always based on a hexagon.

## Salt crystals (below)

Common salt (sodium chloride) forms cubic crystals. The sodium (Na) and chlorine (Cl) atoms are arranged alternately in rows at right angles to each other.

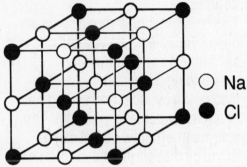

○ Na
● Cl

## Colored crystals

Here we list some examples of colored crystals that may be found in a laboratory. Although it is the presence of impurities that gives some crystals their characteristic colors, the substances listed here are among many that are colored even when they are pure.

Potassium ferricyanide, red
Potassium ferrocyanide, yellow
Copper carbonate, green
Copper sulfate, blue
Potassium permanganate, purple

© DIAGRAM

# Volume, mass, density, weight

**How big and how heavy?** These questions can be answered by finding out the volume, mass, density and weight of an object. Here we look at the scientific meanings of these terms, the units in which they are measured, and how they are related to one another.

## Volume

This measures how much space an object occupies. The volume of a solid object can be found by suspending it in water in a measuring cylinder and seeing how much the water level rises (**a**). The volume of a hollow object can be found by measuring the amount of water needed to fill it.

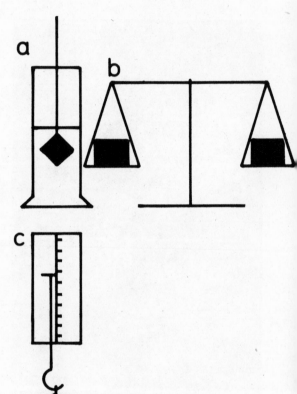

## Mass

This measures how much matter an object contains. The greater an object's mass, the more difficult it is to move. The mass of an object remains the same wherever the object is. An unknown mass can be measured by using a beam balance (**b**) to compare it with objects whose mass is known.

## Density

If an object with a small volume has the same mass as another object with a larger volume, the smaller object is said to have a greater density. The definition of density is "mass per unit volume". It is calculated by dividing the mass of an object by its volume.

## Weight

In scientific language, weight is the term for the force with which gravity pulls an object against the ground. It varies with the force of gravity, so where gravity is less than on Earth (e.g. on the Moon) an object weighs less. Weight is measured with a spring balance (**c**).

## Units

| | |
|---|---|
| Volume | Cubic meter ($m^3$, cu.m), cubic centimeter ($cm^3$, cu.cm) |
| Mass | Kilogram (kg), gram (g) |
| Density | Kilograms per cubic meter ($kg/m^3$, kg/cu.m), grams per cubic centimeter ($g/cm^3$, g/cu.cm) |
| Weight | Newton (N) |

## Gold and silver

We can compare gold and silver ingots to show how volume, mass, density and weight are related.

**1** A gold ingot and a silver ingot of equal volume can be seen to have different masses when compared on a beam balance. The gold ingot has nearly twice the mass of the silver because gold is nearly twice as dense as silver.

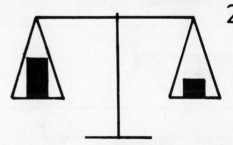

1

**2** A gold ingot and a silver ingot of the same mass have different volumes. Because gold is nearly twice as dense as silver, the silver ingot has nearly twice the volume of the gold ingot.

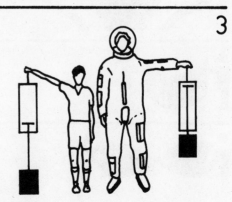

2

**3** The weight of an ingot on the Moon will be about 1/6th of the weight of an ingot on Earth that is identical in mass, volume and density. This is because the Earth's gravity is roughly six times greater than that of the Moon.

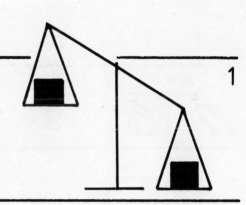

3

© DIAGRAM

# Pushing and pulling

**Forces** A force can change the shape or size of an object, or the speed or direction in which an object is traveling. The unit of force is the newton, which is the amount of force needed to give a mass of one kilogram an acceleration of one meter per second per second (abbreviated as $1m/sec^2$), i.e. with every second that passes the mass travels 1m/sec faster than it did the second before.

**Forces in action**
All forces are basically pushes or pulls.

**1** Pushing can change the speed and/or direction of an object.

**2** Compressing an object to change its shape and size is a form of pushing.

**3** Pulling can change the speed and/or direction of an object.

**4** Stretching an object to change its shape and/or size is a form of pulling.

**5** Bending may be a form of either pushing or pulling.

**6** Twisting is pushing or pulling in a spiral.

## Equilibrium

If two equal forces act in exactly opposite directions on a stationary object, the object will not move. The resultant (i.e. total effect) of the forces is zero. An object is said to be in equilibrium whenever the resultant of two or more forces acting on it is zero. This may be when it is stationary or when it is moving at constant velocity.

## Forces in equilibrium

**a** Two equally matched tug-of-war teams will reach stalemate and neither will be able to pull the marker over the line. The marker does not move because the resultant of the forces is zero.
**b** If two people push a swing door in opposite directions with equal force, the door will not open because the resultant force on it is zero.

a

b

## Gravity

This is the natural force that pulls one object toward another. Its strength depends on the mass of the objects involved. Because the Earth is so massive, objects on it are pulled toward it more than they are pulled toward each other. On Earth, the force of gravity exerts a pull of 9.8 newtons on a mass of 1kg. The weight of a 1kg mass on Earth is therefore 9.8 newtons.

## Newton

The unit of force is called the newton after the great 17th century scientist, Isaac Newton. Among his many discoveries were the laws governing the force of gravity. The original idea which led him to these laws came to him when he was sitting in an orchard and saw an apple fall from a tree. By coincidence, an average apple weighs about one newton.

# Pressure

**Pressure** A force acting over a small area has a greater effect than the same force acting over a large area. The force is said to exert greater pressure when it acts over the smaller area. The definition of pressure is "force per unit area", and it is calculated by dividing the force by the area over which it is acting. Because the Earth's atmosphere has weight (1m³ of air weighs about 12¼ newtons), it exerts pressure. Atmospheric pressure can be measured with a barometer.

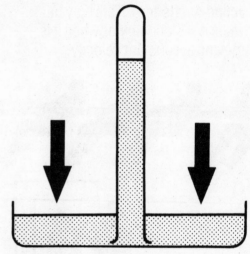

**Barometer** (right)
One of the simplest barometers is a glass tube that is sealed at one end, filled with mercury and turned upside down to stand in a dish of mercury.
The pressure of the atmosphere on the mercury in the dish supplies enough force to support the weight of a column of mercury in the tube. Provided that there is no air above the mercury in the tube, the height of the column of mercury is a measure of the atmospheric pressure.
At sea level, the column of mercury will on average be 760mm (30.4in) high. As the atmospheric pressure changes (e.g. because of changes in the weather), so the height of the column will rise or fall.
Mercury is used in barometers for convenience because it is a dense, heavy liquid. If water were used instead, at sea level the average height of the column would be 10.33m (33.99ft).

**Units**
The basic unit of pressure is called the pascal. One pascal is the pressure exerted by a force of one newton over an area of one square meter. One bar is 100,000 pascals. High pressures can be given in kilobars (1000 bars) or megabars ($10^6$) bars.
Barometric pressure is often given in millibars (0.001 bars). It can also be expressed as the height of a column of mercury. The pressure needed to support a column of mercury 1mm (0.039in) high is called a torr. One torr is 133.3 pascals.

## Falling pressure

Atmospheric pressure decreases with height. Close to the Earth's surface, the height of the column of mercury supported by the atmosphere falls by about 1mm (0.039in) for every 11m (0.433in) increase in height above sea level. Atmospheric pressure at 16,000 (52,493ft) is roughly one tenth as great as it is at sea level. At 100km (62mi) it has fallen to about one millionth of its sea level pressure. Listed below and shown on the diagram right are pressures in millibars and the approximate heights above sea level at which they are found.

| Pressure | Height | |
|----------|--------|--------|
| 1013.25mb | 0m | (0ft) |
| 1000mb | 110m | (361ft) |
| 900mb | 990m | (3248ft) |
| 800mb | 1950m | (6398ft) |
| 700mb | 3010m | (9875ft) |
| 600mb | 4200m | (13,779ft) |
| 500mb | 5575m | (18,290ft) |
| 250mb | 10,350m | (33,956ft) |
| 100mb | 16,180m | (53,083ft) |
| 10mb | 30,000m | (98,424ft) |
| 1mb | 50,000m | (164,040ft) |

© DIAGRAM

# Energy (1)

**What is energy?** A man climbing a flight of stairs, a car driving along a road and a crane lifting a load are all examples of actions that involve energy and work. In science, the terms energy and work have a particular meaning. Work is done whenever a force causes movement, i.e. work involves moving something (whether it be as tiny as an atom or as large as an elephant) from one place to another, however minute the distance. Energy is the capacity for doing work.

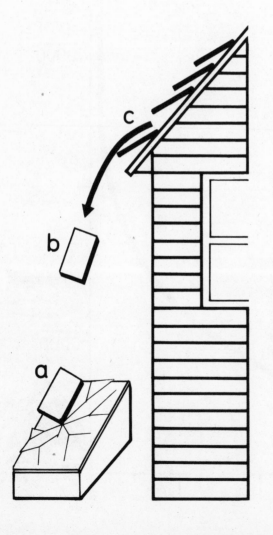

## Kinetic and potential energy

In scientific terms, a slate falling off a roof and breaking a pane of glass is doing work (**a**). The slate therefore has energy.

When the slate is actually falling (**b**), it is said to have kinetic energy, from the Greek word *kinesis*, meaning movement. All moving objects have kinetic energy.

The slate also had energy before it fell off the roof (**c**), because it had the potential to move and do work, i.e. it had potential energy. The term potential energy describes the energy a stationary object has because of its state or position. The slate had potential energy because of its position above the ground – the force of gravity could act on it and make it move. Potential energy is converted into kinetic energy when the object moves.

## From potential to kinetic

These examples show how potential energy changes to kinetic energy.

**1** A roller coaster car at the top of a slope has potential energy because of its position. The force of gravity can act on it and make it move down the slope. As it slides down the slope it loses its potential energy, but at the same time gains kinetic energy because it is moving. This kinetic energy enables it to move up the next incline. As it climbs up it uses up its kinetic energy by working against the force of gravity, but at the same time it gains potential energy as it gains height.

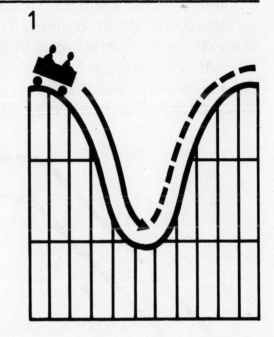

**2** The wound up spring of a clockwork mouse has potential energy because of its state. This changes to kinetic energy as the mouse moves around the floor.

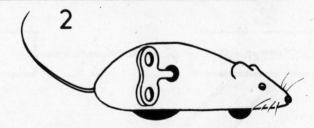

**3** A stretched bowstring has potential energy because of its state. When the string is released, the potential energy of the string changes to the kinetic energy of the arrow.

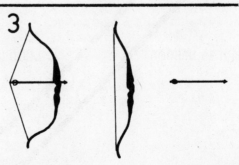

**Energy (2)**

**Energy changes** There are many different forms of energy. Given the right equipment, any one form of energy can be changed into any other form of energy. Sometimes this conversion is easy and people can make use of it in their homes, schools or offices. Sometimes it requires large, complex pieces of equipment. In some cases the conversion is extremely difficult and can only be done in specialized laboratories. Here we look at some important forms of energy and at some of the ways in which energy changes can be made.

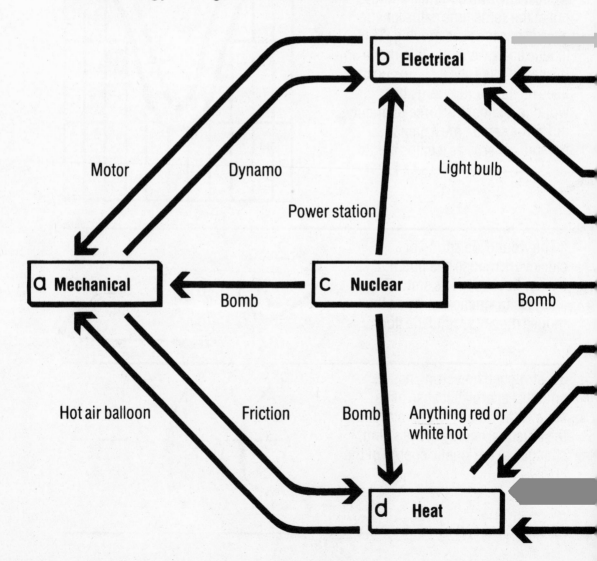

## Types of energy

**a** Mechanical energy is the energy of things that move, and includes both kinetic energy and potential energy.
**b** Electrical energy is provided by an electric current, which is produced by the movement of electrons from one atom to another.
**c** Nuclear energy uses the energy stored in the nucleus of an atom.

**d** Heat energy is produced by the random movement of the atoms in a substance. The more the atoms move, the hotter the substance.
**e** Radiant energy is the energy of light, microwaves, radio waves and other forms of radiation.
**f** Chemical energy is produced by chemical reactions. It is stored in fuels (e.g. coal, oil) and in food.

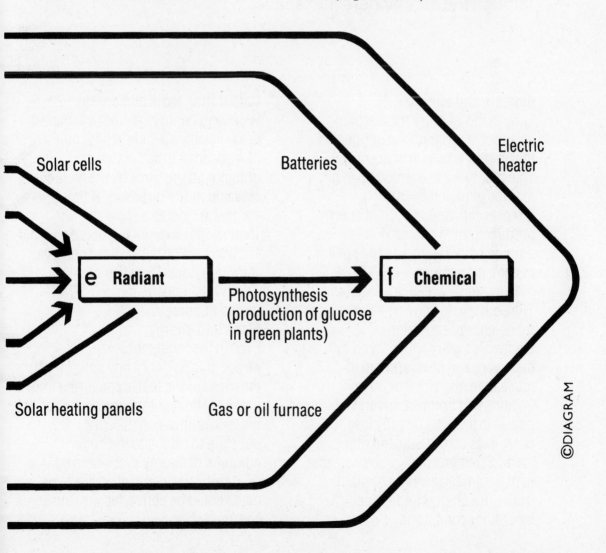

Solar cells

Batteries

Electric heater

**e  Radiant**

**f  Chemical**

Photosynthesis (production of glucose in green plants)

Solar heating panels

Gas or oil furnace

©DIAGRAM

# Energy (3)

**Conservation of energy** Energy cannot be created or destroyed – it can only be changed from one of its forms into another. Although it cannot be destroyed, energy can be wasted, usually in the form of heat. Heat energy is produced whenever an energy change takes place. For example, a flashlight uses the chemical energy in the battery to produce radiant energy from the bulb, and at the same time the battery and bulb get hot. This heat energy often cannot be used and so is wasted. The wasted heat produced on Earth gradually diffuses out through the atmosphere into space.

### Einstein and energy

Early in this century the German scientist Albert Einstein suggested that matter was a form of energy. This theory was summed up in his famous equation $E = mc^2$. E represents the amount of energy produced, m the mass (i.e. the amount of matter) and c the speed of light in a vacuum – $2.997925 \times 10^8$ m/sec – which is a constant. The equation is known as the mass-energy equivalence.

Einstein's theory was proved by the discovery and development of nuclear power. Nuclear power stations and bombs convert the matter in an atom directly into energy, as do the Sun and other stars. Scientists have also been able to make small amounts of matter from pure energy under specialized laboratory conditions.

### Calculating work and energy

Work and energy are both measured in a unit called a joule. The amount of work done is calculated by multiplying the force by the distance traveled in the direction of the force, i.e. joules = newtons × meters. For example, a person who moves a weight of 10 newtons over 3 meters does 30 joules of work. To do this work he needed 30 joules of energy.

### Mass into energy

Even in the most efficient nuclear power station only a tiny amount of the mass of the fuel is converted into energy. The rest remains as matter. Einstein's equation makes it possible to calculate the huge amounts of energy that would be released if the whole of an available mass could be converted into pure energy.

**2**   **3**

**1kg**

**1**   **4**

## Amounts of energy

If one kilogram of any substance could be completely converted into pure energy it would yield $8.99 \times 10^{16}$ joules. This is roughly equal to:

**1**) an earthquake registering 7–8 points on the Richter scale; or

**2**) a severe hurricane; or

**3**) exploding a 20 megaton thermonuclear bomb (a megaton is equivalent to 1,000,000 tons of TNT).

Even one milligram (0.000001kg) of any substance completely converted into pure energy would provide enough energy to send a rocket into space (**4**).

**1mg**

**Moving molecules** Heating a substance increases the amount of vibration in its atoms and molecules. The more heat energy a substance is given, the greater the movement. Because of this increased movement, heated atoms and molecules take up more space than unheated ones, and so a heated substance expands. All substances expand when heated but by different amounts. On average, gases expand about 100 times more than liquids, and liquids about 10 times more than solids.

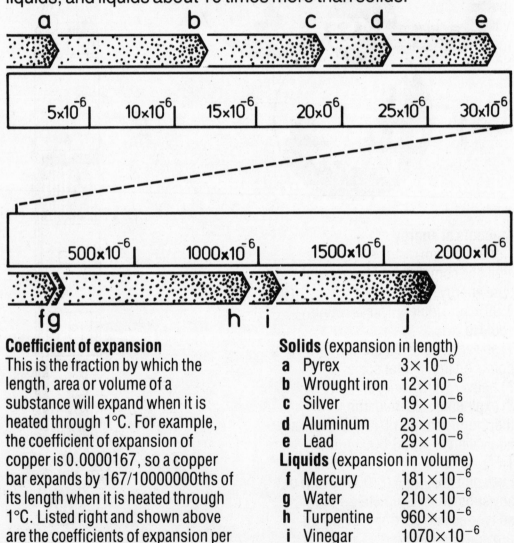

**Coefficient of expansion**
This is the fraction by which the length, area or volume of a substance will expand when it is heated through 1°C. For example, the coefficient of expansion of copper is 0.0000167, so a copper bar expands by 167/10000000ths of its length when it is heated through 1°C. Listed right and shown above are the coefficients of expansion per °C of 10 substances.

**Solids** (expansion in length)
a  Pyrex         $3 \times 10^{-6}$
b  Wrought iron  $12 \times 10^{-6}$
c  Silver        $19 \times 10^{-6}$
d  Aluminum      $23 \times 10^{-6}$
e  Lead          $29 \times 10^{-6}$

**Liquids** (expansion in volume)
f  Mercury       $181 \times 10^{-6}$
g  Water         $210 \times 10^{-6}$
h  Turpentine    $960 \times 10^{-6}$
i  Vinegar       $1070 \times 10^{-6}$
j  Ether         $1630 \times 10^{-6}$

## Heat transfer

Heat can be transferred from a hotter to a cooler body in three ways.

**1** Heat is transferred by conduction when it is transferred directly from molecule to molecule. The heated molecules pass on their increased vibration to their neighboring molecules, so making them hotter. Some substances conduct heat much better than others. For example, silver and copper conduct heat:

3 times as well as aluminum or brass;
10 times as well as iron or steel;
1000 times as well as glass;
10,000 times as well as air.

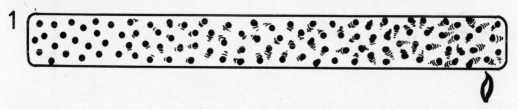

**2** Convection takes place in liquids and gases. As the heated liquid or gas rises, so the cooler liquid or gas falls to be heated in turn. This circulation of liquid or gas is called a convection current.

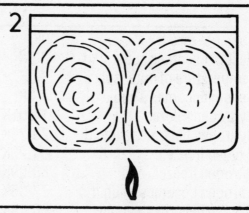

**3** Heat energy can behave like light and other forms of radiant energy, i.e. it can be transferred by radiation. Heat can be radiated even when there is no matter present (i.e. in a vacuum); conduction and convection can only take place when there is matter present.

©DIAGRAM

**Absolute zero** This is the temperature at which molecules have no heat energy at all, $-459.67°F$. It is the zero point on the scale of absolute temperature: temperatures on this scale are given in kelvins (K). It is impossible for a substance to be cooled to absolute zero, but temperatures as low as $5 \times 10^{-8}K$ have been reached in specialized laboratories.

**Kelvin and Fahrenheit**
An interval of one kelvin on the absolute temperature scale is equal to an interval of one degree on the Celsius scale. Temperatures on the Fahrenheit scale can be expressed as kelvins by first converting to degrees Celsius (°F-32) ÷ 1.8) and then adding 273.15.

| | | K | °F |
|---|---|---|---|
| 1 | Absolute zero | 0K | $-459.67°F$ |
| 2 | Helium becomes superfluid | 2.2K | $-455.71°F$ |
| 3 | Temperature of outer space | 3K | $-454°F$ |
| 4 | Helium becomes a liquid | 4.2K | $-450.4°F$ |
| 5 | Hydrogen freezes | 14.01K | $-434.2°F$ |
| 6 | Hydrogen becomes a liquid | 20.28K | $-423.17°F$ |
| 7 | Oxygen freezes | 54.25K | $-362.02°F$ |
| 8 | Nitrogen freezes | 63.29K | $-345.75°F$ |
| 9 | Nitrogen becomes a liquid | 77.35K | $-320.44°F$ |
| 10 | Oxygen becomes a liquid | 90.15K | $-297.4°F$ |
| 11 | Methane freezes | 90.55K | $-296.68°F$ |
| 12 | Methane becomes a liquid | 111.75K | $-258.52°F$ |
| 13 | Alcohol freezes | 159.05K | $-173.38°F$ |
| 14 | Coldest temperature recorded in Antarctica | 184.85K | $-126.94°F$ |
| 15 | Mercury freezes | 234.28K | $-37.97°F$ |
| 16 | Pure water freezes | 273.15K | 32°F |

## Superfluid helium

At 2.2K, helium becomes a "superfluid" which can flow up as well as down, and can leak through spaces that are too tiny for normal liquids or gases to pass through. If an empty test-tube is lowered into superfluid helium (**a**), the helium flows up into the tube until the levels of helium inside and outside the tube are the same. If the tube is then lifted up out of the container of helium, the helium in the tube flows up and out of the tube and back into the container (**b**).

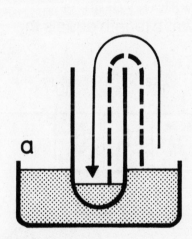

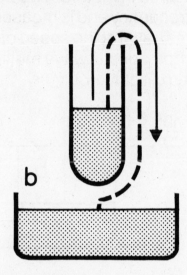

## Superconductors

Some metals and alloys allow an electric current to flow through them more easily than others, but at normal temperature all offer some resistance to the flow, and some of the electrical energy is lost as heat. But below 20K, some metals (e.g. tin and lead) and alloys become "superconductors" and allow an electric current to flow indefinitely without losing any of its strength and without producing any heat.

## Water and ice

Most substances contract and become more dense as they freeze. Water is an exception – it is at its most dense as a liquid at 39.2°F (227.15K). Because of the way in which water molecules are arranged and linked together, they take up more space in ice than they do in water – so water expands by almost one-tenth of its volume and becomes less dense when it freezes. (This is why ice floats and frozen pipes burst.)

# Electromagnetic waves

**Radiant energy** Light, radio waves, X-rays and other forms of radiant energy are transmitted through space as waves of energy called electromagnetic waves. Electromagnetic waves have alternating crests and troughs, like the waves formed when a stone is dropped into a pool of still water. The distance between the crests of the waves is called the wave length and is measured in meters. The number of waves per second is called the frequency and is measured in hertz (Hz). All electromagnetic waves travel at the speed of light; the frequency of an electromagnetic wave multiplied by its wave length equals the speed of light.

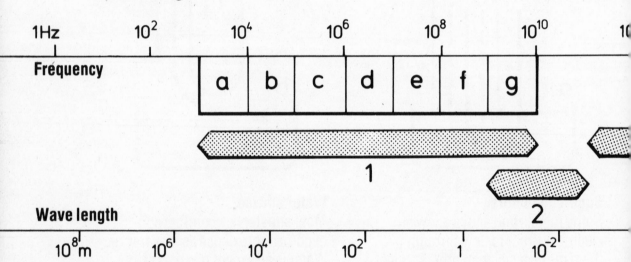

**Electromagnetic spectrum** (above) The diagram above shows the forms of radiant energy arranged in order of their frequency and wave length. The upper scale gives the frequency in hertz (Hz); the lower scale gives the wave length in meters.

**1** Radio waves These are used for transmitting radio and television (see top of facing page).

**2** Radar and microwaves Radar is used to detect unseen objects by bouncing waves off them. Microwaves are used to cook food very quickly.

**3** Infrared waves These are waves of radiant heat and are emitted by all hot objects.

**4** Visible light This part of the spectrum can be detected by the eye.

## Radio waves
This section of the spectrum is divided into bands. By international agreement, each band has specific uses. Here we give the name of each band and examples of the ways in which they may be used.

**a** VLF (very low frequency), special time signals for scientists
**b** LF (low frequency or "long wave"), ships' radio signals, AM radio
**c** MF (medium frequency or "medium wave"), police radios, AM radio
**d** HF (high frequency or "shortwave"), amateur "ham" radio
**e** VHF (very high frequency), FM radio, black and white television
**f** UHF (ultrahigh frequency), color television
**g** SHF (superhigh frequency), space and satellite communications

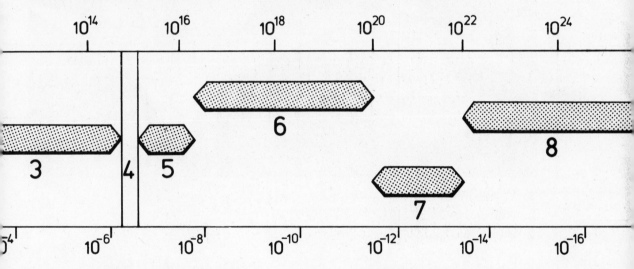

**5** Ultraviolet light
This cannot be detected by the eye. In small amounts it produces vitamin D in the body and causes the skin to tan. In larger amounts it damages body cells.
**6** X-rays
These are used to photograph bones inside the body and to detect flaws in metal structures. Overexposure to X-rays damages body cells.

**7** Gamma rays
These are emitted during the decay of some radioisotopes.
**8** Cosmic rays
These are caused by nuclear explosions and nuclear reactions in outer space. Nearly all cosmic rays are absorbed by the Earth's atmosphere.

©DIAGRAM

# Light (1)

**Visible light** Ordinary light, often called white light, is made up of electromagnetic waves in a range of wave lengths and frequencies. The human eye sees these waves as the seven colors of the rainbow – red, orange, yellow, green, blue, indigo and violet. These colors make up the visible spectrum. Their wave lengths are usually given in nanometers (nm): $1nm = 10^{-9}m$.

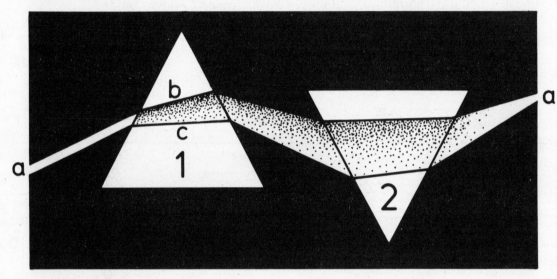

**a** White light
**b** Red end of spectrum
**c** Blue end of spectrum

## Wave lengths of colors

Everyone sees colors differently, but tests have shown that, for most people, the colors have the following wave lengths.

| | |
|---|---|
| Red | 770–622nm |
| Orange | 622–597nm |
| Yellow | 597–577nm |
| Green | 577–492nm |
| Blue | 492–455nm |
| Indigo | 455–430nm |
| Violet | 430–390nm |

## Visible spectrum (above)

If a beam of visible light shines through a triangular glass prism (**1**), it splits into the seven colors of the visible spectrum. A second prism (**2**) will recombine the colors to give white light again. Raindrops in the atmosphere can also act like prisms: when sunlight shines through them, it is split up to form a large scale spectrum, i.e. a rainbow.

## Colored substances (below)
When white light falls on a substance, some of the wave lengths in the spectrum are absorbed by the substance and others are reflected. The reflected wave lengths give the substance its color.

**1** A red substance appears red because it reflects the red wave lengths in the spectrum but absorbs the other colors.

**2** White substances reflect all the colors of the spectrum.

**3** Black substances absorb all the colors of the spectrum.

## Mixing colors of light
The three primary colors of light are red, green and blue. These three colors can be mixed to make all the other colors or to form white light. Mixtures of any two primary colors of light are called secondary colors. The secondary colors of light are yellow (red + green), magenta (red + blue) and cyan (blue + green).

## Mixing colors of paint
The three primary colors of paint are red, blue and yellow. These three colors and white paint can be mixed to make all the other colors. Mixtures of any two primary colors of paint are called secondary colors. The secondary colors of paint are orange (red + yellow), green (blue + yellow) and purple (red + blue).

# Light (2)

**Redirecting light** Mirrors and lenses change the direction in which rays of light travel. Mirrors and other shiny surfaces reflect light; lenses and other transparent substances refract (bend) light. Here we look at the different images produced by some different shapes of mirrors and lenses.

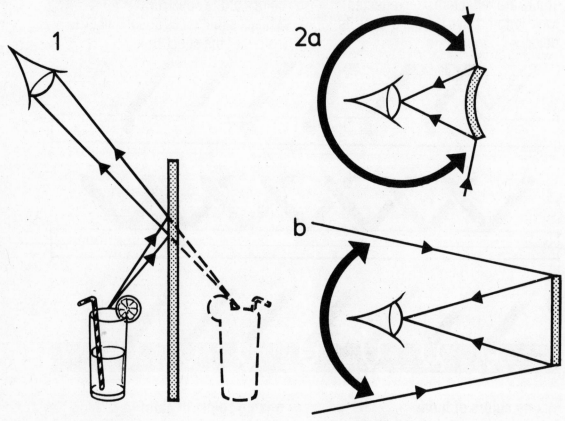

## 1 Flat mirror
The image seen in a flat mirror appears to be as far behind the mirror as the original object is in front of the mirror. It is upright and the same size as the object. The image is laterally inverted, i.e. the left of the object becomes the right of the image and vice versa.

## 2 Convex mirror
A convex mirror (**a**) has a larger field of view than a flat mirror (**b**) the same size. Because of this, convex mirrors are often used as rear view mirrors in cars. The image seen in a convex mirror is upright and laterally inverted. It appears smaller than the original object.

## A Concave lenses

These lenses are thinner at the center than they are at the edges. They make rays of light that pass through them diverge (spread out). The image produced by a concave lens is upright and diminished (i.e. the size of the image is smaller than the size of the original object). It appears to be on the same side of the lens as the object.

## B Convex lenses

These are thicker at the center than at the edges, and make rays of light converge. When the object is close to the lens, the image is upright and magnified, and on the same side of the lens as the object. If the object is far away from the lens, the image is upside down, diminished and on the opposite side of the lens to the object.

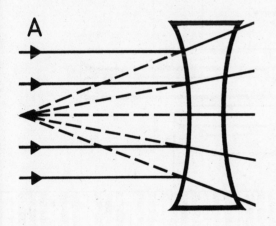

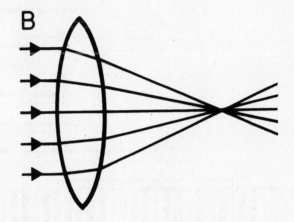

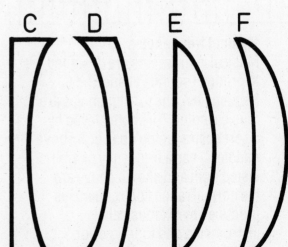

## Shapes of lenses

The concave lens shown above (**A**) is, strictly speaking, a double concave lens; the convex lens (**B**) is a double convex lens. Other lens shapes are shown right.

**C**  Plano-concave (divergent)
**D**  Convexo-concave (divergent)
**E**  Plano-convex (convergent)
**F**  Concavo-convex (convergent)

**Sound**

**Pitch and loudness** Sound is produced by anything that is vibrating. The vibrations in the sound source cause changes of pressure in the surrounding air: these changes of pressure are sound waves. The number of vibrations per second gives the frequency of the sound, which is measured in hertz (Hz). The pitch of a sound (how high or low it is) depends on its frequency. The size of the vibrations gives the loudness of the sound, which is measured in decibels (dB).

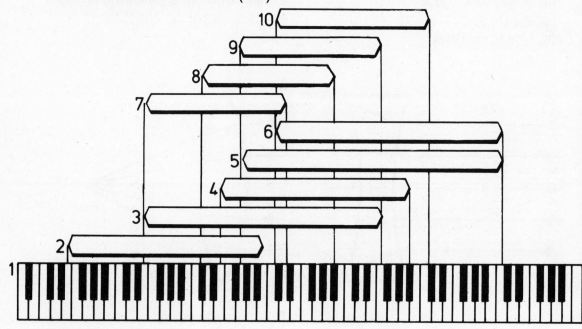

## Musical frequencies

Musical instruments are designed to produce sounds at specific frequencies. These frequencies are musical notes. The note played by an orchestra tuning up (i.e. A above middle C) has a frequency of 440Hz. Listed right and shown above are the normal ranges of frequencies produced by six musical instruments and four types of human voice.

### Instruments

| 1 | Piano | 27.5–4186Hz |
|---|---|---|
| 2 | Double bass | 41.2–247Hz |
| 3 | Guitar | 82.4–698Hz |
| 4 | Trumpet | 165–932Hz |
| 5 | Violin | 196–2093Hz |
| 6 | Flute | 262–2093Hz |

### Voices

| 7 | Bass | 82.4–294Hz |
|---|---|---|
| 8 | Tenor | 147–466Hz |
| 9 | Alto | 196–698Hz |
| 10 | Soprano | 262–1046Hz |

## Noises

The quietest sounds that a person with normal hearing in both ears can hear are rated at 0dB. Noises rated at 120–130dB cause pain; those rated at 140dB and over can cause permanent ear damage. Listed right and shown on the scale below are the decibel ratings of some common noises. (The distance away from the noise is given in brackets.)

| | | |
|---|---|---|
| **A** | Whisper (15ft) | 30dB |
| **B** | Inside an urban home | 50dB |
| **C** | Light traffic (50ft) | 55dB |
| **D** | Normal conversation (3ft) | 60dB |
| **E** | Pneumatic drill (50ft) | 85dB |
| **F** | Heavy traffic (50ft) | 90dB |
| **G** | Loud shout (50ft) | 100dB |
| **H** | Jet taking off (2,000ft) | 105dB |
| **I** | Discotheque at full volume | 117dB |
| **J** | Jet taking off (200ft) | 120dB |

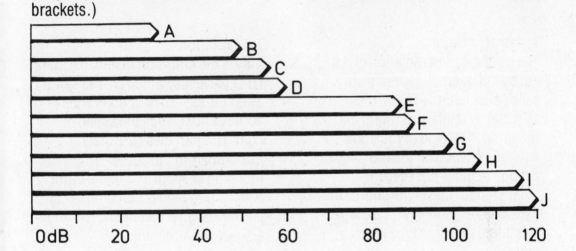

## Speed of sound

Sound can only be transmitted through matter; it cannot travel in a vacuum. Sound travels at different speeds in different materials. Its speed in air at 68°F is about 1135ft /sec; in water it is 4750–4950ft/sec, depending on temperature. "Supersonic" means traveling faster than the speed of sound; "subsonic" means slower than the speed of sound.

## Infrasonic and ultrasonic

The human ear hears sounds with frequencies of about 20–20,000Hz. Sounds with frequencies below 20Hz are called infrasonic: these frequencies are produced by earthquakes and erupting volcanoes. Sounds above 20,000Hz are called ultrasonic. Ultrasonics can be used to examine unborn babies in the womb, clean machinery and detect flaws in metals.

# Radioactivity (1)

**Radioactive elements** These are elements in which some of the nuclei break up to form new atoms, at the same time giving out radiation. This process is known as radioactive decay. Some naturally occurring elements (e.g. those with atomic numbers 84–92) are naturally radioactive, i.e. their nuclei break down spontaneously (of their own accord). Other elements can be made artificially radioactive under special conditions, e.g. by bombarding them with a stream of neutrons in a nuclear reactor. Manmade elements produced in nuclear reactors are also radioactive.

## Types of radiation
The three types of radiation given out by radioactive elements are called after letters of the Greek alphabet: $\alpha$ (alpha), $\beta$ (beta) and $\gamma$ (gamma). The type of radiation emitted depends on the radioactive isotope (usually abbreviated to radioisotope) that is the source of the radiation. Some radioisotopes emit more than one type of radiation.

## $\alpha$ radiation
This is the emission of $\alpha$-particles, which are the same as helium atoms that have lost their electrons. An $\alpha$-particle thus consists of 2 protons and 2 neutrons. The speed of a particle is about 5–7% of the speed of light. $\alpha$-particles can travel through air for about 2.4–3.9in, but they cannot pass through a sheet of paper.

## $\beta^-$ radiation
This is the emission of negative beta ($\beta^-$) particles, which are the same as electrons. Their speed varies – some almost reach the speed of light. $\beta^-$-particles can travel through air for about 6ft. $\beta^-$ radiation is about 100 times more penetrating than $\alpha$ radiation: it can pass through paper but not through a sheet of aluminum.

## $\gamma$ radiation
$\gamma$ radiation is similar to X-rays. $\gamma$ rays travel at the speed of light and can travel long distances through air. $\gamma$ radiation is about 1000 times more penetrating than $\alpha$ radiation: it can pass through paper and aluminum and is only stopped by a thick sheet of lead.

**1**

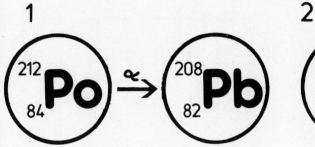

**2**

## Distinguishing isotopes

The total number of protons and neutrons in the nucleus of an atom is called the mass number. It is used to distinguish one isotope of an element from another. For example, uranium (U) has 92 protons in the nucleus. Uranium-238 represents the isotope of uranium with 146 neutrons in the nucleus (92+146=238), while uranium-235 represents the isotope of uranium with 143 neutrons in the nucleus (92+143=235). The abbreviations U-238 and U-235 can be used, or the mass number can be used with the element's symbol and atomic number as shown below.

**Changes**(above)

When an atom of an element loses an $\alpha$-particle (called $\alpha$ decay) it changes to an atom of another element (**1**). The new atom has 2 fewer protons and 2 fewer neutrons, so the atomic number of the element is reduced by 2 and its mass number is reduced by 4. An atom of an element that loses a $\beta^-$-particle (called $\beta^-$ decay) also changes to an atom of another element (**2**). $\beta^-$ radiation occurs when a neutron in the nucleus breaks down to form a proton and an electron: the extra electron is emitted as a $\beta^-$-particle. This means that the new atom has 1 more proton than before and so its atomic number increases by 1. The mass number remains unchanged because the total number of protons and neutrons has not altered. When an atom of an element gives out $\gamma$ radiation it does not change to an atom of another element. $\gamma$ radiation is emitted when a nucleus has more energy than it needs.

**Radioactivity (2)**

### Half life

This is the time it takes for half the number of atoms of a radioactive substance to decay. The diagram right shows what happens to a known amount of Co-60 (**a**), whose half life is 5.2 years. After one half life, half of the Co-60 has decayed (**b**). After another half life (just as long), half of the remaining Co-60 has decayed (**c**), leaving just one quarter of the original amount of Co-60. After the next half life, half of this remaining quarter has decayed (**d**), and so on.

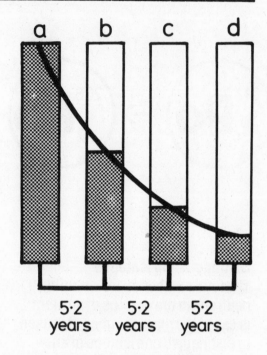

5·2 years    5·2 years    5·2 years

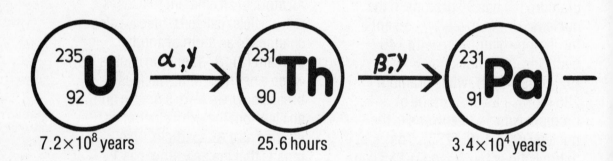

$^{235}_{92}\text{U}$ $\xrightarrow{\alpha,\gamma}$ $^{231}_{90}\text{Th}$ $\xrightarrow{\beta^-,\gamma}$ $^{231}_{91}\text{Pa}$ —

$7.2 \times 10^8$ years          25.6 hours          $3.4 \times 10^4$ years

### Radioactive series

Sometimes the new atoms produced by the decay of a radioisotope are themselves radioactive. They then decay to produce atoms of another element, and so on. The last stage of the series is always an isotope that does not emit radiation, i.e. it is stable.

All the isotopes in the series can exist together at the same time. Here we show the first isotopes in the radioactive series formed by the decay of U-235. The half life and type of decay are given for each isotope. The series continues through several more isotopes until it reaches a stable isotope of lead, Pb-207

## Lengths of half lives

Half lives vary from a fraction of a second (the shortest is Li-5 with a half life of $4.4 \times 10^{-22}$ sec) to several million years. Because a particular radioisotope always has the same half life whatever the conditions around it, scientists can work out how old some substances are by studying the radioisotopes they contain. This is called radiometric dating. For example, the amount of K-40 in rock around a fossil can be used to calculate the fossil's age. Half lives of some radioisotopes with practical uses in medicine, science and industry are given in the table right.

| Radioisotopes | Type of decay | Half life and example of use |
|---|---|---|
| $^{24}_{11}\text{Na}\,\beta^-$ | | 15 hours<br>Studying blood circulation |
| $^{82}_{35}\text{Br}\,\beta^-,\gamma$ | | 35.9 hours<br>Detecting leaks in underground piping |
| $^{198}_{79}\text{Au}\,\beta^-,\gamma$ | | 2.7 days<br>Cancer treatment |
| $^{131}_{53}\text{I}\quad\beta^-,\gamma$ | | 8.05 days<br>Testing thyroid gland activity |
| $^{59}_{26}\text{Fe}\,\beta^-,\gamma$ | | 45.1 days<br>Testing automobile parts |
| $^{60}_{27}\text{Co}\,\beta^-,\gamma$ | | 5.2 years<br>Disinfecting goats' hair |
| $^{238}_{94}\text{Pu}\,\alpha,\gamma$ | | 89.6 years<br>Powering heart pacemakers |
| $^{14}_{6}\text{C}\quad\beta^-$ | | 5570 years<br>Radiometric dating |
| $^{239}_{94}\text{Pu}\,\alpha,\gamma$ | | $2.4 \times 10^4$ years<br>Nuclear reactors |
| $^{235}_{92}\text{U}\quad\alpha,\gamma$ | | $7.2 \times 10^8$ years<br>Nuclear reactors |
| $^{40}_{19}\text{K}\quad\beta^-,\gamma$ | | $1.3 \times 10^9$ years<br>Radiometric dating |

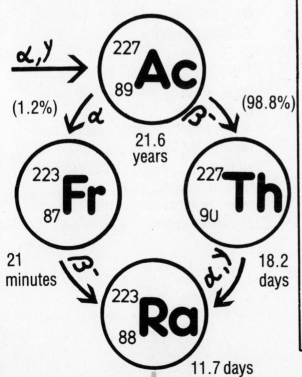

©DIAGRAM

**Properties of air** Air is a mixture of gases, mainly nitrogen and oxygen. The oxygen in the air is essential to support life and to allow fuels to burn. Nitrogen-fixing plants and bacteria use nitrogen from the air to make soil fertile. Because air conducts heat badly it insulates the Earth, preventing it getting too hot during the day or losing too much heat at night. Air also protects the Earth from dangerous radiation from outer space.

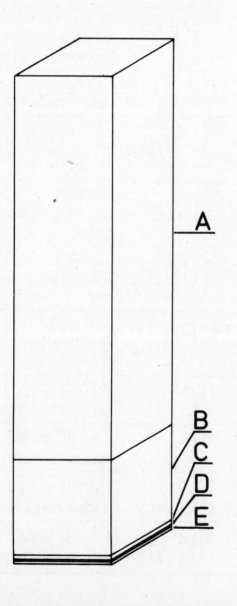

**Clean air**
The exact composition of air varies from place to place around the world. The average percentages (by volume) of the gases in clean, dry air are listed below and shown in the diagram left.

| | | |
|---|---|---|
| **A** | Nitrogen | 78% |
| **B** | Oxygen | 20.8% |
| **C** | Argon | 0.9% |
| **D** | Carbon dioxide | 0.03% |
| **E** | Other gases | 0.27% |

The other gases include helium, neon, krypton, xenon, hydrogen and methane.
Air also contains water vapor, but the amount varies a great deal. Dry air (e.g. in desert regions) contains no water vapor, moist air (e.g. over a tropical jungle) may contain 6% water vapor.

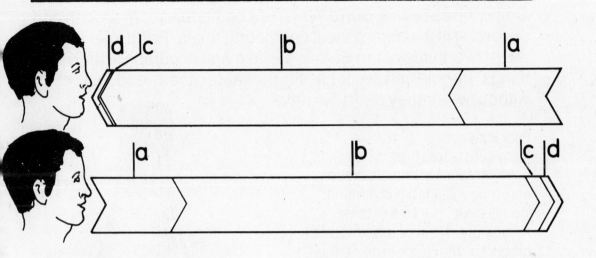

## Carbon dioxide

The percentage of carbon dioxide in air can vary from 0.01% to 0.1% Green plants take carbon dioxide from the air and put back oxygen. People, animals and machines all take oxygen from the air and put back carbon dioxide. Listed below and shown above is the average composition of one quart of air breathed in by a person and of one quart of air breathed out.

### Breathed in

| a | Oxygen | 12.7 cu.in |
|---|---|---|
| b | Nitrogen | 47.6 cu.in |
| c | Carbon dioxide | 0.02 cu.in |
| d | Other gases | 0.71 cu.in |

### Breathed out

| a | Oxygen | 10.4 cu.in |
|---|---|---|
| b | Nitrogen | 47.6 cu.in |
| c | Carbon dioxide | 2.34 cu.in |
| d | Other gases | 0.72 cu.in |

## Dirty air

Dirty or polluted air contains dust, grit, soot and harmful gases. A small town can produce over 10,000lb of air pollution in one day. Listed below are some of the harmful gases found in polluted air and examples of the sources that produce them. Other pollutants, e.g. ozone, are produced when these gases react with each other in sunlight.

Sulfur dioxide, burning coal, oil or gas
Nitrogen dioxide, car exhausts
Carbon monoxide, car exhausts
Lead compounds, car exhausts
Fluorocarbons, aerosols
Hydrocarbons, chemical works

## Speed

The average speed of a molecule of air is 1365.4ft/sec.

# Water

**Commonest compound** Water is a compound of hydrogen and oxygen. It is the commonest compound on the Earth, making up about two-thirds of the Earth's surface and occurring in all living things. People can live for several weeks without food, but without water they die in 3-4 days.

### Pure water

Many substances dissolve easily in water. Because of this, naturally occurring water is never pure – it always contains traces of other substances. The type and amount of these vary from place to place: the label right lists the substances found in one type of bottled spring water. Pure water (called "distilled" or "deionized" water) can only be prepared by removing the dissolved substances under special conditions.

### Heavy water

If some or all of the hydrogen in water is replaced by deuterium (the isotope of hydrogen with a neutron in the nucleus), the water becomes "heavy" water. This is used in nuclear reactors. Its boiling point is 214.56°F and its freezing point is 38.88°F. Naturally occurring water contains about 1 molecule of heavy water for every 6760 molecules of "ordinary" water.

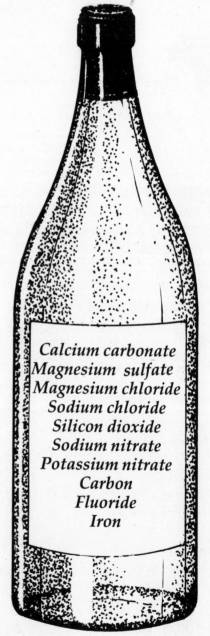

*Calcium carbonate*
*Magnesium sulfate*
*Magnesium chloride*
*Sodium chloride*
*Silicon dioxide*
*Sodium nitrate*
*Potassium nitrate*
*Carbon*
*Fluoride*
*Iron*

## Water content

The human body contains a great deal of water. An average young man (**a**) is about 65% water; a middle-aged woman (**b**) is about 50% water. An average adult needs nearly 2½ quarts of water a day. Some of this can be obtained from food. Listed below and shown right are the average percentages of water in some common foods.

| A | Lettuce | 97% |
|---|---------|-----|
| B | Cucumber | 95% |
| C | Tomato | 94% |
| D | Egg | 74% |
| E | Beef | 70% |
| F | Chicken | 55% |
| G | Bread | 42% |
| H | Ham | 38% |
| I | Cheese | 26% |
| J | Butter | 9% |
| K | Sugar | 0% |
| L | Salt | 0% |

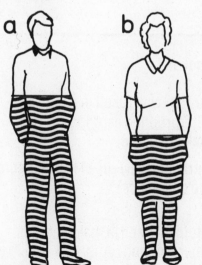

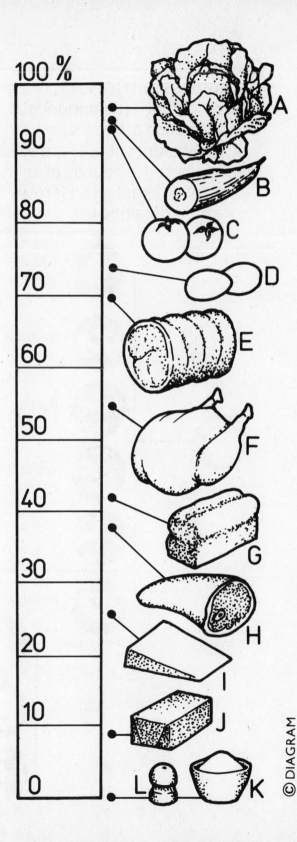

© DIAGRAM

**Composition** Crude oil, or petroleum, is a mixture of hydrocarbons (compounds of hydrogen and carbon). The composition of petroleum varies considerably: no two crude oils from different sources are exactly alike. Petroleum was produced by the decay of animals and plants that lived in the sea millions of years ago. Here we look at some of the thousands of products obtained from the refining of crude oil.

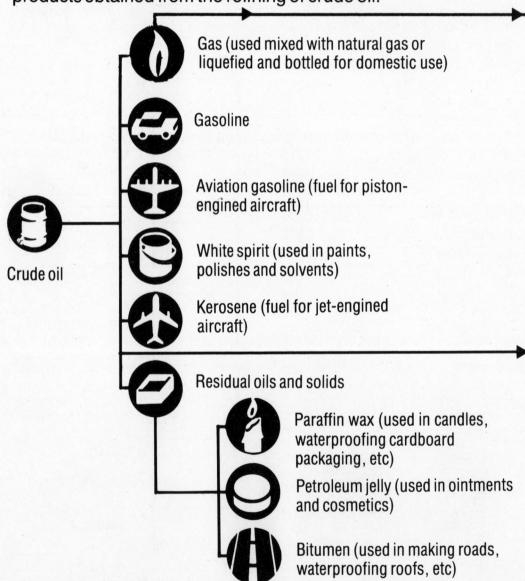

Crude oil

Gas (used mixed with natural gas or liquefied and bottled for domestic use)

Gasoline

Aviation gasoline (fuel for piston-engined aircraft)

White spirit (used in paints, polishes and solvents)

Kerosene (fuel for jet-engined aircraft)

Residual oils and solids

Paraffin wax (used in candles, waterproofing cardboard packaging, etc)

Petroleum jelly (used in ointments and cosmetics)

Bitumen (used in making roads, waterproofing roofs, etc)

Synthetic rubbers, synthetic fibers, plastics, etc

*Combined to make other useful chemicals*

Olefins (used to improve the quality of gasoline)

Benzene (used in drugs, plastics, etc)

Toluene (used in explosives, artificial sweeteners, etc)

*Broken down ("cracked") to form other useful chemicals*

Gas oil (fuel for oil burning furnaces)

Diesel oil (fuel for diesel-engined buses, trains, etc)

Fuel oil (used in oil burning power plants, industrial furnaces)

Lubricating oils and greases (used in engines, gearboxes, machinery, etc)

©DIAGRAM

# Coal

**Coal products** Coal was produced by the decay of forests that covered large areas of the Earth millions of years ago. It is an important fuel and is also used to produce thousands of different chemicals. Nylon, polyesters, polycarbonate, epoxides and other polymers can all be made from coal as well as oil. In some countries synthetic gasoline made from coal is already on sale. As crude oil becomes scarcer and more expensive, so chemicals made from coal are becoming more important.

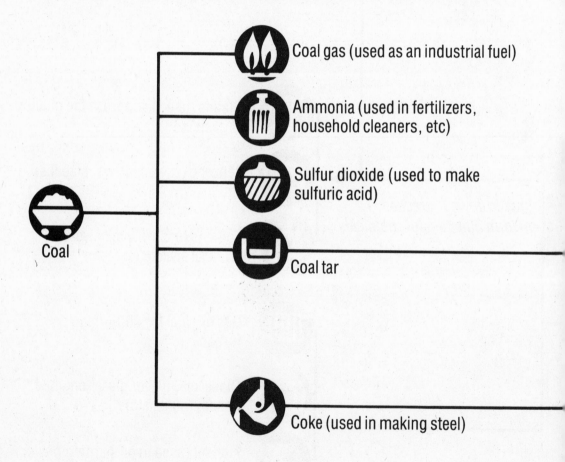

Coal

Coal gas (used as an industrial fuel)

Ammonia (used in fertilizers, household cleaners, etc)

Sulfur dioxide (used to make sulfuric acid)

Coal tar

Coke (used in making steel)

Benzene (used in polystyrene, synthetic rubbers, etc)

Toluene (used in explosives, artificial sweeteners, etc)

Xylene (used in synthetic fibers and resins)

Pyridine (used in drugs, vitamins, etc)

Phenol (used in nylon, epoxides, polycarbonate, etc)

Naphthalene (used in polyesters, aspirin, dyes, drugs, etc)

Creosote (used in dyes, wood preservatives, disinfectants, etc)

Anthracene oil (used in making dyes)

Pitch (used in coating roofs, making bricks for lining furnaces, making clay pigeons, etc)

Asphalt (used in surfacing roads)

Methanol (used in dyes, perfumes, rocket fuels, etc)

Gasoline

Diesel fuel (fuel for diesel -engined machinery)

Synthesis gas

Lubricating oils (used in engines, machinery, etc)

Acetylene (used in acrylic fibers, synthetic rubbers, etc)

Waxes (used in waterproofing packaging, etc)

# Polymers

**Large molecules** Polymers are large molecules made up of hundreds of small molecules joined together to form long chains. (The word polymer comes from two Greek words: *poly*, meaning many and *meros* meaning parts or units.) Some polymers occur naturally but many others are manmade: many plastics and artificial fibers are manmade polymers. Depending on how they are made, polymers can be soft or hard, stretchy or rigid, easily melted or heat resistant, pressed out into flat sheets, spun into thread, or made into foam. The starting materials for making polymers come from petroleum or coal.

**Natural polymers**
Listed here are five naturally occurring types of polymer.

| | |
|---|---|
| Rubber | Starch |
| Proteins | Diamond |
| Cellulose | |

**Textile fibers**
Listed below are five types of polymer textile fibers and some of the names by which they are known commercially.

| Polyamide | **NYLON** |
|---|---|
| Polyvinyl chloride | **Vinyl** |
| Polyester | **DACRON** **FORTREL** **KODEL** |
| Polyurethane | **Lycra** **SPANDEX** |
| Polyacrilonitrile | **ACRYLIC** **Creslan** **ORLON** |

## Manmade polymers

Here we list some common manmade polymers and examples of their uses.

| Polymer | Examples of use |
|---|---|
| Polyethylene | Bottles (**1**) shopping bags, containers, electrical insulation |
| Polypropylene | Carpets, blankets, crates, containers |
| Polystyrene | Pens, toys, insulating tiles |
| Polyvinyl chloride (PVC) | Roofs, pipes, toys (**2**), luggage, upholstery |
| Polymethyl methacrylate (Plexiglass) | Aircraft windows, car lights, baths |
| Polyurethane | Furniture, foam upholstery |
| Polyvinyl acetate | Emulsion paint |
| Polytetrafluoroethylene (PTFE, Teflon) | Nonstick pans (**3**) |
| Polyformaldehyde | Safety steering columns |
| Polyamide | "Cook in the bag" packaging |
| Polyethylene terephthalate | Shrink wrapping |
| Polycarbonate | Safety helmets (**4**), computer parts |
| Polyether urethane | Car seats and armrests |
| Polychloroprene (neoprene) | Adhesives, shoes (**5**), packaging |
| Polyoxyethylene | Coating textiles and paper |
| Epoxide resin | Adhesives |
| Acrylonitrile-butadiene-styrene | Luggage, car doors and bodies, telephones (**6**) |
| Styrene-butadiene rubber | Tires, hoses |
| Silicones | Aircraft and spacecraft lubricants, laminating fiberglass |

© DIAGRAM

# Metals and nonmetals

**Properties of metals** All but 25 of the known elements are metals. Metals are elements that can lose one or more electrons to form positive ions. (An ion is a small electrically charged particle.) Metals are good conductors of heat and electricity. They are malleable (i.e. they can be beaten or rolled into a new shape) and ductile (i.e. they can be pulled out into long wires). All metals are shiny, crystalline solids, except mercury, which is a liquid.

## Alloys

An alloy is a mixture of two or more metals. Here we list some everyday alloys and the metals from which they are made.

| Alloy | Metals | Examples of use |
|---|---|---|
| Bronze | Copper, tin | "Copper" coins |
| Brass | Copper, zinc | Doorhandles, buttons, etc |
| Cupronickel | Copper, nickel | "Silver" coins (**1**) |
| Pewter | Tin, lead | Tankards (**2**) |
| Stainless steel | Iron, chromium, nickel | Cutlery, pots, etc |
| Sterling silver | Silver, copper | Jewelry (**3**) |
| 9, 18, and 22 carat gold | Gold, silver, copper | Jewelry |
| Dental amalgam | Silver, tin, copper, zinc, mercury | Filling teeth |
| Solder | Lead, tin | Joining metals together |

## Activity series (right)

Some metals form positive ions more easily than others, and so are more chemically active. Here we list 16 common metals in the order of their activity. Lithium is the most active of all the metals, and gold is the least active.

## Native metals

Only four of the least active metals – copper, silver, platinum and gold – commonly occur in the Earth's crust as native metals (i.e. as free elements). All the others are found as compounds called ores which must be chemically treated to obtain the pure element.

## Nonmetals (right)

Here we list the 17 nonmetallic elements. They are poor conductors of heat and electricity, i.e. they are good insulators. Some are solids, some are gases, and one is a liquid.

## Metalloids

These are the "halfway" elements between metals and nonmetals. Depending on the way they are treated, they can act as insulators like nonmetals or conduct electricity like metals. They are all solids. The eight metalloid elements are boron, silicon, germanium, arsenic, antimony, tellurium, polonium and astatine.

**Most active**

Lithium
Potassium
Calcium
Sodium
Magnesium
Aluminum
Zinc
Chromium
Iron
Nickel
Tin
Lead
Copper
Silver
Platinum
Gold

**Least active**

| Solid | Liquid | Gas |
|---|---|---|
| Phosphorus | Bromine | Hydrogen |
| Sulfur | | Nitrogen |
| Selenium | | Oxygen |
| Carbon | | Fluorine |
| Iodine | | Chlorine |
| | | Helium |
| | | Neon |
| | | Argon |
| | | Krypton |
| | | Xenon |
| | | Radon |

©DIAGRAM

# Carbon

**Forms of carbon** Some forms of carbon are crystalline and others are amorphous, i.e. the atoms in the substance are not arranged in a regular, crystalline pattern. Charcoal and coke are both amorphous forms of carbon. The most commonly used type of bituminous coal is 80–90% amorphous carbon. The crystalline forms of carbon are diamond and graphite.

**A Diamond**
Carbon atoms in diamond are surrounded by four others, as shown right. This structure makes diamond a very strong substance: it is the hardest substance known.

**B Graphite**
Carbon atoms in graphite are surrounded by three others, as shown far right. The carbon atoms are in flat layers which can slide over each other like cards in a pack. This makes graphite a good lubricant.

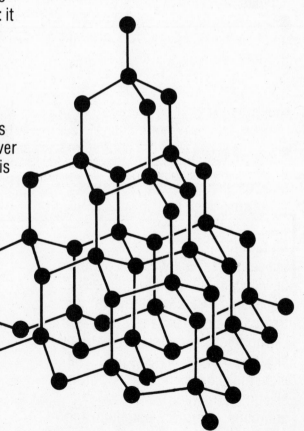
A

## Carbon compounds

Listed right are the common names of just 10 of the many thousands of compounds that contain carbon. The total number of carbon compounds is greater than the total number of compounds formed by all the other elements. Most substances produced by living things are compounds of carbon.

Alcohol
Chalk
Sugar
Soap
Polyethylene
Nylon
Antifreeze
Penicillin
TNT
Vinegar

B

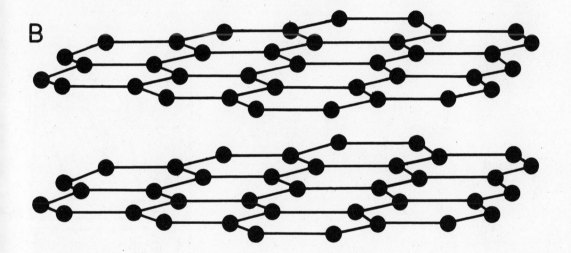

## Properties

Although diamond and graphite are both made up only of carbon atoms, their different structures give them very different properties.

| Diamond | Graphite |
|---|---|
| Hard | Soft |
| Transparent | Grayish-black |
| Does not conduct electricity | Conducts electricity |
| Used in jewelry | Used in pencils |
| Cuts other substances | Easily cut or broken |
| Not a lubricant | Good lubricant |

# Section 5

# Numbers

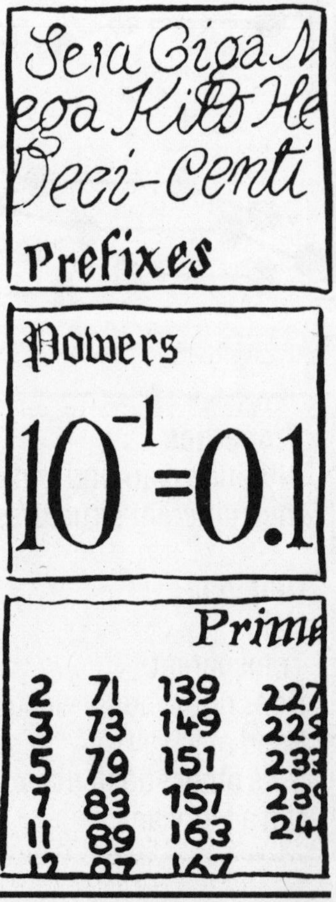

Tera Giga M
ega Kilo He
Deci-Centi

**Prefixes**

**Powers**

$$10^{-1} = 0.1$$

*Prime*

| | | | |
|---|---|---|---|
| 2 | 71 | 139 | 227 |
| 3 | 73 | 149 | 229 |
| 5 | 79 | 151 | 233 |
| 7 | 83 | 157 | 239 |
| 11 | 89 | 163 | 24 |
| 13 | 97 | 167 | |

**Shapes**

**Circles**

**Areas**

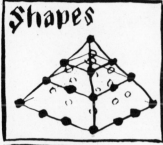

**Shapes**

**Angles**

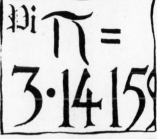

**Pi** $\pi = 3\cdot1415$

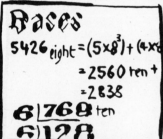

**Bases**

$$5426_{eight} = (5\times8^3) + (4\times8^2$$
$$= 2560_{ten} +$$
$$= 2838$$

$6\overline{)768}_{ten}$
$6\overline{)128}$

**Polygons**

**Formulae**

$V = \frac{4}{3}\pi r^3$

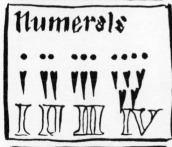

**Numerals**

I II III IV

**Solids**

**Solids**

**Tables** *Base 8*

1 2 3 4 5 6 7
2 4 6 10 12 14
3 6 11 14 17 22

**Semi-regular solids**

**Topology**

# Names for numbers (1)

**Named numbers** Many numbers have names. Some of these names are in everyday use, others apply in more specialized areas such as music and multiple births. Some names for specialized numbers have the same first part (prefix). These prefixes indicate the number to which the name refers.

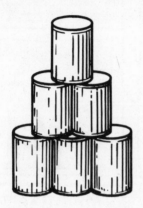

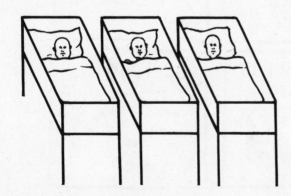

## Everyday use

| | |
|---|---|
| 2 | Pair, couple |
| 6 | Half a dozen |
| 12 | Dozen |
| 13 | Baker's dozen |
| 20 | Score |
| 50 | Half century |
| 100 | Century |
| 144 | Gross |
| 500 | Ream |

## Groups of musicians

| | |
|---|---|
| 1 | Soloist |
| 2 | Duet |
| 3 | Trio |
| 4 | Quartet |
| 5 | Quintet |
| 6 | Sextet |
| 7 | Septet |
| 8 | Octet |

## Multiple births

| | |
|---|---|
| 2 | Twins |
| 3 | Triplets |
| 4 | Quadruplets (quads) |
| 5 | Quintuplets (quins) |
| 6 | Sextuplets |

**Slang for money**

| | |
|---|---|
| 1¢ | Penny |
| 5¢ | Nickel |
| 10¢ | Dime |
| 25¢ | Quarter, two bits |
| $1 | Buck |

**Prefixes in numerical order**

| | |
|---|---|
| 1/10 | Deci- |
| 1/2 | Semi-, hemi-, demi- |
| 1 | Uni- |
| 2 | Bi-, di- |
| 3 | Tri-, ter- |
| 4 | Tetra-, tetr-, tessara-, quadri-, quadr- |
| 5 | Pent-, penta-, quinqu-, quinque-, quint- |
| 6 | Sex-, sexi-, hex-, hexa- |
| 7 | Hepta-, sept-, septi-, septem- |
| 8 | Oct-, octa- |
| 9 | Non-, nona-, ennea- |
| 10 | Deca- |
| 11 | Hendeca-, undec-, undeca- |
| 12 | Dodeca- |
| 15 | Quindeca- |
| 20 | Icos-, icosa-, icosi- |

**Prefixes in alphabetical order**

| | |
|---|---|
| Bi- | 2 |
| Deca- | 10 |
| Deci- | 1/10 |
| Demi- | 1/2 |
| Di- | 2 |
| Dodeca- | 12 |
| Ennea- | 9 |
| Hemi- | 1/2 |
| Hendeca- | 11 |
| Hepta- | 7 |
| Hex-, hexa- | 6 |
| Icos-, icosa-, icosi- | 20 |
| Non-, nona- | 9 |
| Oct-, octa- | 8 |
| Pent-, penta- | 5 |
| Quadr-, quadri- | 4 |
| Quindeca- | 15 |
| Quinqu-, quinque- | 5 |
| Quint- | 5 |
| Semi- | 1/2 |
| Sept-, septem-, septi- | 7 |
| Sex-, sexi- | 6 |
| Ter- | 3 |
| Tessara- | 4 |
| Tetr-, tetra- | 4 |
| Tri- | 3 |
| Undec-, undeca- | 11 |
| Uni- | 1 |

# Names for numbers (2)

**Arithmetical operations** The four basic arithmetical operations are addition, subtraction, multiplication and division. Each part of an arithmetical operation has a specific name.

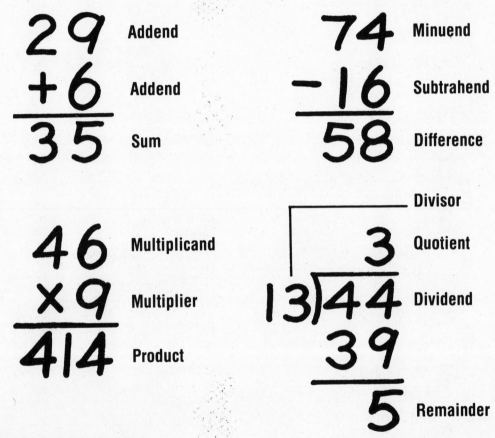

$$
\begin{array}{rl}
29 & \text{Addend} \\
+6 & \text{Addend} \\
\hline
35 & \text{Sum}
\end{array}
$$

$$
\begin{array}{rl}
74 & \text{Minuend} \\
-16 & \text{Subtrahend} \\
\hline
58 & \text{Difference}
\end{array}
$$

$$
\begin{array}{rl}
46 & \text{Multiplicand} \\
\times 9 & \text{Multiplier} \\
\hline
414 & \text{Product}
\end{array}
$$

Divisor
Quotient: 3
$13\overline{)44}$ Dividend
39
Remainder: 5

**Parts of a Fraction** (right)
Fractions express numbers which are parts of a whole. The denominator of a fraction is the number below or after the dividing line: it shows into how many parts the whole has been divided. The numerator is the number above or before the line: it shows how many of these parts there are.

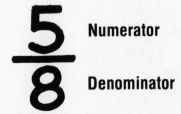

$$\frac{5}{8}$$ Numerator

Denominator

**Factors** The factors of a number are all the numbers which will divide into it exactly without leaving a remainder. For example, 18 has six factors – 1, 2, 3, 6, 9 and 18.

```
    1           1           1              1              1
  + 2         + 2         + 2            + 2            + 2
  + 3         + 4         + 4            + 4            + 4
  ___         + 7         + 8            + 8            + 8
    6         + 1 4       + 1 6          + 1 6          + 1 6
              _____       + 3 1          + 3 2          + 3 2
                2 8       + 6 2          + 6 4          + 6 4
                          + 1 2 4        + 1 2 7        + 1 2 8
                          + 2 4 8        + 2 5 4        + 2 5 6
                          _____        + 5 0 8        + 5 1 2
                            4 9 6        + 1 0 1 6      + 1 0 2 4
                                         + 2 0 3 2      + 2 0 4 8
                                         + 4 0 6 4      + 4 0 9 6
                                         _____        + 8 1 9 1
                                           8 1 2 8      + 1 6 3 8 2
                                                        + 3 2 7 6 4
                                                        + 6 5 5 2 8
                                                        + 1 3 1 0 5 6
                                                        + 2 6 2 1 1 2
                                                        + 5 2 4 2 2 4
                                                        + 1 0 4 8 4 4 8
                                                        + 2 0 9 6 8 9 6
                                                        + 4 1 9 3 7 9 2
                                                        + 8 3 8 7 5 8 4
                                                        + 1 6 7 7 5 1 6 8
                                                        _____
                                                          3 3 5 5 0 3 3 6
```

**Perfect numbers** (above)
A perfect number is a whole number which equals the sum of all its factors other than the number itself. Perfect numbers are rare. Shown above are the factors of the first five perfect numbers. The sixth perfect number is 8,589,869,056. No odd perfect numbers have yet been found.

©DIAGRAM

# Powers, indices, roots

**Powers** When a number is multiplied by itself – for example, $7 \times 7$ – it is said to have been raised to the power of two and can be written $7^2$. The small number is called the "power" or "index" and shows by how many times the number should be multiplied by itself. $7^3$ is seven raised to the power of three ($7 \times 7 \times 7$); $7^4$ is seven raised to the power of four ($7 \times 7 \times 7 \times 7$); and so on.

### Negative powers

A negative power or index shows how many times the number must be divided into the number one. For example, $7^{-1} = 1 \div 7$ (also written 1/7); $7^{-2} = 1 \div 7 \div 7$ (also written $1/7^2$); and so on. Negative powers of 10 ($10^{-1}$, $10^{-2}$, etc) can also be written as decimals, as shown in the examples below.

| | |
|---|---|
| $10^{-1}$ | 0.1 |
| $10^{-2}$ | 0.01 |
| $10^{-3}$ | 0.001 |
| $10^{-4}$ | 0.0001 |
| $10^{-10}$ | 0.0000000001 |

### Multiplying and dividing

Numbers written in their index forms can be multiplied by adding their indices, e.g. $7^2 \times 7^3 = 7^5$. They can be divided by subtracting their indices, e.g. $7^8 \div 7^6 = 7^2$. Expressing large numbers in their index forms (usually as multiples of 10) makes it possible to multiply or divide them quickly. For example, 20,000 can be written as $2 \times 10^4$, and 1,350,000 can be written as $1.35 \times 10^6$. Therefore

$$20,000 \times 1,350,000$$
$$= 2 \times 10^4 \times 1.35 \times 10^6$$
$$= 2.7 \times 10^{10} = 27,000,000,000$$

### Roots

If a larger number can be expressed as a power of a smaller number, the smaller number is called a root of the larger number.

For example, $64 = 2^6$; 2 is therefore the sixth root of 64 and can be written $\sqrt[6]{64}$ or $64^{1/6}$.

Another way of writing 64 is as $4^3$; 4 is therefore the third root of 64 and can be written $\sqrt[3]{64}$ or $64^{1/3}$.

### Special powers

Numbers to the power of one are written without an index, i.e. $7 = 7^1$. A number raised to the power of two is said to be "squared". If it is raised to the power of three it is said to be "cubed". The second root of a number is called the "square root" and is shown by a root sign on its own without an index ($\sqrt{\phantom{x}}$). A third root is called a "cube root".

## Millions and billions

Listed below are the names given to 10 when it is raised to various powers. In some cases, the names used in the USA are different from those used in the rest of the world. It is therefore important to say which system is being used for numbers of a billion or more.

| Power | Number in full | Name in USA | International name |
|---|---|---|---|
| $10^2$ | 100 | Hundred | Hundred |
| $10^3$ | 1000 | Thousand | Thousand |
| $10^6$ | 1,000,000 | Million | Million |
| $10^9$ | 1,000,000,000 | Billion | Milliard |
| $10^{12}$ | 1,000,000,000,000 | Trillion | Billion |
| $10^{15}$ | 1,000,000,000,000,000 | Quadrillion | |
| $10^{18}$ | 1,000,000,000,000,000,000 | Quintillion | Trillion |
| $10^{100}$ | 1 followed by 100 zeroes | Googol | Googol |

The number 1 followed by a googol of zeroes (written $10^{(10^{100})}$) is called a googolplex.

## Prefixes

Listed below are the internationally agreed prefixes used to show multiples of the number 10 raised to various powers. These prefixes are used with units of measurement. For example, a kilogram is one thousand grams; a centimeter is one tenth of a meter; and so on.

| Prefix | Symbol | Power | Multiple in full |
|---|---|---|---|
| Tera | T | $10^{12}$ | 1,000,000,000,000 |
| Giga | G | $10^9$ | 1,000,000,000 |
| Mega | M | $10^6$ | 1,000,000 |
| Kilo | k | $10^3$ | 1,000 |
| Hecto | h | $10^2$ | 100 |
| Deca | da | 10 | 10 |
| Deci | d | $10^{-1}$ | 0.1 |
| Centi | c | $10^{-2}$ | 0.01 |
| Milli | m | $10^{-3}$ | 0.001 |
| Micro | μ | $10^{-6}$ | 0.000001 |
| Nano | n | $10^{-9}$ | 0.000000001 |
| Pico | p | $10^{-12}$ | 0.000000000001 |
| Femto | f | $10^{-15}$ | 0.000000000000001 |
| Atto | a | $10^{-18}$ | 0.000000000000000001 |

# Prime and composite numbers

**Prime numbers** These are whole numbers that have only two factors – the number itself and the number one. The only even prime number is two: all other prime numbers are odd.

**2 3 5 7 11 13 17 19 23**
**29 31 37 41 43 47 53 59**
**61 67 71 73 79 83 89 97 101 103 107 109 113 127**
**131 137 139 149 151 157 163 167 173 179 181 191**
**193 197 199 211 223 227 229 233 239 241**

**Primes to 250**
Here we list all the prime numbers below 250.

**Composite numbers** These are all the whole numbers greater than one that are not primes. Here we look at quick ways to check if a composite number is exactly divisible by numbers from 2 to 13.

**2**
A number is divisible by 2 if its last digit is even, e.g. the last digit of 256 is 6, which is even, so 256 is exactly divisible by 2.
**3**
A number is divisible by 3 if the sum of its digits is a multiple of 3, e.g. 531 is exactly divisible by 3 because $5+3+1=9=3\times3$.
**4**
A number is divisible by 4 if its last two digits are a multiple of 4, e.g. 1932 is exactly divisible by 4 because $32=4\times8$.
**5**
A number is exactly divisible by 5 if its last digit is 5 or 0.
**6**
A number is exactly divisible by 6 if it is divisible by both 2 and 3.
**7**
To check for divisibility by 7, start at the right and separate the digits into groups of three. Beginning at the right with a +, write + and – alternately in front of each group. Do the sum. If the answer is a multiple of 7, then the original number can be divided by 7. For example, 14294863492 is exactly divisible by 7 because $-14+294-863+492=-91=7\times-13$.

**Largest prime**

Listed right are six prime numbers which have held the record as the largest known prime and the years in which they were discovered. The largest prime known in 1952 is written out in full below. The largest prime known in September 1983 has 39,751 digits.

| | |
|---|---|
| 1952 | $2^{127}-1$ |
| 1963 | $2^{11213}-1$ |
| 1978 | $2^{21701}-1$ |
| February 1979 | $2^{23209}-1$ |
| April 1979 | $2^{44497}-1$ |
| September 1983 | $2^{132049}-1$ |

**170141183460469231731687303715884105727**

**8**
A number is exactly divisible by 8 if its last three digits are a multiple of 8.
**9**
A number is exactly divisible by 9 if the sum of its digits is a multiple of 9.
**10**
A number is exactly divisible by 10 if its last digit is 0.
**11**
To check for divisibility by 11, start at the left and add together the first, third, fifth, etc digits. Then add the second, fourth, sixth, etc digits. Subtract the second sum from the first. If the answer is 0 or 11, the original number can be divided by 11. For example, 1254649 is exactly divisible by 11 because $1+5+6+9=21$, $2+4+4=10$, and $21-10=11$.
**12**
A number is exactly divisible by 12 if it is divisible by both 3 and 4.
**13**
To check for divisibility by 13, group the digits as if testing for divisibility by 7 and do the sum. If the answer is a multiple of 13, then the original number can be divided exactly by 13.

# Number shapes (1)

**Polygonal numbers** When a number is represented by a group of dots, the dots can be arranged in a geometric shape (polygon). If the dots form a triangle, the number is called a triangular number; if they form a square, it is called a square number, and so on. The general name is "polygonal numbers".

**Triangular numbers** (right)
The dots representing these numbers can be arranged into triangles with the same number of dots on each side. Each row has one more dot than the row above it. A triangular number is the sum of all the whole numbers from 1 up to the number of rows of dots in the triangle, e.g. $6 = 1 + 2 + 3$.

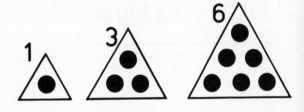

**Square numbers** (right)
The dots representing these numbers can be arranged into squares with the same number of dots on each side. When a number is multiplied by itself, it is said to have been "squared" because the product is always a number which can be formed into a square.

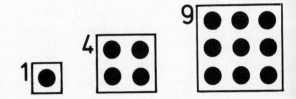

**Some other polygonal numbers**
Examples are shown right.
**a** The pentagonal numbers are 1, 5, 12, 22, 35, 51, 70, etc.
**b** The hexagonal numbers are 1, 6, 15, 28, 45, 66, 91, etc.
**c** The heptagonal numbers are 1, 7, 18, 34, 55, 81, 112, etc.
**d** The octagonal numbers are 1, 8, 21, 40, 65, 96, 133, etc.

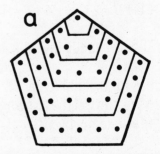

# Different shapes

Some numbers have more than one shape. For example, 6, 15, 28, 45, 66 and 91 can be triangular or hexagonal numbers; 21 can be triangular or octagonal; 36 can be triangular or square; 55 can be triangular or heptagonal; 81 can be square or heptagonal.

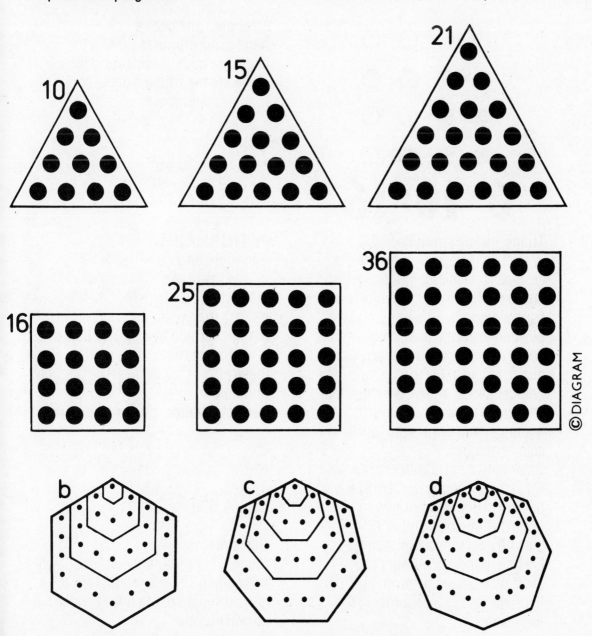

# Number shapes (2)

## Identifying polygonal numbers

Polygonal numbers are usually identified by their position in their series. For example, the series of triangular numbers is 1, 3, 6, 10, 15, etc. The number 6 is referred to as the third triangular number, 15 as the fifth triangular number, and so on.

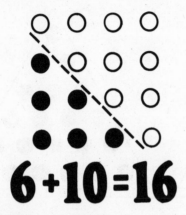

$6+10=16$

## Triangles and squares

When two triangular numbers that are next to each other in the series are added together, their sum is a square number. This has the same position in the square number series as the higher of the two triangular numbers had in the triangular number series. Above we show that the sum of the third and fourth triangular numbers is the fourth square number.

Other polygonal numbers are also linked by triangular numbers, e.g. the fourth triangular number (10) + the fifth square number (25) = the fifth pentagonal number (35); the fifth triangular number (15) + the sixth hexagonal number (66) = the sixth heptagonal number (81); and so on.

## Triangles and cubes

If the cubic numbers (see facing page) are added up in order, the sums are the squares of the series of triangular numbers.

$1=1^2$
$1+8=9=3^2$
$1+8+27=36=6^2$
$1+8+27+64=100=10^2$
$1+8+27+64+125=225=15^2$

## Perfect triangles

Although not all the triangular numbers are perfect numbers, all the perfect numbers (6, 28, 496, etc) are triangular. Each side of the triangle formed by a perfect number is a prime number. Here we list these primes for the first five perfect numbers.

| Perfect number | Side of triangle |
|---|---|
| 6 | 3 |
| 28 | 7 |
| 496 | 31 |
| 8128 | 127 |
| 33,550,336 | 8191 |

## Odd squares

Multiplying a triangular number by 8 and adding 1 to the product always gives a square number that is also an odd number.

# Polyhedral numbers

Some numbers can be represented as a three-dimensional geometric shape (polyhedron). Shown below are examples of cubic (**a**), tetrahedral (**b**) and pyramidal (**c**) numbers. A tetrahedral number is formed of layers of triangular numbers and a pyramidal number of layers of square numbers.

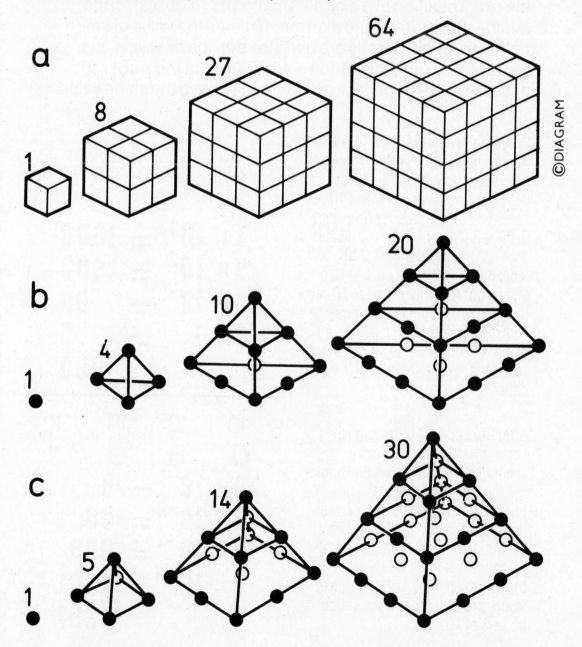

# Number bases (1)

**Decimal system** The full name of our everyday counting system is the "decimal positional notational system". A decimal system has a number base of 10, i.e. the number on which the decimal system is constructed is 10. In a positional notational system, the exact position of a digit determines its value, e.g. in the number 22 the left-hand digit has 10 times the value of the right-hand digit. Zeroes are used to keep the positions and values of the other digits correct, e.g. without the zeroes the numbers 20200 and 22 would appear to have the same value.

**Counting in powers of 10** (right)
When a number is written in base 10 (the decimal system), the value of a digit in the number increases 10 times whenever it moves one place to the left. For example, 2 indicates $2 \times 1$; 20 indicates $2 \times 10$; 200 indicates $2 \times 10 \times 10$ (i.e. $2 \times 10^2$); and so on. A number in base 10 can therefore be set out in columns, with each column representing a power of 10. These powers of 10 are called the "place values" of the digits.

| $10^3$ | $10^2$ | $10$ | $1$ |
|---|---|---|---|
| **1** | **9** | **8** | **0** |

$$1 \times 10^3 = 1000$$
$$9 \times 10^2 = \phantom{0}900$$
$$8 \times 10 = \phantom{00}80$$
$$0 \times 1 = \phantom{000}0$$
$$\overline{\phantom{0}1980}$$

**After the decimal point** (right)
In base 10, the decimal point separates the numbers 1 and above (on the left-hand side of the point) from numbers less than 1 (on the right-hand side of the point). Each column to the right of the decimal point has one tenth of the value of the column before it. These place values are expressed as negative powers of 10.

| $10^{-1}$ | $10^{-2}$ | $10^{-3}$ | $10^{-4}$ |
|---|---|---|---|
| $\cdot 0$ | $8$ | $9$ | $1$ |

$$0 \times 10^{-1} = \cdot 0$$
$$8 \times 10^{-2} = \cdot 08$$
$$9 \times 10^{-3} = \cdot 009$$
$$1 \times 10^{-4} = \cdot 0001$$
$$\overline{\cdot 0891}$$

**Binary system** This is a positional notational system with a number base of 2. The only digits used are 0 and 1. Computers use the binary system as their basic operating code ("machine code"). When a computer processes coded signals it does so in a series of electronic pulses. The presence or absence of a pulse can be represented by the digits 1 and 0. When talking about computers, these digits are referred to as "bits" (an abbreviation for "binary digits"). A group of eight bits is called a "byte".

## Binary place values

The place values in the binary system are the powers of 2 (**a**). When a number is written in base 2, the value of the digit in the number increases by one power of 2 whenever it moves one place to the left.

Odd numbers in base 2 always end in 1; even numbers end in 0.

To double a binary number, add 0 to its right-hand side (**b**).

To halve an even binary number, remove the final 0 (**c**).

## Bicimals

In the binary system, a point separates numbers of 1 and above from numbers less than 1. In base 2, numbers less than 1 are called "bicimals". The place values to the right of the bicimal point are expressed as negative powers of 2, i.e. each column to the right of the point has one half of the value of the column before it (**d**).

a
$$2^4 \quad 2^3 \quad 2^2 \quad 2^1 \quad 1$$
$$1 \quad 0 \quad 0 \quad 1 \quad 1$$

b
$$10011 \times 2$$
$$= 100110$$

c
$$101010 \div 2$$
$$= 10101$$

d
$$2^{-1} \quad 2^{-2} \quad 2^{-3} \quad 2^{-4}$$
$$.1 \quad 1 \quad 0 \quad 1$$

© DIAGRAM

# Number bases (2)

**Other number bases** Any number can be used as the base of a number system. The decimal system is probably the most commonly used in the world today simply because we have 10 fingers and thumbs. Computers use the binary system, but some can also be programmed in base 16 (the hexagesimal system, usually called "hex") or base 8 (the octal system). We use base 60 (the sexagesimal system) for time (60 seconds = 1 minute, 60 minutes = 1 hour), and for measuring angles.

**Place values and symbols**
Listed in the table below are the place values and digits used in systems with number bases from 2 to 10. Because there are only 10 different digits (i.e. 0 to 9 inclusive), systems which have a number base greater than 10 need additional symbols. Letters of the alphabet can be used as these symbols. For example, in hex the letters A to F are used as well as the digits 0 to 9, with A representing 10, B representing 11, and so on.

## $1011$ two
## $41203$ $_5$

**Identifying the base** (above)
The base in which a number is written can be identified by a "subscript", i.e. by writing the number of the base in words or figures below and to the right of the final digit. Numbers written without a subscript are normally assumed to be in base 10.

| Place values | Base | System | Digits used |
|---|---|---|---|
| ...$2^5, 2^4, 2^3, 2^2, 2, 1$ | 2 | Binary | 0, 1 |
| ...$3^5, 3^4, 3^3, 3^2, 3, 1$ | 3 | Ternary | 0, 1, 2 |
| ...$4^5, 4^4, 4^3, 4^2, 4, 1$ | 4 | Quaternary | 0, 1, 2, 3, |
| ...$5^5, 5^4, 5^3, 5^2, 5, 1$ | 5 | Quinary | 0, 1, 2, 3, 4 |
| ...$6^5, 6^4, 6^3, 6^2, 6, 1$ | 6 | Senary | 0, 1, 2, 3, 4, 5 |
| ...$7^5, 7^4, 7^3, 7^2, 7, 1$ | 7 | Septenary | 0, 1, 2, 3, 4, 5, 6 |
| ...$8^5, 8^4, 8^3, 8^2, 8, 1$ | 8 | Octal | 0, 1, 2, 3, 4, 5, 6, 7 |
| ...$9^5, 9^4, 9^3, 9^2, 9, 1$ | 9 | Nonary | 0, 1, 2, 3, 4, 5, 6, 7, 8 |
| ...$10^5, 10^4, 10^3, 10^2, 10, 1$ | 10 | Decimal | 0, 1, 2, 3, 4, 5, 6, 7, 8, 9 |

**Changing to base 10** (below)
To change a number from any other base to base 10, multiply each digit in the number by its place value and add the products together.

$$5426_{eight} = (5 \times 8^3) + (4 \times 8^2) + (2 \times 8) + (6 \times 1)$$

$$= 2560_{ten} + 256_{ten} + 16_{ten} + 6_{ten}$$

$$= 2838_{ten}$$

**Changing from base 10** (below)
To change a number from base 10 to another base, divide the base 10 number repeatedly by the new base and record the remainders in reverse order.

$6\underline{\smash{\big)}768}_{ten}$

$6\underline{\smash{\big)}128}$ remainder  0

$6\underline{\smash{\big)}\,21}$ remainder  2

$6\underline{\smash{\big)}\,\,3}$ remainder  3

$\phantom{6}\,\,0$ remainder  3

$768_{ten} = 3320_{six}$

**1980** (below)
Here we show the number 1980 in base 10 and then as it appears when written in other bases.

$1980_{10}$

$11110111100_2$

$2201100_3$

$132330_4$

$30410_5$

$13100_6$

$5526_7$

$3674_8$

$2640_9$

$7BC_{hex}$

**Other people's numbers**

**Written numerals** Different civilizations have developed their own systems for writing numbers. Here we show numerals from four such systems. The earliest known written numerals were used by the Egyptians and Babylonians about 5000 years ago. The Egyptians used 10 as their number base: the Babylonians used 60. The Romans used both five and 10 as number bases, and used letters to represent some of their numerals. None of these three systems has a symbol for zero. The Mayans of Central America included a zero in their system, which used number bases of five and 20. At the bottom of the page we show the number 1980 written in each of these systems.

| | **0** | **1** | **2** | **3** | **4** | **5** | **6** |
|---|---|---|---|---|---|---|---|
| **A Egyptian** | | I | II | III | IIII | III II | III III |
| **B Babylonian** | | Y | YY | YYY | YYYY | YYY YY | YYY YYY |
| **C Roman** | | I | II | III | IV | V | VI |
| **D Mayan** | ⬯ | • | •• | ••• | •••• | — | ≐ |

A

B

## Hindu-Arabic numerals

Modern Western numerals have developed from the Hindu numerals brought from India to Europe by the Arabs.

**a** Hindu numerals of about 800AD
**b** Arabic numerals of about 900AD
**c** Numerals used in Spain in about 1000AD
**d** Numerals used in Italy in about 1400AD

| 7 | 8 | 9 | 10 | 50 | 100 | 500 | 1000 |
|---|---|---|----|----|-----|-----|------|
| \|\|\|\| | \|\|\|\| | \|\|\| | ∩ | | | | |
| VII | VIII | IX | X | L | C | D | M |

C MCMLXXX

 D

©DIAGRAM

# Tables

**Using the tables** Here we give multiplication tables for base 10, base 2, base 5 and base 8. Similar tables can be made for all number bases. To multiply two factors together, find the first factor in the extreme left-hand column of the table for the correct number base. Follow that row of figures across the table until it crosses the column headed by the second factor. The number at the point where the row and column cross is the product of the two factors.

**Base 10**

| × | 1 | 2 | 3 | 4 | 5 | 6 | 7 | 8 | 9 | 10 | 11 | 12 |
|---|---|---|---|---|---|---|---|---|---|---|---|---|
| 1 | 1 | 2 | 3 | 4 | 5 | 6 | 7 | 8 | 9 | 10 | 11 | 12 |
| 2 | 2 | 4 | 6 | 8 | 10 | 12 | 14 | 16 | 18 | 20 | 22 | 24 |
| 3 | 3 | 6 | 9 | 12 | 15 | 18 | 21 | 24 | 27 | 30 | 33 | 36 |
| 4 | 4 | 8 | 12 | 16 | 20 | 24 | 28 | 32 | 36 | 40 | 44 | 48 |
| 5 | 5 | 10 | 15 | 20 | 25 | 30 | 35 | 40 | 45 | 50 | 55 | 60 |
| 6 | 6 | 12 | 18 | 24 | 30 | 36 | 42 | 48 | 54 | 60 | 66 | 72 |
| 7 | 7 | 14 | 21 | 28 | 35 | 42 | 49 | 56 | 63 | 70 | 77 | 84 |
| 8 | 8 | 16 | 24 | 32 | 40 | 48 | 56 | 64 | 72 | 80 | 88 | 96 |
| 9 | 9 | 18 | 27 | 36 | 45 | 54 | 63 | 72 | 81 | 90 | 99 | 108 |
| 10 | 10 | 20 | 30 | 40 | 50 | 60 | 70 | 80 | 90 | 100 | 110 | 120 |
| 11 | 11 | 22 | 33 | 44 | 55 | 66 | 77 | 88 | 99 | 110 | 121 | 132 |
| 12 | 12 | 24 | 36 | 48 | 60 | 72 | 84 | 96 | 108 | 120 | 132 | 144 |

## Base 2

| X | 0 | 1 |
|---|---|---|
| 0 | 0 | 0 |
| 1 | 0 | 1 |

## Base 5

| X | 1 | 2 | 3 | 4 |
|---|---|---|---|---|
| 1 | 1 | 2 | 3 | 4 |
| 2 | 2 | 4 | 11 | 13 |
| 3 | 3 | 11 | 14 | 22 |
| 4 | 4 | 13 | 22 | 31 |

## Base 8

| X | 1 | 2 | 3 | 4 | 5 | 6 | 7 |
|---|---|---|---|---|---|---|---|
| 1 | 1 | 2 | 3 | 4 | 5 | 6 | 7 |
| 2 | 2 | 4 | 6 | 10 | 12 | 14 | 16 |
| 3 | 3 | 6 | 11 | 14 | 17 | 22 | 25 |
| 4 | 4 | 10 | 14 | 20 | 24 | 30 | 34 |
| 5 | 5 | 12 | 17 | 24 | 31 | 36 | 43 |
| 6 | 6 | 14 | 22 | 30 | 36 | 44 | 52 |
| 7 | 7 | 16 | 25 | 34 | 43 | 52 | 61 |

# Circles

**Definition of a circle** A circle is a plane (flat) figure enclosed by one curved line. Every point on this curve is at the same distance from the circle's center. The line marking the boundary of the circle is called the circumference. Here we look at the names of some other features of a circle.

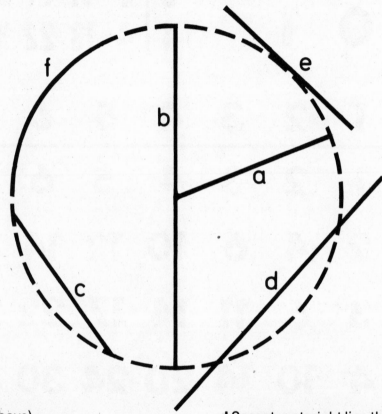

**Lines** (above)

**a** Radius (plural radii): a straight line joining the center of a circle to any point on its circumference.

**b** Diameter: a straight line through the center of a circle that joins two opposite points on the circumference.

**c** Chord: a straight line joining any two points on the circumference.

**d** Secant: a straight line that cuts across the circumference of a circle at any two points.

**e** Tangent: a straight line that touches the circumference of a circle at one point only.

**f** Arc: a section of the circumference of a circle.

**Spaces** (below)
**A** Semicircle: the space between a diameter and the circumference.
**B** Sector: the space between any two radii.
**C** Segment: the space between a chord and the circumference.

**Annulus** (bottom)
The space between the circumferences of two circles with different radii is called an annulus (**a**). If the circles are concentric, i.e. if they share the same center, the annulus is ring-shaped (**b**).

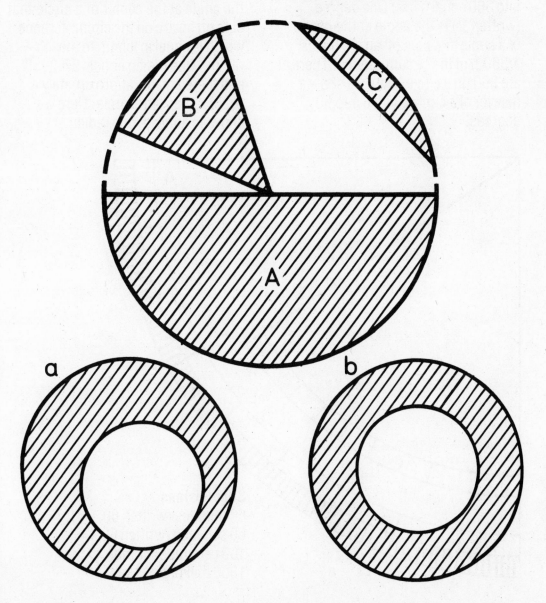

# Angles

**Measuring angles** Here we look at two units used for measuring angles, both of which are based on divisions of a circle. The degree is the more widely used of the two units, but the radian is preferred for some forms of mathematics.

### Degrees (A)
The degree system divides a circle into 360 equal parts. One degree (written 1°) is the angle at the center of a circle that cuts off an arc that is 1/360th of the circumference. There are 360° in a circle. Here we show a quarter of a circle divided into 90 degrees.

### Radians (B)
One radian (abbreviated to 1 rad) is the angle at the center of a circle that cuts off an arc on the circumference which is equal in length to the radius. One radian equals 57.2958°, and there are 2π (approximately 6.28) radians in a circle. Here we show an angle of one radian.

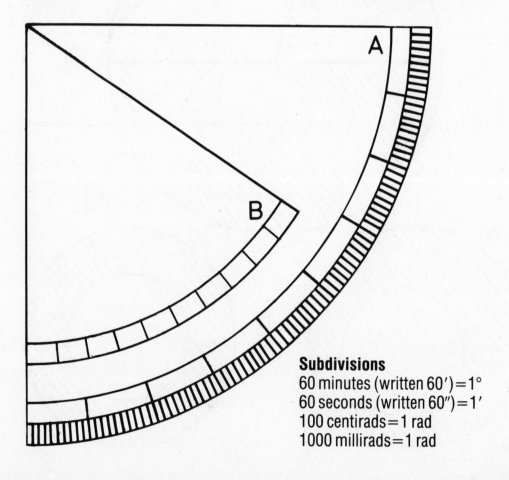

**Subdivisions**
60 minutes (written 60′)=1°
60 seconds (written 60″)=1′
100 centirads=1 rad
1000 millirads=1 rad

**Names for angles** (above)
Angles are named according to their size.
**a** An acute angle measures more than 0° but less than 90°.
**b** A right angle measures 90°. Two lines at right angles are said to be perpendicular to one another.
**c** An obtuse angle measures more than 90° but less than 180°.

**d** A straight angle measures 180°.
**e** A reflex angle measures more than 180° but less than 360°.
**f** Complementary angles are two angles whose sum is 90°.
**g** Supplementary angles are two angles whose sum is 180°.
**h** Conjugate angles are two angles whose sum is 360°.

©DIAGRAM

# Plane figures (1)

**Polygons** A plane figure enclosed by straight lines is called a polygon, from the Greek word *poly*, meaning many, and *gonia*, meaning angles. Here we look at the names, shapes and angles of polygons with from 3 to 12 sides.

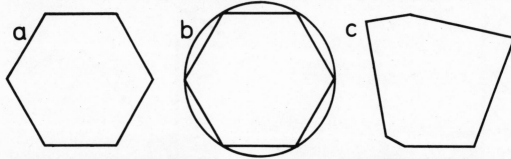

### Regular and irregular polygons
All the sides of a regular polygon (**a**) are the same length and all its angles are the same size. A regular polygon will fit into a circle with all its vertices (i.e. the points where two sides of the polygon meet) touching the circumference (**b**). The sides of an irregular polygon (**c**) are of different lengths and its angles are of different sizes.

### Names and angles
The table below gives the names and numbers of sides of the first 10 regular polygons. Also listed are the sizes of the internal angles made by the sides where they join around the edges of the polygon, and the sum of all the internal angles in the polygon. On the facing page we show the 10 polygons all drawn with sides of the same length.

| Name of polygon | Number of sides | Each internal angle | Sum of internal angles |
|-----------------|-----------------|---------------------|------------------------|
| Triangle | 3 | 60° | 180° |
| Square | 4 | 90° | 360° |
| Pentagon | 5 | 108° | 540° |
| Hexagon | 6 | 120° | 720° |
| Heptagon | 7 | 128.6° | 900° |
| Octagon | 8 | 135° | 1080° |
| Nonagon | 9 | 140° | 1260° |
| Decagon | 10 | 144° | 1440° |
| Undecagon | 11 | 147.3° | 1620° |
| Dodecagon | 12 | 150° | 1800° |

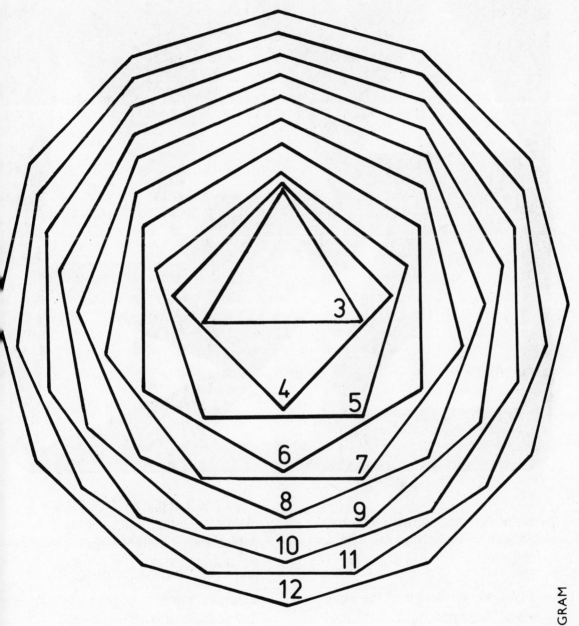

# Plane figures (2)

### Triangles

Listed here and shown above are six different types of triangles . The sum of the internal angles of any flat triangle is always 180°.

**a** Equilateral triangle: all the sides are of the same length and all the angles are equal.

**b** Isosceles triangle: two sides are of the same length and two angles are of equal size.

**c** Scalene triangle: all the sides are of different lengths and all the angles are of different sizes.

**d** Right-angled triangle: a triangle that contains one right angle.

**e** Obtuse-angled triangle: a triangle that contains one obtuse angle.

**f** Acute-angled triangle: a triangle with three acute angles.

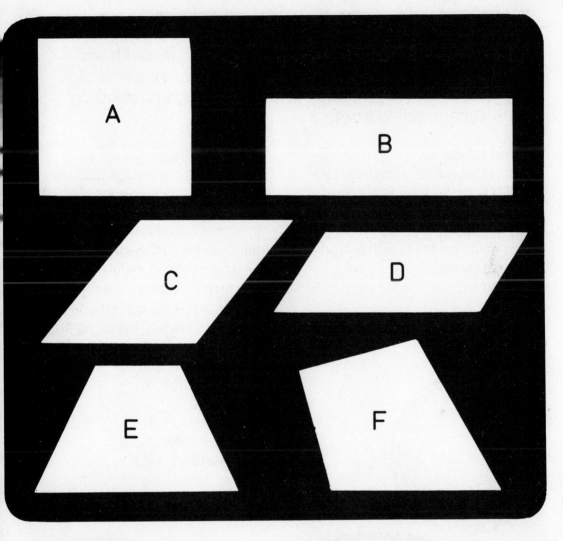

## Quadrilaterals

A quadrilateral is a four-sided polygon. Listed here and shown above are six different types of quadrilaterals.

**A** Square: all the sides are the same length and all the angles are right angles.

**B** Rectangle: opposite sides are the same length and all the angles are right angles.

**C** Rhombus: all the sides are the same length but none of the angles are right angles.

**D** Parallelogram: opposite sides are parallel to each other and of the same length.

**E** Trapezium: one pair of opposite sides is parallel.

**F** Kite: adjacent sides are the same length and the diagonals intersect at right angles.

# Solid figures (1)

**Three dimensions** Solid figures (sometimes called space figures) are three dimensional: they have length, width and depth. A polyhedron (plural polyhedra) is a solid figure with polygons as faces. Opening out and flattening a polyhedron gives a shape called a net.

## Curved solids

A sphere (**a**) is a solid enclosed by a single curved surface. Every point on its surface is at the same distance from the sphere's center. Four other common solids with curved surfaces are also shown below.

**b** Spheroid
**c** Torus
**d** Cone
**e** Cylinder

## Regular solids

All the faces of a regular solid are identical regular polygons of equal size. A regular polyhedron will fit into a sphere with all its vertices touching the surface of the sphere. There are only five regular solids. The names of these solids and the numbers of sides are listed below. They are shown on the facing page with examples of their nets.

**A** Tetrahedron, 4
**B** Cube, 6
**C** Octahedron, 8
**D** Dodecahedron, 12
**E** Icosahedron, 20

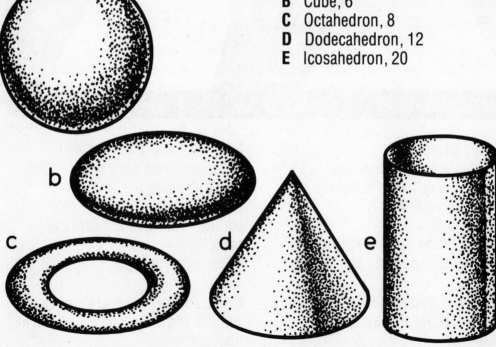

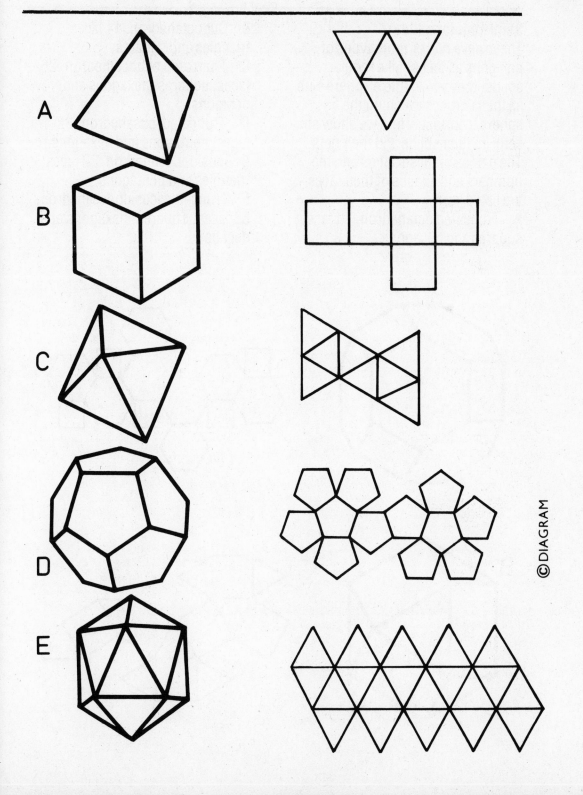

A

B

C

D

E

©DIAGRAM

# Solid figures (2)

## Semi-regular solids

These have two or more types of polygons as faces. Like regular solids, they will fit into a sphere with all their vertices touching the sphere's surface. Here we show six semi-regular solids and their nets. The names of these solids and the numbers and shapes of their faces are listed here.

**A** Truncated octahedron, 14 faces, squares and hexagons

**B** Cuboctahedron, 14 faces, triangles and squares

**C** Truncated cuboctahedron, 26 faces, squares, hexagons and octagons

**D** Truncated icosahedron, 32 faces, pentagons and hexagons

**E** Icosidodecahedron, 32 faces, triangles and pentagons

**F** Truncated icosidodecahedron, 62 faces, squares, hexagons and decagons

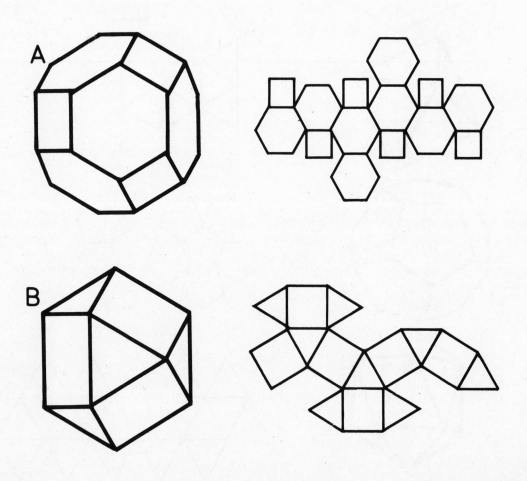

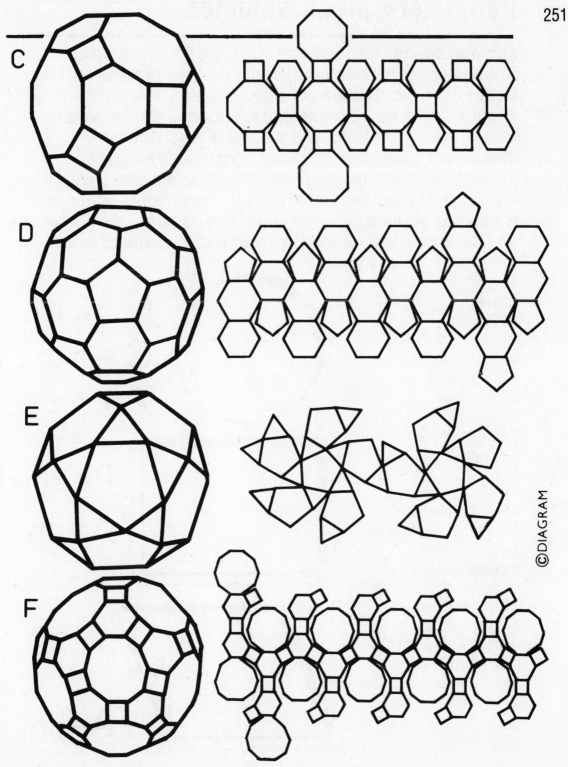

# Perimeters, areas, volumes

**Size and space** The perimeter of a plane figure is the distance around its edge or boundary. It is measured in linear units, i.e. inches, feet, etc. The area of a figure is a measure of the size of its surface. Areas are measured in square units, i.e. square inches, square feet, etc. The volume of a solid figure is a measure of the amount of space it occupies. Volume is measured in cubic units, i.e. cubic inches, cubic feet, etc. Here we give the formulae used to calculate perimeters, areas and volumes of some common figures. The names of the figures and the abbreviations used in the formulae are listed below.

**Figures**
1 Circle
2 Rectangle
3 Parallelogram
4 Triangle
5 Trapezium
6 Cuboid
7 Cone
8 Cylinder
9 Sphere

**Abbreviations**
A=area of plane figure
a=length of top
b=length of base
C=length of circumference
d=length of diameter
h=perpendicular height
P=length of perimeter
r=length of radius
S=area of surface of solid
V=volume
w=width
$\pi$=3.1416

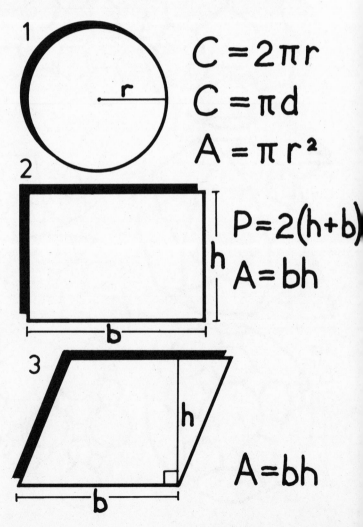

$$C = 2\pi r$$
$$C = \pi d$$
$$A = \pi r^2$$

$$P = 2(h+b)$$
$$A = bh$$

$$A = bh$$

## Pi

Whatever the size of a circle, the ratio of its circumference to its diameter is always the same. The Greek letter π (pi) is used as a symbol for this ratio: π=circumference÷diameter.

The value of π has been calculated to 16 million places of decimals (below we show it to the first 120 places) but the value usually used in calculations is 3.1416. π is used in calculating the perimeters, areas and volumes of circular figures and solids.

$$\pi = 3.141592653589793238462643383279502884197169399375105820974944592307816406286208998628034825342117067982148086513282306647$$

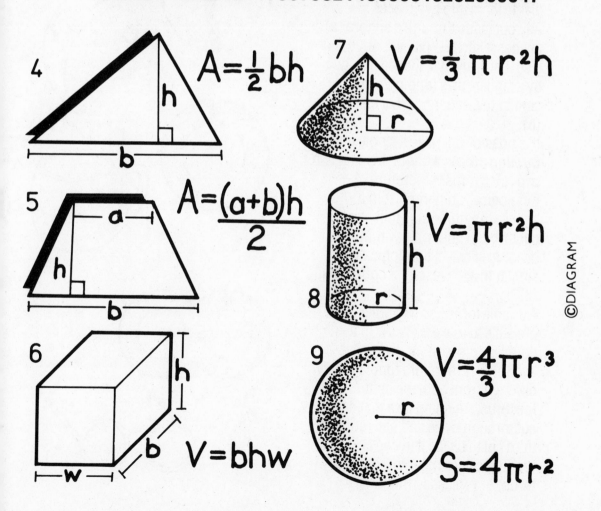

4   $A=\frac{1}{2}bh$

7   $V=\frac{1}{3}\pi r^2 h$

5   $A=\frac{(a+b)h}{2}$

8   $V=\pi r^2 h$

6   $V=bhw$

9   $V=\frac{4}{3}\pi r^3$

$S=4\pi r^2$

©DIAGRAM

**Topology** This form of geometry looks at the way surfaces and objects behave if they are transformed by, for example, bending, twisting or stretching. Topology is concerned with geometrical properties that are not altered by these transformations, e.g. with the number of edges, surfaces and holes in an object and not with their sizes.

**Grouping solids**

Solids may be grouped topologically by the number of cuts needed to divide them into two pieces.

Any cut made through a sphere (**a**) divides it into two pieces. Anything else that is always divided into two by a single cut is topologically similar to a sphere, e.g. a banana (**b**).

It is possible to make a single cut through a torus without dividing it in two (**c**); a torus is therefore topologically different from a sphere. Anything else that can be cut through once only without dividing in two is topologically similar to a torus, e.g. a coffee mug (**d**).

A double torus has two holes. It is possible to make two cuts in a double torus without dividing it in two (**e**); it is therefore topologically different from both the sphere and the torus. Anything else that can be cut through twice and still require a third cut to divide it in two is topologically similar to a double torus, e.g. glasses frame (**f**).

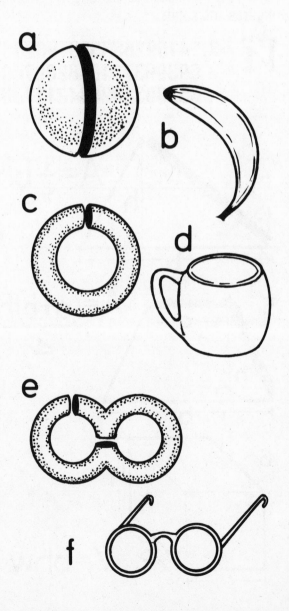

## Topologically similar

Another way to demonstrate that two solids are topologically similar is to show that it is possible to transform the first solid into the second without tearing, breaking or puncturing extra holes in it. These types of transformations have earned topology its nickname of "rubber sheet geometry".

A Sphere to banana
B Torus to coffee mug
C Double torus to glasses frame

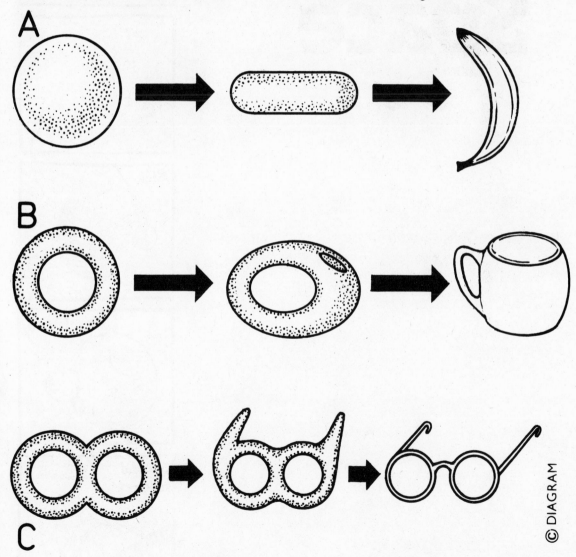

© DIAGRAM

# Section 6
# Space

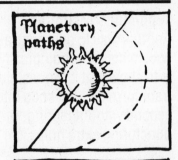

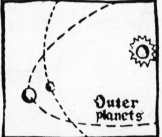

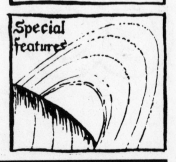

Tides

Stars

Nearest galaxies

Minor planets

Brightness

Unmanned satellites

Comets

Constellations

Probes

Sun

Galaxies

Manned spaceflight

Solar eclipse

Milky way

Reusable spacecraft

# Earth in the solar system (1)

**Third planet** The solar system contains nine major planets as well as enormous numbers of asteroids (minor planets), comets and meteoroids. Earth is the third planet out from the Sun. Five of the planets – Mercury, Venus, Mars, Jupiter and Saturn – can be seen from Earth with the naked eye (i.e. without using a telescope or binoculars), and astronomers have been studying them for thousands of years. The other three planets – Uranus, Neptune and Pluto – were discovered after the invention of the telescope. Uranus was discovered in 1781, Neptune in 1846 and Pluto in 1930. Some astronomers think that there may be a tenth planet which has not yet been discovered.

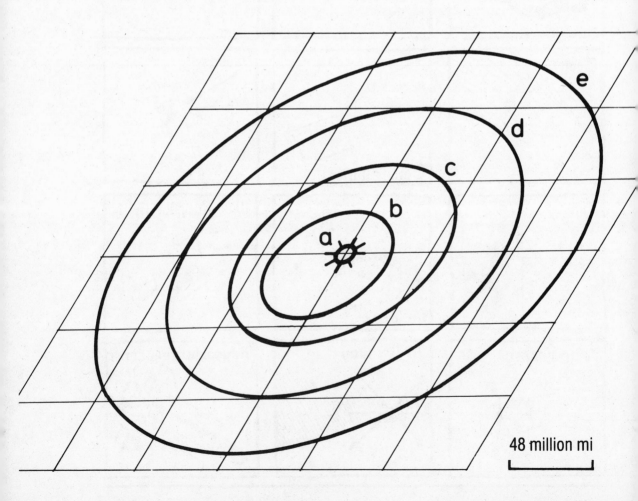

48 million mi

## Paths of the planets

Shown to scale in the diagrams below are the orbits (paths) around the Sun of the nine known planets. We have used two different scales to make it possible to show the complete orbits of all the planets. Except for Pluto, all the planets have orbits that are tilted at roughly the same angle in space: Pluto's orbit is tilted much more steeply. The planets are listed here in order going outward from the Sun.

**a** Sun
**b** Mercury
**c** Venus
**d** Earth
**e** Mars
**f** Jupiter
**g** Saturn
**h** Uranus
**i** Neptune
**j** Pluto

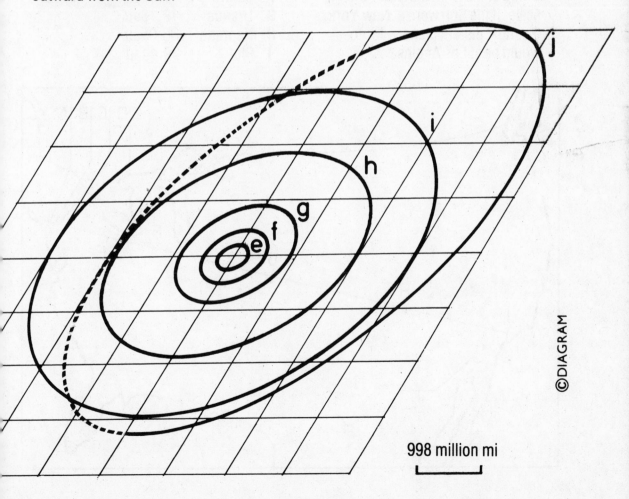

998 million mi

©DIAGRAM

# Earth in the solar system (2)

**Distances in the solar system** The planets in the solar system are millions of miles apart. For convenience, astronomers measure the distances between planets in astronomical units (au). An astronomical unit is the average distance between Earth and the Sun, and equals 93,000,000 mi.

**Distances from the Sun**
The average distances of the nine planets from the Sun are listed in order of distance in the table right. In the diagram below these distances are shown to scale against a map of the United States. On this scale, if the Sun were at New York, the most distant planet – Pluto – would be at Los Angles.

| | Planet | Average distance from Sun |
|---|---|---|
| A | Mercury | 0.39au |
| B | Venus | 0.72au |
| C | Earth | 1.00au |
| D | Mars | 1.52au |
| E | Jupiter | 5.20au |
| F | Saturn | 9.54au |
| G | Uranus | 19.18au |
| H | Neptune | 30.06au |
| I | Pluto | 39.44au |

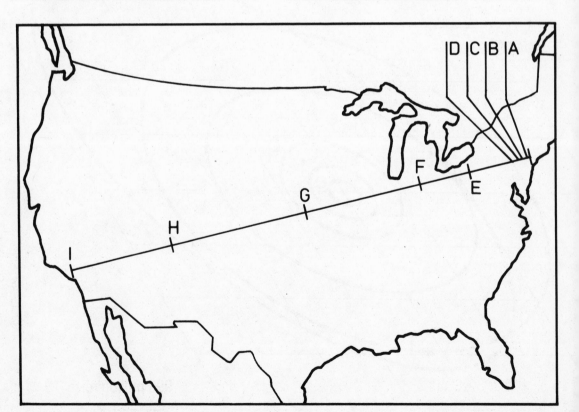

### Close to Earth

The closest distances between Earth and the other planets are listed in order of distance in the table right. The distances to the three closest planets are shown to scale above. We would need to continue this scale for another 32 pages to show the distance from Earth to Pluto (**g**) or Neptune (**h**).

| | Planet | Closest distance |
|---|---|---|
| a | Venus | 0.27au |
| b | Mars | 0.38au |
| c | Mercury | 0.54au |
| d | Jupiter | 3.95au |
| e | Saturn | 8.00au |
| f | Uranus | 17.28au |
| g | Pluto | 28.72au |
| h | Neptune | 28.80au |

### Orbit shape (right)

A planet's orbit around the Sun is shaped like an ellipse. Because of this, each planet is closer to the Sun at some times than at others. The shortest distance between a planet and the Sun (**1**) is called "perihelion"; the greatest distance (**2**) is called "aphelion". These distances are listed below.

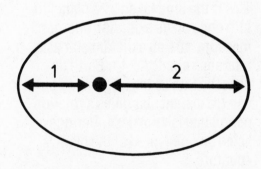

| Planet | Perihelion | Aphelion |
|---|---|---|
| Mercury | 0.31au | 0.47au |
| Venus | 0.72au | 0.73au |
| Earth | 0.98au | 1.02au |
| Mars | 1.38au | 1.67au |
| Jupiter | 4.95au | 5.46au |
| Saturn | 9.01au | 10.07au |
| Uranus | 18.28au | 20.09au |
| Neptune | 29.80au | 30.32au |
| Pluto | 29.58au | 49.14au |

### Outermost planets

Pluto is usually the outermost planet in the solar system: on average it is over 840 million mi farther from the Sun than Neptune. Sometimes Pluto's orbit crosses inside Neptune's orbit, and Neptune becomes the outermost planet. Neptune is the outermost planet from 1979 to 1999.

© DIAGRAM

# Planets: speed, time

**Moving through space** Although we are not usually aware of it, Earth and the other planets are moving around the Sun at high speeds. Each planet is also rotating on its axis (the imaginary line through the center of a planet that joins its north pole to its south pole).

## Orbital speeds

The average speeds at which the planets orbit the Sun are listed in the table right. The closer a planet's orbit is to the Sun, the faster its average speed. A planet does not travel at the same speed through the whole of its orbit: it travels faster at perihelion than it does at aphelion.

| Planet | Average orbital speed |
|--------|----------------------|
| Mercury | 28.74mi/sec |
| Venus | 21mi/sec |
| Earth | 17.88mi/sec |
| Mars | 14.46mi/sec |
| Jupiter | 7.86mi/sec |
| Saturn | 5.76mi/sec |
| Uranus | 4.08mi/sec |
| Neptune | 3.24mi/sec |
| Pluto | 2.82mi/sec |

## Rotation period

This is the time taken by a planet to turn once on its axis. Astronomers measure it using a distant star as a reference point. A 24hr Earth day uses the Sun as the reference point; using a distant star gives a rotation period that is 4min less. Periods listed are measured at the planets' equators.

| Planet | Rotation period |
|--------|----------------|
| Mercury | 58 days 15hr |
| Venus | 243 days |
| Earth | 23hr 56min |
| Mars | 24hr 37min |
| Jupiter | 9hr 50min |
| Saturn | 10hr 14min |
| Uranus | 16hr 10min |
| Neptune | 18hr 26min |
| Pluto | 6 days 9hr |

## Sidereal period

This is the time taken by a planet to orbit the Sun once. For Earth this period is approximately 365 days, i.e. one year. Sidereal periods on other planets are often referred to as planetary "years": outer planets have longer "years" than inner planets. Earth time is used in the list right.

| | Planet | Sidereal period |
|---|--------|----------------|
| a | Mercury | 88 days |
| b | Venus | 224.7 days |
| c | Earth | 365.256 days |
| d | Mars | 687 days |
| e | Jupiter | 11.86 years |
| f | Saturn | 29.46 years |
| g | Uranus | 84.01 years |
| h | Neptune | 164.8 years |
| i | Pluto | 247.7 years |

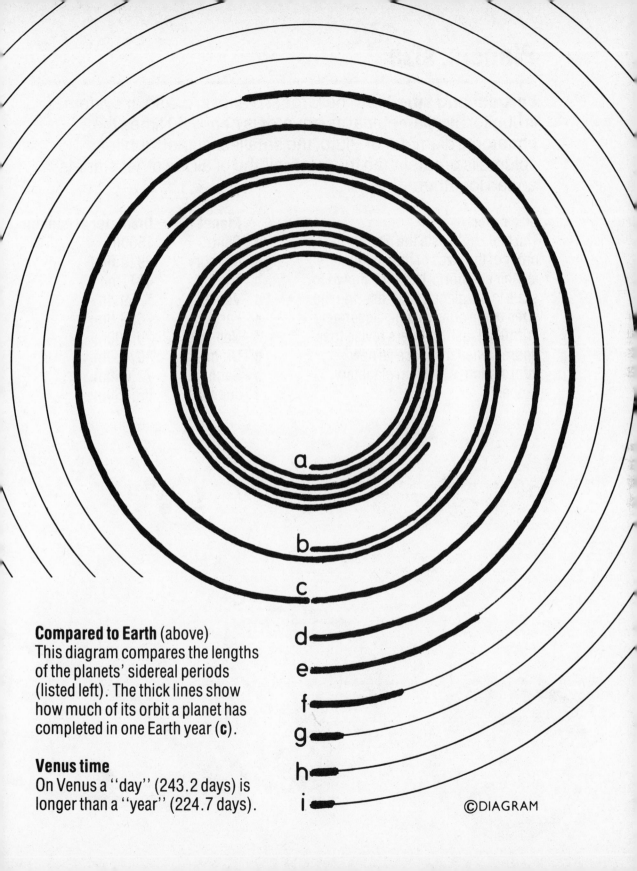

a

b

c

d

e

f

g

h

i

**Compared to Earth** (above)
This diagram compares the lengths
of the planets' sidereal periods
(listed left). The thick lines show
how much of its orbit a planet has
completed in one Earth year (**c**).

**Venus time**
On Venus a ''day'' (243.2 days) is
longer than a ''year'' (224.7 days).

©DIAGRAM

# Planets: size

**Largest and smallest** The largest planet in the solar system is Jupiter: its diameter at its equator is nearly 50 times the equatorial diameter of Pluto, the smallest planet. Jupiter's volume is greater than the total volume of all the other planets added together.

**Size order**
The table right lists the planets in order of the sizes of their diameters at their equators. They are shown to scale in the diagram. Measuring the sizes of the outer planets accurately is difficult: astronomers revise their figures when they receive new information, e.g. from planetary probes.

| | Planet | Diameter at equator |
|---|---|---|
| a | Pluto | 1800mi |
| b | Mercury | 2926.8mi |
| c | Mars | 4077mi |
| d | Venus | 7269.4mi |
| e | Earth | 7653.6mi |
| f | Neptune | 29,100mi |
| g | Uranus | 30,480mi |
| h | Saturn | 72,000mi |
| i | Jupiter | 85,650mi |

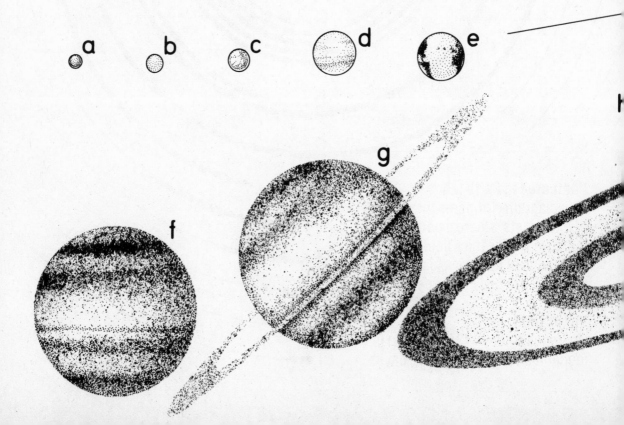

i

# Planets: mass, temperature, gravity

**Composition** The four inner planets are rocky and contain a lot of iron. The next four – Jupiter, Saturn, Uranus and Neptune – are sometimes called the "gas giants". They have small rocky cores but are mainly made up of gases such as hydrogen and helium. Pluto is thought to be a ball of rock and ice.

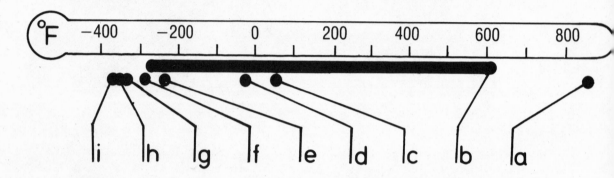

## Mass
The total mass of all the planets is about 2,670,000,000,000,000, 000,000,000,000kg. This is less than 1% of the mass of the whole solar system. In the list below we compare the mass of each of the planets with Earth's mass of $5.98 \times 10^{24}$kg. Jupiter, the most massive planet, has over twice the mass of all the other planets put together.
Jupiter, 317.9 times Earth's mass
Saturn, 95.2 times Earth's mass
Neptune, 17.2 times Earth's mass
Uranus, 14.6 times Earth's mass
Venus, 0.82 times Earth's mass
Mars, 0.11 times Earth's mass
Mercury, 0.06 times Earth's mass
Pluto, estimated to be 0.002–0.003 times Earth's mass

## Temperature
Average surface temperatures of the planets are listed below and shown on the diagram above. For the four inner planets these are the temperatures at the solid surface; for the gas giants and Pluto they are the temperatures at the surface of the clouds. Only Mercury has a huge variation between day and night temperatures.
**a** Venus, 896°F
**b** Mercury, 662°F (day), −274°F (night)
**c** Earth, 71°F
**d** Mars, −9.4°F
**e** Jupiter, −238°F
**f** Saturn, −292°F
**g** Uranus, −346°F
**h** Neptune, −364°F
**i** Pluto, −382°F

# Gravity

In the list below we compare the gravity on other planets with Earth's gravity. The greater the force of gravity, the harder it becomes to leave a planet's surface. Here we take a 3ft high jump on Earth and show how high a similar jump would be when made on another planet. Pluto's gravity is not yet known.

**A** Jupiter: gravity 2.64 times Earth's, jump of 1ft 3½in

**B** Neptune: gravity 1.2 times Earth's, jump of 2ft 6½in

**C** Uranus: gravity 1.17 times Earth's, jump of 2ft 6¾in

**D** Saturn: gravity 1.15 times Earth's, jump of 2ft 7¼in

**E** Earth: jump of 3ft

**F** Venus: gravity 0.88 times Earth's, jump of 3ft 4¾in

**G** Mars: gravity 0.38 times Earth's, jump of 7ft 10¾in

**H** Mercury: gravity 0.38 times Earth's, jump of 8ft 1¼in

© DIAGRAM

A B C D E F G H

# Planets: satellites

**Satellite** A satellite is a companion body that orbits a planet. The name comes from the Latin word *satelles*, meaning an attendant. Earth's satellite is the Moon, and satellites of other planets are sometimes referred to as moons. Venus and Mercury are the only planets without satellites.

## Names and numbers

Listed below and shown in the diagram right are the number of known satellites orbiting each of the planets from Mars out to Pluto. The names or identifying numbers of the satellites are also given. They are listed in order of their distance from the planet, closest first.

**A   Mars** 2 satellites – Phobos, Deimos

**B   Jupiter** 16 satellites – Metis, Adrastea, Amalthea, Thebe, Io, Europa, Ganymede, Callisto, Leda, Himalia, Lysithea, Elara, Ananke, Carme, Pasiphaë, Sinope

**C   Saturn** 19 satellites – 1980 S.28, 1980 S.27, 1980 S.26, Epimetheus, Janus, Mimas, Mimas co-orbital, Enceladus, Tethys, Calypso, Telesto, Dione, 1980 S.6, Dione co-orbital, Rhea, Titan, Hyperion, Iapetus, Phoebe

**D   Uranus** 11 satellites – the five closest are Miranda, Ariel, Umbriel, Titania and Oberon.

**E   Neptune** 2 satellites – Triton, Nereid (The existence of a third satellite orbiting even closer to Neptune than Triton is suspected but unconfirmed.)

**F   Pluto** 1 satellite – Charon

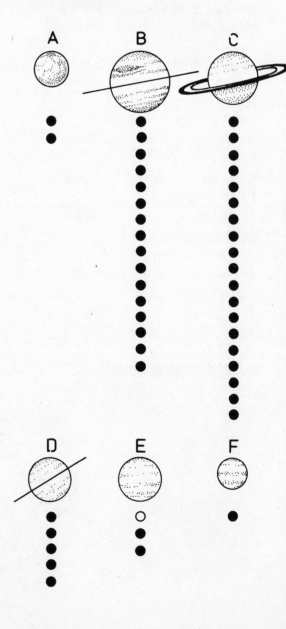

## Bigger than a planet

Some of the larger satellites are bigger than a small planet. In the list below and the diagram right we compare the sizes of five large satellites with the two smallest planets.

| | Name | Diameter at equator |
|---|---|---|
| a | Ganymede | 3165.6mi |
| b | Titan | 3084mi |
| c | Mercury | 2926.8mi |
| d | Callisto | 2892mi |
| e | Io | 2179.2mi |
| f | Europa | 1875.6mi |
| g | Pluto | 1800mi |

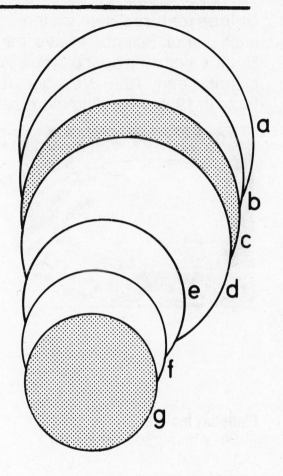

## Small satellites (below)

Some satellites are very small, as little as 6–9mi in diameter. Among the smallest are Mars' two satellites, Phobos and Deimos, which can be compared in size to islands on Earth. Here we show Phobos (**1**) to scale against Grenada and Deimos (**2**) to scale against Kahoolawe (Hawaii).

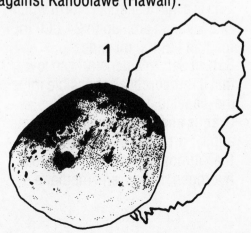

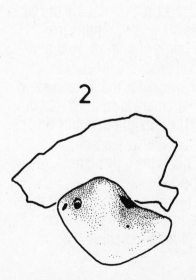

# Planets: special features

**Unique features** Here we look at some features unique to each planet. Scientists have learned many new things about Uranus since the space probe Voyager 2 passed close to this planet in early 1986. Voyager 2 should reach Neptune and Pluto in 1989, revealing more secrets of our solar system.

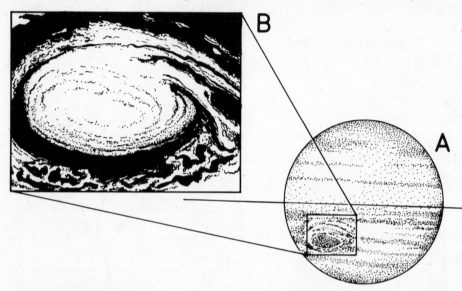

## Planetary features

**Mercury** The atmosphere is so thin that for most purposes it can be considered nonexistent.

**Venus** Here the Sun rises in the west and sets in the east. There are clouds made of sulfuric acid and the rain is probably the most corrosive liquid in the solar system. The atmosphere is so thick that only 20% of the sunlight that falls on Venus reaches its surface.

**Earth** This is the only planet known to support life.

**Mars** The red soil (colored by the rust it contains) gives Mars its characteristic red color. The highest volcano in the solar system, Olympus Mons, is on Mars: it is about three times as high as Mount Everest.

**Jupiter** (**A**) The most noticeable feature is the Great Red Spot (**B**). This is a hurricane-like storm which can cover an area up to 24,000 mi long and 2,400 mi wide.

**Saturn** Saturn's density is so low that it is theoretically possible for the planet to float on water.

**Uranus and Neptune** These planets appear greenish in color because their atmospheres are a mixture of hydrogen, helium and methane.

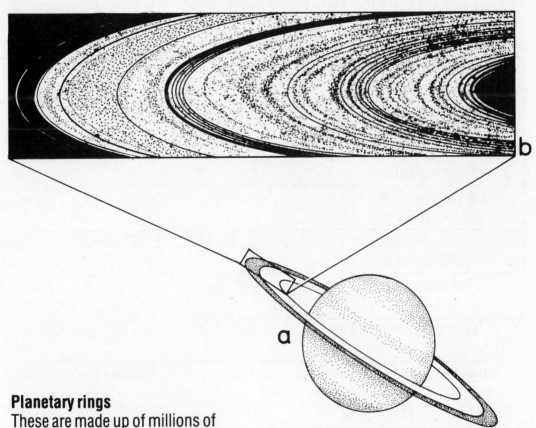

## Planetary rings

These are made up of millions of small particles orbiting the planet. They are rarely more than some 500ft in thickness but may be many miles wide. So far rings are known around only three planets – Jupiter, Saturn and Uranus. Jupiter has one ring divided into a bright outer section and a dimmer inner section. The particles that make up the ring are only a few millionths of an inch across. The ring is almost 156,000 mi in diameter at its outermost part. Saturn (**a**) may have more than 1000 separate rings (**b**). These rings are further divided into thin ringlets. The particles making up the rings are made of dust and ice and measure from a fraction of an inch to 30ft across. The diameter of the outermost ring is over 300,000 mi. Uranus has at least 10 rings, mostly made up of tiny fragments. One ring is v-shaped. The outermost and largest ring is 60 mi wide with a diameter of over 60,000 mi.

# Planets: summary

**Planetary data** The table on these pages summarizes the data available on the nine planets.

| | Mercury | Venus | Earth | Mars |
|---|---|---|---|---|
| **Average distance from Sun** | 0.39au | 0.72au | 1.00au | 1.52au |
| **Distance at perihelion** | 0.31au | 0.72au | 0.98au | 1.38au |
| **Distance at aphelion** | 0.47au | 0.73au | 1.02au | 1.67au |
| **Closest distance to Earth** | 0.54au | 0.27au | — | 0.38au |
| **Average orbital speed** | 28.74 mi/sec | 21.0 mi/sec | 17.88 mi/sec | 14.46 mi/sec |
| **Rotation period** | 58 days 15hr | 243 days | 23hr 56min | 24hr 37min |
| **Sidereal period** | 88 days | 224.7 days | 365.256 days | 687 days |
| **Diameter at equator** | 2926.8 mi | 7262.4 mi | 7653.6 mi | 4077 mi |
| **Mass (Earth's mass=1)** | 0.06 | 0.82 | 1 | 0.11 |
| **Surface temperature** | 662°F (day) −274°F (night) | 896°F | 71.6°F | −9.4°F |
| **Gravity (Earth's gravity=1)** | 0.38 | 0.88 | 1 | 0.38 |
| **Density (density of water=1)** | 5.5 | 5.25 | 5.517 | 3.94 |
| **Number of satellites known** | 0 | 0 | 1 | 2 |
| **Number of rings known** | 0 | 0 | 0 | 0 |
| **Main gases in atmosphere** | no atmosphere | Carbon dioxide | Nitrogen, oxygen | Carbon dioxide |

| Jupiter | Saturn | Uranus | Neptune | Pluto |
|---------|--------|--------|---------|-------|
| 5.20au | 9.54au | 19.18au | 30.06au | 39.44au |
| 4.95au | 9.01au | 18.28au | 29.80au | 29.58au |
| 5.46au | 10.07au | 20.09au | 30.32au | 49.14au |
| 3.95au | 8.00au | 17.28au | 28.80au | 28.72au |
| 7.86 mi/sec | 5.76 mi/sec | 4.08 mi/sec | 3.24 mi/sec | 2.82 mi/sec |
| 9hr 50min | 10hr 14min | 16hr 10min | 18hr 26min | 6 days 9hr |
| 11.86 years | 29.46 years | 84.01 years | 164.8 years | 247.7 years |
| 85,680 mi | 72,000 mi | 30,480 mi | 29,100 mi | 1800 mi |
| 317.9 | 95.2 | 14.6 | 17.2 | 0.002–0.003 |
| −238°F | −292°F | −346°F | −364°F | −382°F |
| 2.64 | 1.15 | 1.17 | 1.2 | not known |
| 1.33 | 0.71 | 1.7 | 1.77 | not known |
| 16 | 19 | 11 | 2 | 1 |
| 1 | 1000+ | 10+ | 0 | 0 |
| Hydrogen, helium | Hydrogen, helium | Hydrogen, helium, methane | Hydrogen, helium, methane | Methane |

©DIAGRAM

# Earth and the Moon (1)

**Moon origins** Astronomers believe that Earth and the Moon were formed separately, but at the same time and close to each other in space. Tests on Moon rocks brought back to Earth by astronauts show that Earth and the Moon are both about the same age – about 4.6 billion years old.

### Moon statistics

Average distance from the center of Earth to the center of the Moon: 238,840 mi
Distance at perigee (i.e. the shortest distance between Earth and the Moon): 213,846 mi
Distance at apogee (i.e. the greatest distance between Earth and the Moon): 244,018 mi
Average orbital speed: 2,288 mph
Diameter at equator: 2158 mi
Surface area: 14,660,000 mi$^2$
Volume: 7,734 $\times$ 10$^{12}$ft$^3$
Mass: 7.37$\times$10$^{22}$kg
Surface temperature: 248°F (day), −256°F (night)
Gravity: 0.1653 times Earth's gravity
Density: 3.34 times the density of water

### Gravity (right)

Because the Moon's gravity is only about one-sixth of Earth's gravity, a jump 3ft high on Earth (**A**) would be a jump 18ft 9in high on the Moon (**B**). Weight also depends on gravity: an astronaut who measured his weight on the Moon would find it was only about one-sixth of his weight on Earth.

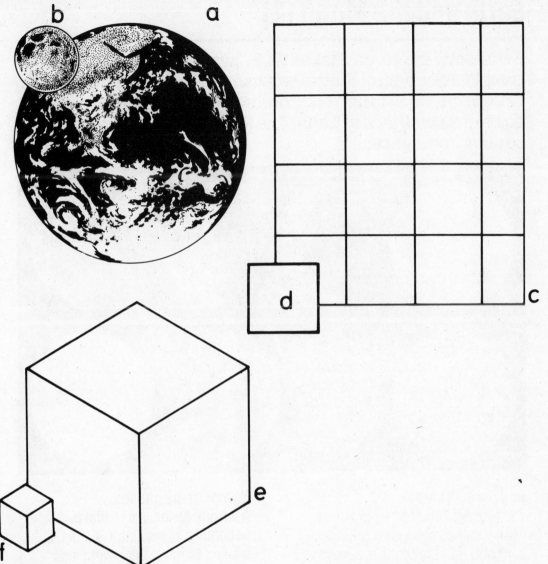

## Comparative sizes

Above we show Earth (**a**) and the Moon (**b**) drawn to the same scale. The Moon's diameter is just over one-quarter of Earth's diameter. Also drawn to the same scale are squares representing the surface areas of Earth (**c**) and the Moon (**d**). Earth's surface area is over 13 times the Moon's surface area.

The cubes, again to the same scale, represent the volumes of Earth (**e**) and the Moon (**f**). Earth's volume is nearly 50 times the Moon's volume.

## Mass and density

The Moon's mass is about 1/100th of Earth's mass, and its density is about 2/3rds of Earth's density.

# Earth and the Moon (2)

**Far side of the Moon** It takes 27.3 days for the Moon to complete one orbit of Earth. Because it takes exactly the same time for the Moon to turn once on its own axis, the Moon always points the same face at Earth. The far side of the Moon can only be seen from space.

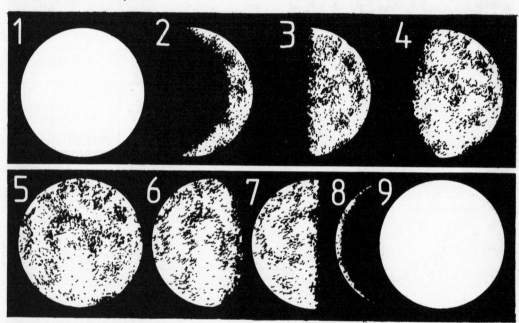

## Phases of the Moon

The Moon produces no light of its own: it shines because it reflects sunlight. Half the Moon is always in sunlight. The amount of the lit half that can be seen from Earth changes from day to day. These regular changes are known as the phases of the Moon. Above we show how the Moon appears from Earth on selected nights within a month. The interval between one new Moon and the next is 29 days 12 hours 44 minutes 3 seconds.

## Names of the phases

A waxing Moon is one that is becoming increasingly visible; a waning Moon is becoming less visible; and a gibbous ("humped") Moon is between half and full.
1 New Moon
2 Waxing crescent Moon
3 Half Moon, first quarter
4 Waxing gibbous Moon
5 Full Moon
6 Waning gibbous Moon
7 Half Moon, last quarter
8 Waning crescent Moon
9 New Moon

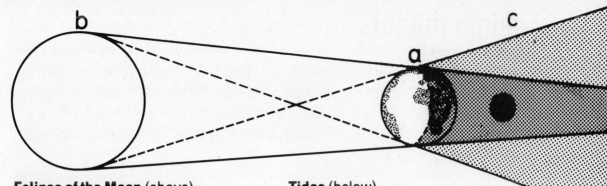

## Eclipse of the Moon (above)

This occurs when the Earth (**a**) is in a direct line between the Sun (**b**) and Moon (**c**). The Moon is then in Earth's shadow and cannot receive any direct sunlight. It becomes dim and appears coppery-red in color. There are never more than three eclipses of the Moon in a year.

## Tides (below)

The pull of the Moon's gravity is the main cause of the tides in Earth's seas and oceans, although the Sun also has an influence. The highest (''spring'') tides occur when the Moon and Sun pull along the same line (**A** and **B**); the lowest (''neap'') tides when they pull at right angles (**C** and **D**).

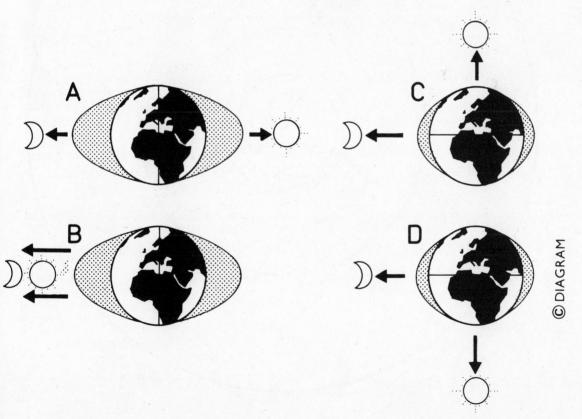

**Minor planets**

**Asteroids** The minor planets are also referred to as asteroids or planetoids. A newly discovered asteroid is given a temporary number that identifies its date of discovery. When its orbit has been plotted it is given its permanent number, and its discoverer may then give it a name.

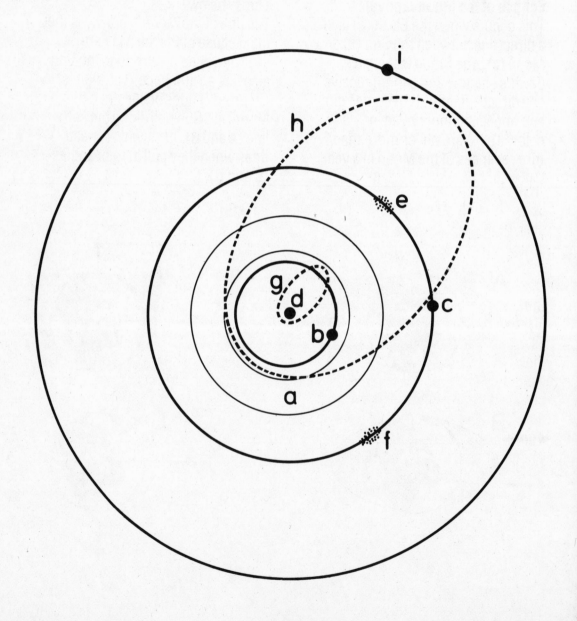

## Main belt

Most of the minor planets are found in the main asteroid belt (**a**), which lies between the orbits of Mars (**b**) and Jupiter (**c**), about 2.2–3.3au from the Sun (**d**). It is estimated that there are 40,000–50,000 asteroids in this belt; so far the orbits of less than 3000 of them have been plotted.

## Trojans

The two groups of Trojan asteroids (whose members are named after the legendary heroes of the Trojan War) move in similar orbits to Jupiter, outside the main asteroid belt. It is estimated that there are over 700 asteroids in the Achilles group (**e**) and over 300 in the Patroclus group (**f**).

## Close-approach asteroids

Listed below are three types of asteroids that come much closer to the Sun than the main belt. It is estimated that there are over 1000 close-approach asteroids, with diameters in the range 0.3–21.7mi.
Apollo type, called after 1862 Apollo, whose orbits cross Earth's orbit.
Amor type, called after 1221 Amor, whose orbits do not cross Earth's orbit.
Aten type, called after 2062 Aten, whose orbits usually lie inside Earth's orbit.

## Record asteroids

Listed below with their numbers are six record-holding named asteroids. The orbits of Icarus (**g**) and Hidalgo (**h**) are shown on the diagram far left.
1 Ceres: first asteroid discovered (1801), largest asteroid (estimated diameter 601.8–624mi).
4 Vesta: brightest asteroid, only asteroid visible with naked eye.
95 Arethusa: darkest asteroid.
944 Hidalgo: asteroid whose orbit takes it farthest from the Sun (9.7au).
1566 Icarus: asteroid whose orbit takes it closest to the Sun (16,800,000mi ot 0.19au).
1937 Hermes: asteroid whose orbit brings it closest to Earth (468,000mi or 0.006au).

## Mass

The total mass of the asteroid belt is estimated at $2.4–3 \times 10^{21}$kg. This is roughly equal to 1/25th of the Moon's mass or 1/2500th of Earth's mass. The largest asteroid, 1 Ceres, has an estimated mass of $11.1–12.3 \times 10^{20}$kg, nearly half the total mass of all the asteroids.

## 2060 Chiron

Although most of its orbit lies outside that of Saturn (**i**), it is thought that this unusual object may be an exceptional asteroid.

# Comets and meteoroids

**Comets** It has been estimated that 1000 comets pass close to the Sun each century. Of these, only a few are bright enough to be seen with the naked eye. The most famous of these is Halley's comet, which passes close to the Sun every 76 years, appearing this century in 1910 and 1986.

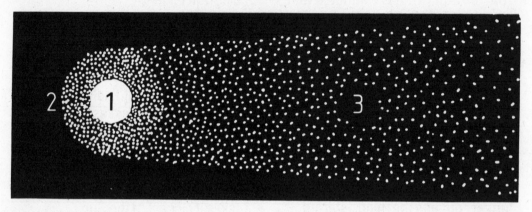

**Parts of a comet** (above)
**1 Nucleus:** the very bright center of a comet's head. Nucleii may be from 300–30,000ft in diameter: the diameter of Halley's comet is estimated to be 16,500ft. Astronomers believe that the nucleus may be a "dirty snowball" made up of dust, rocky fragments, frozen methane, frozen ammonia, frozen carbon dioxide and other ices. Planned research into Halley's comet may provide more definite information about cometary nucleii.
**2 Coma:** the visible sphere of gas and dust around the nucleus. It is formed when the Sun's radiation melts part of the nucleus. The coma may be up to 6.6 million mi in diameter and appears when the comet comes within 3au of the Sun.

The coma is surrounded by a cloud of hydrogen gas which cannot be seen from Earth.
**3 Tail:** this is formed of material streaming away from the head of the comet. It appears when the comet comes close to the Sun. Comets have two types of tail – a dust tail from 0.5–50 million mi long and a plasma (very hot ionized gas) tail up to 50 million mi long. A comet's tail may vary greatly in shape but always points away from the Sun. Many of the comets that are visible only through a telescope do not have tails, either because they do not come close enough to the Sun for one to form or because there is not enough cometary material present to stream out into a tail.

**Meteoroids** These are fragments of material that orbit the Sun. Meteoroids that enter Earth's atmosphere and vaporize to form "shooting stars" are called meteors. Meteoroids that survive the fall through the atmosphere and land on Earth's surface are called meteorites.

## Meteors
It is estimated that over 75 million meteors enter Earth's atmosphere every day, traveling at 21–57mi/sec. An average meteor takes about one second to vaporize completely. Most meteors are about the size of the head of a pin (**a**); the largest may be the size of a grape (**b**).

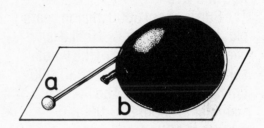

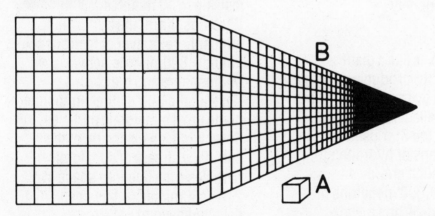

## Meteorites
Every year about six meteorites are observed as they fall, and a further 12–24 are discovered whose fall was not observed. It is estimated that up to 500 meteorites reach Earth's surface each year, as well as up to 1000 tons of micrometeorites (meteorites about the size of specks of dust).

**Largest and smallest** (above)
The diagram shows relative weights.
**A** The smallest meteorite known is the Ras Tanura meteorite, which landed in Saudi Arabia in 1961. It weighs 0.212oz.
**B** The largest meteorite known landed at Hoba West, Grootfontein, in south-west Africa in prehistoric times. It weighs about 60 tons.

# Profile of the Sun (1)

**Average star** The Sun is a star, which only appears different from the other stars in the sky because it is so close to Earth. It is an average star, similar in size and temperature to many millions of other stars in the universe. Like them, it is a sphere of very hot gas that gives out light.

## Age and size

The Sun is about 5000 million years old. Its mass of $1.99 \times 10^{30}$kg is over 99% of the mass of the whole solar system and is about 330,000 times Earth's mass. The Sun's diameter is about 840,000mi, more than 100 times Earth's diameter. Its gravity is about 27 times Earth's gravity.

## Energy

The Sun behaves like a giant hydrogen bomb, producing energy by converting hydrogen into helium in a process called nuclear fusion. Every second the Sun uses up 4–5 million tons of hydrogen to produce as much energy as exploding 100,000 megatons of TNT (a megaton is one million tons). Earth receives only a tiny fraction of this energy: in one second the Sun gives out in all directions as much energy as Earth receives from it in 100 years.

## Traveling light

It takes on average 8 minutes 18 seconds for light from the Sun to reach Earth.

## Some solar features

**Photosphere:** The Sun's visible surface, temperature about 10,000°F.

**Limb:** the edge of the Sun's disc.

**Granulation (1):** the mottled appearance of the surface, caused by clouds of hotter gases rising from inside the Sun. A granule measures 180–780mi across and lasts up to 10 minutes.

**Chromosphere:** the Sun's inner atmosphere, a layer of hydrogen about 4,800mi wide between the photosphere and the corona.

**Corona:** the Sun's outer atmosphere, made up of subatomic particles.

**Solar wind:** an extension of the corona, a stream of subatomic particles traveling into space at 210–480mi/sec. It has been detected beyond Saturn.

**Prominences (2):** huge clouds of hydrogen about 120,000mi high. They may be eruptive (short lived) or quiescent (lasting many months).

**Flares:** disturbances in the lower part of the corona that appear as brilliant flashes of light.

**Spicules (3):** groups of jets of hydrogen, 4,800–6,000mi high, rising from the chromosphere. Each spicule lasts up to 15 minutes.

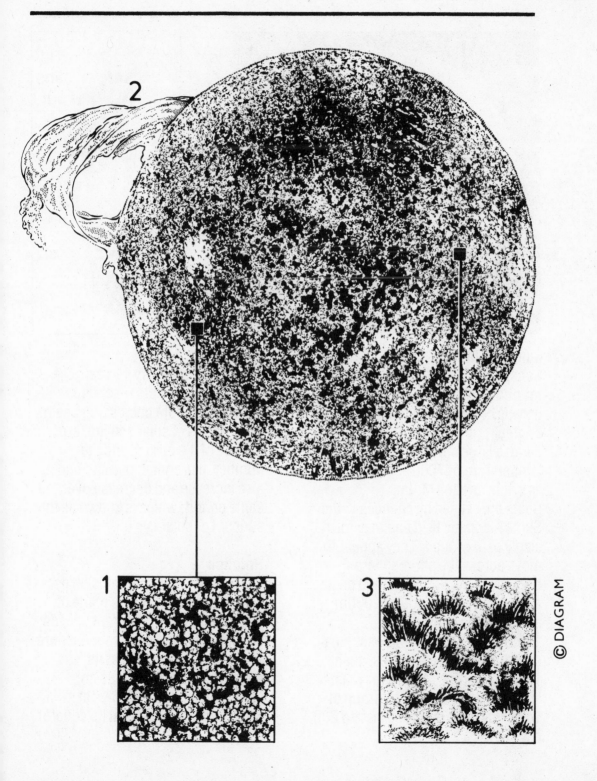

# Profile of the Sun (2)

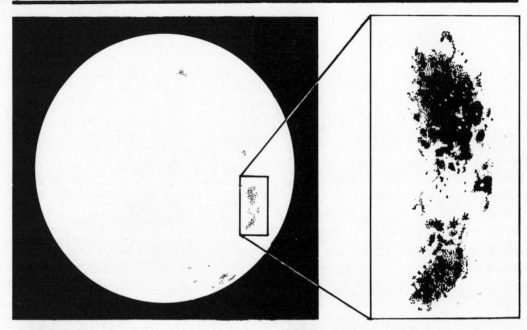

## Sunspots (above)

Sunspots are seen as dark areas on the photosphere. They appear dark only by contrast with the hotter, brighter photosphere surrounding them: a large sunspot has a temperature of 7000–9000°F and is as bright as a full Moon.

Spots are caused by changes in the Sun's magnetic field and may form singly or in groups, They appear to move across the photosphere because of the Sun's rotation on its axis. An average spot is 6,000mi across; large spots can be 120,000–180,000mi across; small spots (called pores) are less than 1,800mi across. A pore may last less than an hour; a large group of spots has been recorded lasting 200 days.

## Solar cycle

Approximately every 11 years the number of sunspots reaches a maximum before decreasing again. Other forms of solar activity, e.g. the size of the corona and the number of prominences and flares, also increase and decrease over the same period, which is known as the sunspot or solar cycle.

## Rotation

The Sun, like Earth, rotates on its axis. Because the Sun is made of gas it can rotate at different speeds at different latitudes: it rotates more slowly at its poles than at its equator. Rotation periods are approximately 24–26 days at its poles and 34–37 days at its equator.

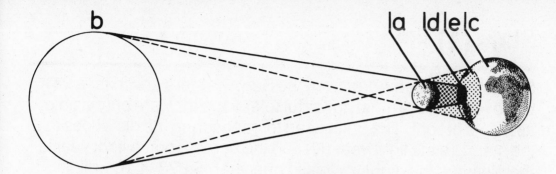

b a d e c

## Eclipses of the Sun (above)

From Earth, the Sun and the Moon appear to be about the same size: the Sun is about 400 times as big as the Moon but is also 400 times farther away from Earth.

When the Moon (**a**) is in a direct line between the Sun (**b**) and Earth (**c**), the Moon's disc appears to cover the Sun's photosphere. The part of Earth directly in the Moon's shadow (**d**) sees a total eclipse of the Sun; areas around it (**e**) see a partial eclipse.

## Types of eclipse (right)

**1 Total** This can last from a split second up to a maximum of 7min 31sec. The area over which it can be seen has a maximum width of 163.2mi but is usually much less. The corona is visible to the naked eye.

**2 Partial** The Moon's disc only obscures part of the photosphere.

**3 Annular** Named from the Latin word *annulus*, meaning ring. This type of eclipse occurs if the Moon is at its farthest point from Earth and Earth is at its nearest point to the Sun. The Moon's disc then appears slightly smaller than the photosphere.

**1**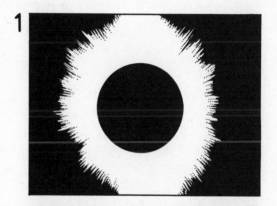

**2**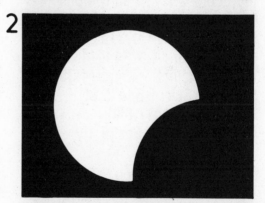

**3**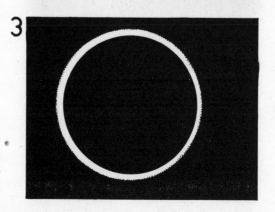

# Stars (1)

**Stellar distances** Apart from the Sun, the stars are so far away that even with the most powerful telescope they are only visible as points of light. The units used for measuring the distances to the stars are the light year (ly) and the parsec (pc). A light year is the distance that light travels in one year, $5.878 \times 10^{12}$mi, which equals 63,290au. A parsec is 3.26 light years, i.e. $19.174 \times 10^{12}$mi or 206,265au.

## Near and far
Listed below are the 11 stars nearest Earth (excluding the special case of the Sun). They are the only stars within 3 parsecs or 10 light years. The most distant stars in our galaxy are estimated to be 19,325pc (63,000ly) away – nearly 4 billion times as far away as the Sun.

Proxima Centauri, 1.31pc (4.28ly)
Alpha Centauri A, 1.34pc (4.35ly)
Alpha Centauri B, 1.34pc (4.35ly)
Barnard's Star, 1.8pc (5.8ly)
Wolf 359, 2.3pc (7.6ly)
Lalande 21185, 2.5pc (8.1ly)
Sirius A, 2.65pc (8.7ly)
Sirius B, 2.65pc (8.7ly)
UV Ceti A, 2.7pc (8.8ly)
UV Ceti B, 2.7pc (8.8ly)
Ross 154, 2.9pc (9.5ly)

## Distant light
The light now reaching Earth from these stars left them at about the time of these historic events.

Rigel, Battle of Hastings (1066)
Polaris (the Pole Star), Outbreak of Black Death (1348)
Capella, Pearl Harbor (1941)

## Color and size
Stars are often referred to in terms of their color (red, orange, yellow, blue, white) and comparative size and brightness (dwarf, giant, supergiant). The Sun is a yellow dwarf star. Blue and white stars are hotter than the Sun, orange and red stars are cooler. In the list below, five types of star are compared in size and brightness with the Sun. The diagram on the facing page shows their comparative sizes.

**1** Sirius B, white dwarf, diameter 1/100th of Sun's, brightness 1/400th of Sun's
**2** Barnard's Star, red dwarf, diameter 1/10th of Sun's, brightness 1/2000th of Sun's
**3** Sun, yellow dwarf
**4** Capella, yellow giant, diameter 16 times Sun's, brightness 150 times Sun's
**5** Rigel, blue-white giant, diameter 80 times Sun's, brightness 60,000 times Sun's
**6** Betelgeux, red supergiant, diameter 300–400 times Sun's, brightness 15,000 times Sun's

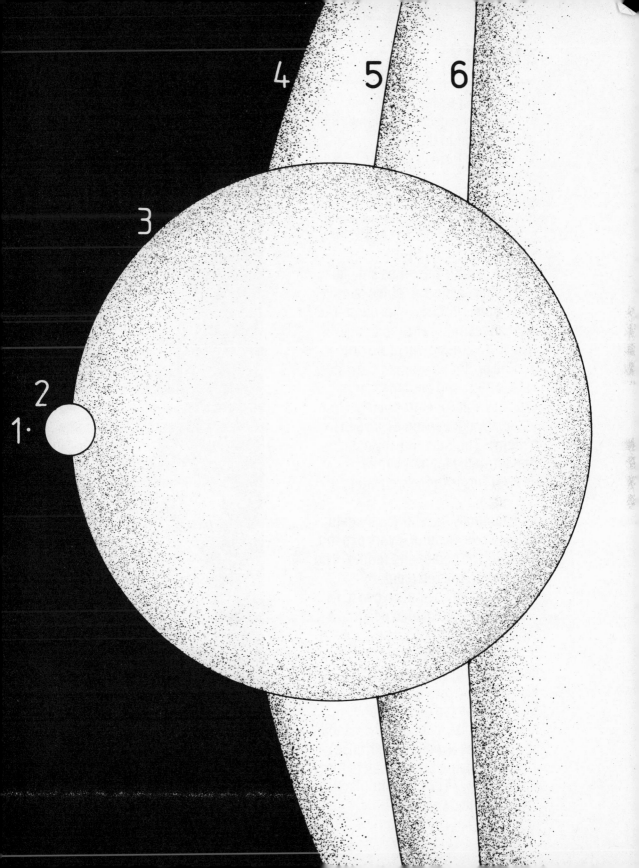

# Stars (2)

**Life cycle of a star** (right)
This is the life cycle of a star with a mass similar to the Sun.

**1** All stars form in nebulae (clouds of gas and dust). Denser, smaller clouds called globules gradually form within a nebula. (A globule the size of the solar system will form a star the size of the Sun.)

**2** The globule becomes smaller and hotter, begins to shine faintly, and forms a large red "protostar" (star ancestor). "Protoplanets" may form around the protostar.

**3** The protostar contracts further, gets hotter, and becomes an ordinary star (one producing energy by converting hydrogen to helium). The star and any planets remain stable for many million years. (This is the current state of the Sun.)

**4** Eventually the star's core gets hotter while its outer layers expand and become cooler and redder. The star becomes a red giant, destroying any planets close to it. (The Sun is expected to become a red giant, 100 times its present size, in about 5 billion years. It will engulf Mercury, Venus and possibly Earth.)

**5** When the red giant reaches its maximum size it becomes unstable and pulsates (swells and shrinks). The outer layers break away to form a ring nebula. The core shrinks to form a white dwarf star.

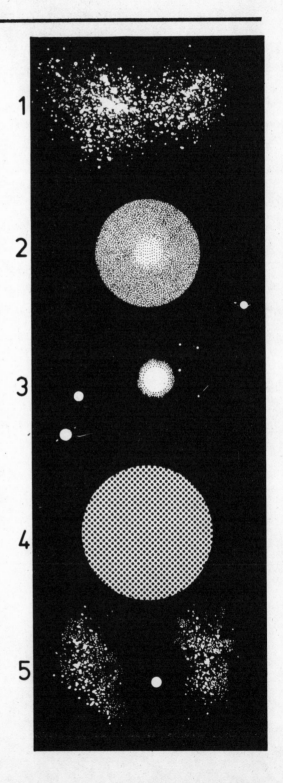

## Larger than the Sun

Stars whose mass is more than 1½ times the Sun's burn out faster. (A star with 10 times the Sun's mass lasts only 1/10th as long.) These stars end their life cycle by burning up in a violent nuclear explosion, forming a supernova (**a**). The outer layers are thrown off to form a nebula. The core collapses to form a small very dense star called a neutron star; very massive stars may collapse further to form a black hole.

In seven days a supernova can become 10 billion times as bright as the Sun. The last supernova observed in our galaxy was seen in 1604. The Crab Nebula (**b**) is the remains of a supernova explosion observed on July 4, 1054.

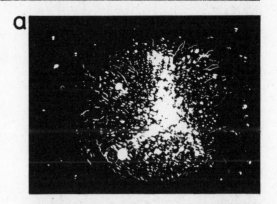

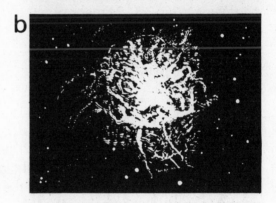

## Smaller than the Sun

A globule whose mass is about 1/10th of the Sun's mass forms a red dwarf star. A red dwarf lasts much longer than the Sun, and may have a lifetime of a million million years.

A globule whose mass is less than 1/10th of the Sun's mass will not form a star.

## Stars and planets

Perhaps 10% of stars may have planets, but none has definitely been detected. Barnard's Star is thought to have two planets.

## Multiple stars

A globule may break up as it contracts and form more than one star. Globules that form close together may stay close together when they become stars and form groups of stars. It is estimated that there are more groups of two, three or more stars than there are single stars like the Sun. Perhaps over 50% of stars are in binary systems. (In a binary system two stars are in orbit around each other.) The Sun may once have been a member of a group of stars which have since moved apart.

# Stars (3)

## Brightness

The brightness of a star is described in terms of its magnitude. The brighter the star, the smaller its magnitude; very bright stars have negative magnitudes. The dimmest stars visible to the naked eye are of magnitude +6; the most powerful telescopes can detect stars of magnitude +23. The ratio between magnitudes is 2.512 (i.e. a star of magnitude +3 is 2.512 times as bright as a star of magnitude +4, which in turn is 2.512 times as bright as a star of magnitude +5, etc).

## Apparent and absolute magnitude

The apparent magnitude of a star is its brightness as seen from Earth. Apparent magnitude is affected by distance: stars that are farther away from Earth appear less bright than those that are closer. For more accurate comparison, astronomers calculate the absolute magnitude of a star. This is the brightness that a star would have if it were at a distance of 10pc (32.6ly) from Earth. The Sun has an apparent magnitude of −26.8 and an absolute magnitude of +4.7.

## Brightest stars

The ten stars which observers on Earth see as the brightest stars in the sky are listed below in order of their apparent magnitude. Of these stars, only Canopus compares in absolute magnitude with the brightest star in the sky, R136a, which has an absolute magnitude of about −10.4. R136a is about 75 million times as bright as the Sun but cannot be seen from Earth with the naked eye.

| | Star | Apparent magnitude | Absolute magnitude | Number of times brighter than Sun | Distance ly | pc |
|---|---|---|---|---|---|---|
| 1 | Sirius | −1.46 | +1.4 | 26 | 8.7 | 2.6 |
| 2 | Canopus | −0.72 | −8.5 | 200,000 | 1200 | 360 |
| 3 | Alpha Centauri | −0.27 | +4.1 | 1.5 | 4.35 | 1.3 |
| 4 | Arcturus | −0.04 | −0.2 | 115 | 36 | 11 |
| 5 | Vega | +0.03 | +0.5 | 52 | 26 | 8.1 |
| 6 | Capella | +0.08 | +0.3 | 70 | 42 | 13 |
| 7 | Rigel | +0.12v | −7.1v | 60,000 | 900 | 280 |
| 8 | Procyon | +0.38 | +2.6 | 11 | 11.4 | 3.5 |
| 9 | Archernar | +0.46 | −1.6 | 780 | 85 | 26 |
| 10 | Betelgeux | +0.85v | −5.6v | 15,000 | 310 | 95 |

v=variable star, average figure given

©DIAGRAM

## Brightness and distance

The star Alnilan (**A**) has an absolute magnitude of −6.2 (about 26,000 times as bright as the Sun) and is 1200ly (370pc) away. The star Bellatrix (**B**) has an absolute magnitude of −3.6 (about 2200 times as bright as the Sun) and is 360ly (110pc) away. Although Alnilan is nearly 12 times as bright as Bellatrix, it is over three times as far from Earth (**C**). The two stars therefore appear about the same in brightness when seen from Earth. Apparent magnitudes are: Alnilan, +1.70; Bellatrix, +1.64.

## Variable stars

Intrinsically variable stars are stars that vary in brightness because they alter in diameter. Some pulsate (swell and shrink) regularly and it is possible to predict changes in their size and brightness. Others vary irregularly and unpredictably. So far over 25,000 variable stars are known.

## Nova

A nova is a dim star that suddenly becomes 100–1,000,000 times as bright for a few days before fading away again. The sudden brightness is caused by the star exploding a shell of gas into space. The star is not destroyed and keeps shining. The same star may erupt as a nova many times.

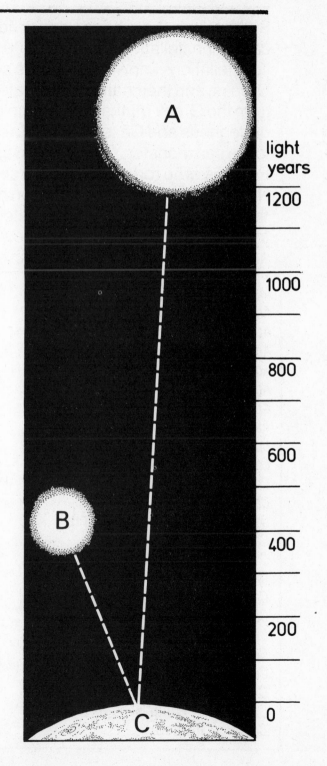

light years

1200

1000

800

600

400

200

0

# Constellations

**Star groups** Stars have been divided into the artificial groups called constellations for over 2,000 years. Many of the constellations known today were suggested by the ancient Greeks, and their names celebrate characters and monsters from the Greek myths. For example, Andromeda, the daughter of Cepheus and Cassiopeia, was chained to a rock as a sacrifice to the sea monster, Cetus. She was rescued by the hero Perseus, who rode the flying horse Pegasus.

No new constellations have been named since the middle of the eighteenth century. 88 constellations are recognized by astronomers and are usually known by their Latin names. These are listed below with their English equivalents.

*Andromeda*, Andromeda
*Antlia*, the air pump
*Apus*, the bird of paradise
*Aquarius*, the water-bearer
*Aquila*, the eagle
*Ara*, the altar
*Aries*, the ram
*Auriga*, the charioteer
*Boötes*, the herdsman
*Caelum*, the sculptor's tools
*Camelopardus*, the giraffe
*Cancer*, the crab
*Canes Venatici*, the hunting dogs
*Canis Major*, the great dog
*Canis Minor*, the little dog
*Capricornus*, the goat
*Carina*, the keel*
*Cassiopeia*, Cassiopeia
*Centaurus*, the centaur
*Cepheus*, Cepheus
*Cetus*, the sea monster, the whale
*Chamæleon*, the chameleon
*Circinus*, the compasses
*Columba*, the dove

*Coma Berenices*, Berenice's hair
*Corona Australis*, the southern crown
*Corona Borealis*, the northern crown
*Corvus*, the crow
*Crater*, the cup
*Crux Australis*, the southern cross
*Cygnus*, the swan
*Delphinus*, the dolphin
*Dorado*, the swordfish
*Draco*, the dragon
*Equuleus*, the foal
*Eridanus*, the river
*Fornax*, the furnace
*Gemini*, the twins
*Grus*, the crane
*Hercules*, Hercules
*Horologium*, the clock
*Hydra*, the water snake
*Hydrus*, the little snake
*Indus*, the Indian
*Lacerta*, the lizard
*Leo*, the lion
*Leo Minor*, the little lion
*Lepus*, the hare

## Record constellations

As seen from Earth, the largest constellation in area is Hydra; the smallest in area is Crux Australis; the brightest is Orion; the dimmest is Mensa; and the constellation containing the greatest number of stars visible to the naked eye (at least 94) is Centaurus.

## Naming stars

Only the best-known stars have proper names. Bright stars are referred to by a form of their constellation's name following a letter of the Greek alphabet – $\alpha$ (alpha), $\beta$ (beta), etc. For example, Capella is $\alpha$ Aurigae; Rigel is $\beta$ Orionis. Faint stars are known by their numbers in star catalogs.

*Libra*, the scales, the balance
*Lupus*, the wolf
*Lynx*, the lynx
*Lyra*, the lyre
*Mensa*, the table
*Microscopium*, the microscope
*Monoceros*, the unicorn
*Musca Australis*, the southern fly
*Norma*, the rule
*Octans*, the octant
*Ophiuchus*, the serpent-bearer
*Orion*, Orion the hunter
*Pavo*, the peacock
*Pegasus*, the flying horse
*Perseus*, Perseus
*Phoenix*, the phoenix
*Pictor*, the painter
*Pisces*, the fishes
*Piscis Austrinus*, the southern fish
*Puppis*, the poop*
*Pyxis*, the mariner's compass*
*Reticulum*, the net
*Sagitta*, the arrow
*Sagittarius*, the archer

*Scorpio*, the scorpion
*Sculptor*, the sculptor
*Scutum*, the shield
*Serpens*, the serpent
*Sextans*, the sextant
*Taurus*, the bull
*Telescopium*, the telescope
*Triangulum*, the triangle
*Triangulum Australe*, the southern triangle
*Tucana*, the toucan
*Ursa Major*, the great bear
*Ursa Minor*, the little bear
*Vela*, the sails*
*Virgo*, the virgin
*Volans*, the flying fish
*Vulpecula*, the fox

*Once part of a much larger constellation, *Argo Navis*, the ship "Argo", which was divided into smaller groupings for convenience.

©DIAGRAM

# Celestial poles

**Poles in the sky** The north and south celestial poles are the equivalents in the sky of the north and south poles on Earth. Earth's axis joins the north and south poles: extended northward it points to the north celestial pole, and extended southward it points to the south celestial pole.

**North celestial pole** (below)
The north celestial pole is roughly marked by the star Polaris (**a**) in the constellation Ursa Minor (**A**). Polaris is only three-quarters of one degree away from the true pole. To find Polaris, find the Big Dipper (**B**) and extend the imaginary line joining the two stars known as the Pointers (**b** and **c**).

**South celestial pole** (below)
There is no star marking the south celestial pole; the nearest star visible with the naked eye is Sigma Octantis (**d**). To find the south celestial pole (**e**), find the constellation of the Southern Cross (**C**) and extend the imaginary line joining the two stars that form its longer arm (**f** and **g**).

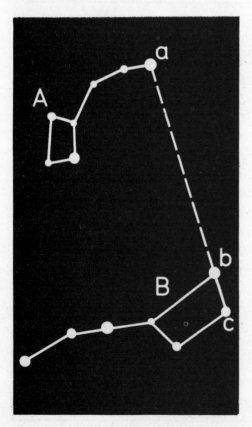

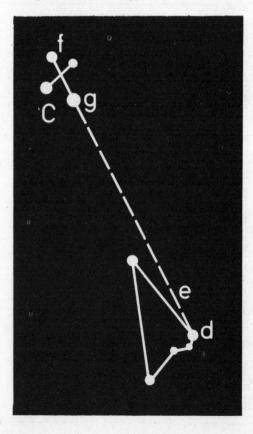

**Polar changes** (below)
Earth's movement is similar to that of a slowly spinning top – it rotates on its axis and wobbles at the same time. Because of this movement (called precession), Earth's axis appears to trace two circles in the sky (one to the north and one to the south) and the celestial poles move around these circles. The diagram shows how the north celestial pole moves in its circle through the constellations Draco (**A**), Ursa Minor (**B**), Cepheus (**C**), Cygnus (**D**) and Lyra (**E**). It takes 25,800 years to complete the circle.

Because the celestial pole's position in the sky changes, the star that is the pole star also changes. In 3000BC the pole star was Thuban (**a**); currently it is Polaris (**b**); in about 10,000AD it will be Deneb (**c**); in about 14,000 AD it will be Vega (**d**); and in about 23,800AD it will again be Thuban.
Precession also affects the timing of the seasons. By 15,000AD, December will be a summer month in the northern hemisphere and a winter month in the southern hemisphere.

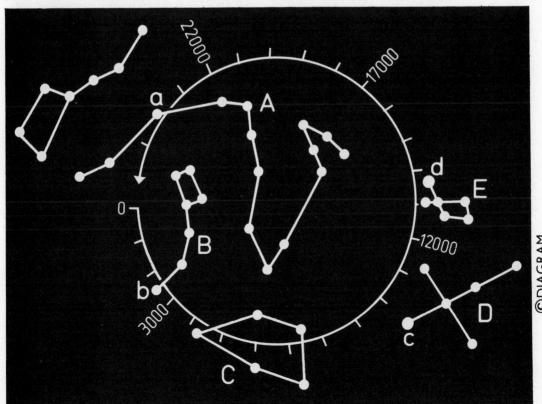

©DIAGRAM.

# Galaxies (1)

**Star islands** Galaxies are collections of stars, planets, gas, dust, nebulae, etc, that form "islands" in the emptiness of space. Powerful telescopes can detect 1 billion galaxies, measuring from 1000ly to 10 million ly across. Most galaxies are found in groups; very few are found on their own.

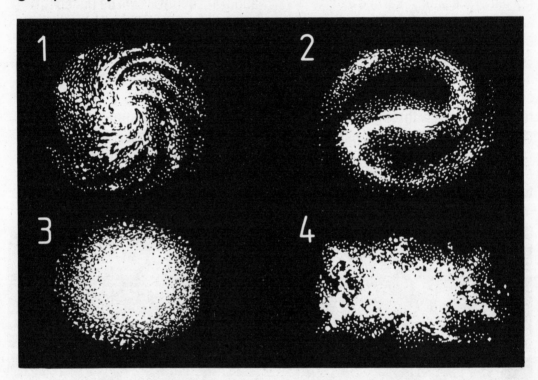

**Galactic shapes**
Galaxies are classified by their shape. The four main classes are listed here and illustrated above.
**1 Spiral** These galaxies resemble pinwheels, with spiral arms trailing out from a bright center.
**2 Barred spiral** Here the spiral arms trail from the ends of a central bar. About 30% of galaxies are spirals or barred spirals.

**3 Elliptical** These galaxies do not have spiral arms. About 60% of galaxies are elliptical, varying in shape from almost spherical (like a soccer ball) to very flattened (like a football)
**4 Irregular** About 10% of galaxies are irregular with no definite shape.

A

|— 100,000ly —|

## Our Galaxy

Our Galaxy is a spiral galaxy about 100,000ly (30,600pc) in diameter. The diagram above shows it as seen from the side. The older stars are found in the central bulge, which is about 20,000ly (6100pc) thick. The younger stars are found in the spiral arms. The center of the Galaxy is in the constellation Sagittarius; its north pole is in Coma Berenices; its south pole is in Sculptor. The Sun(**A**) is on the inner edge of the Carina-Cygnus spiral arm, about 32,000ly (9800pc) from the center of the Galaxy.

It is estimated that the Galaxy is 12–14 billion years old and that it contains about 100 billion stars.

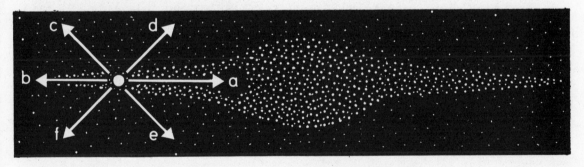

## Milky Way

Observers looking towards the center of the Galaxy (arrow **a**) or through its rim (arrow **b**) see many thousand million stars at once. To the naked eye these stars appear as the faint band of light in the night sky called the Milky Way. Observers looking out of the Galaxy (arrows **c**,**d**,**e**,**f**) see fewer stars.

## Galactic rotation

The Galaxy is rotating on its axis. It rotates more quickly at the center than at the edges. The central region turns on its axis once in about every 50,000 years. The Sun, traveling at about 150mi/sec, takes about 225 million years (called a "cosmic year") to complete one rotation.

# Galaxies (2)

### Galactic clusters

Our Galaxy belongs to a small cluster called the "Local Group", which is estimated to include 30–50 galaxies. Other galactic clusters may be much larger, e.g. the Virgo cluster, which includes over 1000 galaxies. There are also superclusters – clusters of clusters of galaxies.

### Shapes and sizes

Three members of the Local Group are spiral galaxies; a few members are irregular galaxies; and the remaining members are dwarf elliptical galaxies measuring less than 5000ly across. The three spiral galaxies are the largest members of the Local Group. Largest of all is M31, the Andromeda galaxy, which is 1½ times the size of our Galaxy. Our Galaxy is the second largest. The third largest is M33, the Triangulum galaxy, which is half the size of our Galaxy.

### Naked eye galaxies

The three Local Group members which can be seen from Earth with the naked eye are the Large Magellanic Cloud, the Small Magellanic Cloud, and M31, the Andromeda galaxy. M31 is the brightest galaxy in the Local Group and the most remote object visible with the naked eye.

### Group distances (facing page)

The relative positions of some members of the Local Group are shown in the diagram. Distances are in millions of light years. The whole Local Group is estimated to measure five million light years across.

- **a** The Galaxy, spiral
- **b** Large Magellanic Cloud, irregular
- **c** Small Magellanic Cloud, irregular
- **d** Ursa Minor, elliptical
- **e** Draco, elliptical
- **f** Sculptor, elliptical
- **g** Fornax, elliptical
- **h** Leo I, elliptical
- **i** Leo II, elliptical
- **j** NGC 6822, irregular
- **k** NGC 185, elliptical
- **l** NGC 147, elliptical
- **m** NGC 205, elliptical
- **n** M31 (Andromeda galaxy), spiral
- **o** M32, elliptical
- **p** IC 1613, irregular
- **q** M33 (Triangulum galaxy), spiral

### Receding galaxies

Apart from Local Group galaxies, all other galaxies are receding (moving away) from Earth at high speed. The farther away the galaxy, the faster the speed at which it is receding. The most distant galaxy known, 3C 295 in Boötes, is receding from Earth at half the speed of light.

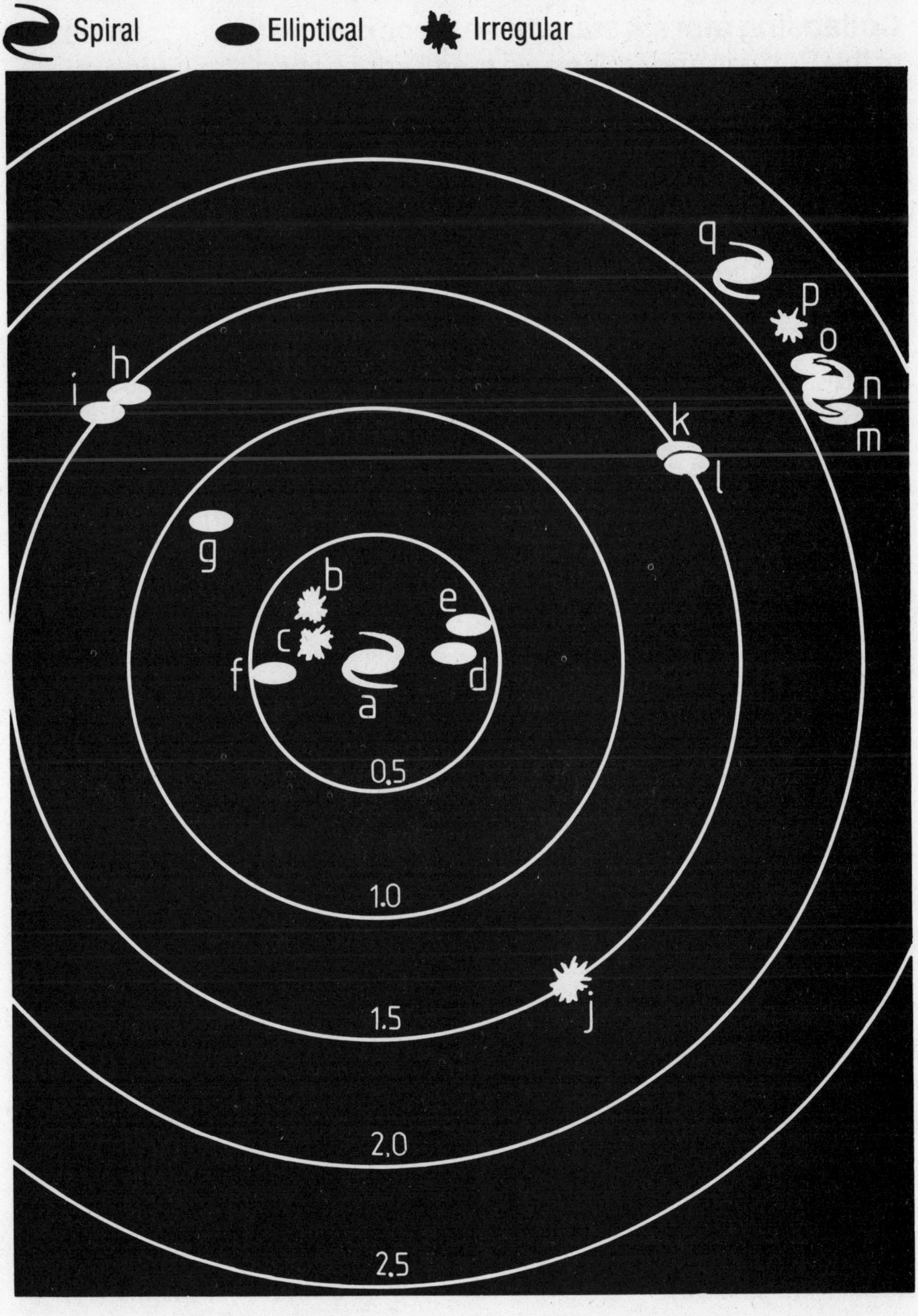

Spiral Elliptical Irregular

©DIAGRAM

# Pulsars, black holes, quasars

**Collapsing stars** A star whose mass is more than 1½ times that of the Sun will end its life as a small very dense star called a pulsar or neutron star. A very massive star – one whose mass is more than three times that of the Sun – may collapse further and become a black hole.

## Pulsars

Neutron stars are called "pulsars" because they give out radio waves which are received on Earth as regular, rapid pulses. The pulse rate slows down as the neutron star ages. The youngest and fastest pulsar known is NP 0532 in the Crab Nebula, pulsing at over 30 times a second. The oldest and slowest pulsar known is NP 0527, pulsing once every 3.7 seconds.
Pulsars are detected with radio telescopes. The average diameter of a neutron star is 6mi, and so they are almost undetectable with optical telescopes. Only two pulsars have so far been seen with optical telescopes – NP 0532 in the Crab Nebula and PSR 0833-45 in the Gum Nebula.

## Black holes

Black holes are invisible and can only be detected by their effect on stars near them. Black holes warp space and time: time stops at their edges. The gravity in black holes is so great that not even light can escape from them. Anything coming close to a black hole is pulled into it and vanishes from our universe forever.
No one has yet proved that black holes definitely exist. It is thought that there may be a black hole in the binary system Cygnus X-1. One member of this system is a blue-white supergiant star, HDE 226868. Its companion is invisible, has a mass 14 times that of the Sun, is not a neutron star, and may be a black hole.

a

## Heavy star

A pinhead-sized piece of a neutron star weighs more than the liner Queen Elizabeth II (**a**).

## Hole size

It has been calculated that a black hole with the same mass as Earth would be 0.273in in diameter.

**Quasars** The name "quasar" is an abbreviation of "quasi-stellar object", i.e. an object that appears to be a star. When seen by optical telescopes, quasars look like ordinary faint stars. When seen by radio telescopes, they are clearly not stars but distant objects that give out massive amounts of energy.

### Quasar mystery

Quasars are the remotest, fastest-moving and brightest objects in the universe and some of the most puzzling. A typical quasar is 1/100,000th the size of our Galaxy but 100–200 times as bright. Quasars also give out enormous amounts of energy in the form of radio waves and X-rays. Astronomers are puzzled as to how such small objects can be so powerful, and have been trying to work out what quasars really are ever since the first one (quasar 3C 273 in Virgo) was discovered in the early 1960s. It is currently thought that they may be the nucleii (central parts) of very young, very active galaxies, possibly powered by massive black holes.

### Distance away

Quasars are the most distant objects in the universe and are receding at high speed. The most remote object known is the quasar PKS 2000-330, which is estimated to be 11–13 billion ly away and to be moving away from Earth at 90% of the speed of light.

### Comparative sizes (below)

The diameter of our Galaxy is 100,000ly. The diameter of a typical quasar is less than 1ly. If the diameter of our Galaxy is represented by the distance by air from London (**A**) to New York (**B**), then the diameter of the quasar would be less than the length of a Concorde (**C**) flying the route.

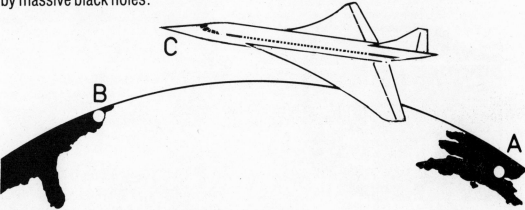

# The universe

**Age and size** Astronomers estimate that the universe is 13–20 billion years old. No one knows how large the universe is or how large it will become — it is still expanding as the galaxies and clusters of galaxies move farther away from each other.

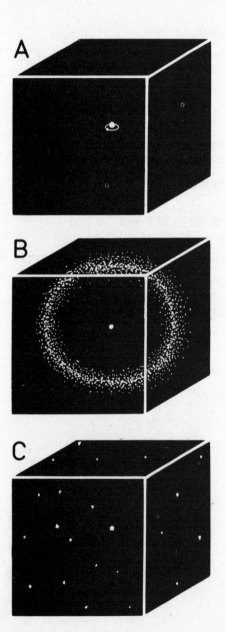

### The scale of the universe

In these diagrams we use cubes to give some idea of the enormous scale of the universe. Each cube has sides 100 times as long as the sides of the cube before it. This means that each cube represents a section of space with a volume 1,000,000 times greater than the section of space represented by the cube before it. The volume of the last cube in the series is 1,000,000,000, 000,000,000,000,000,000,000, 000,000 times the volume of the first cube. On the facing page we list the length of the sides of each cube and the planets, stars, galaxies, etc, which would fit into it.

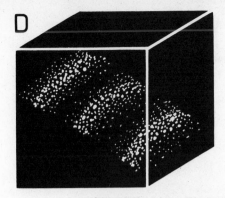

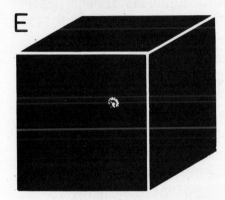

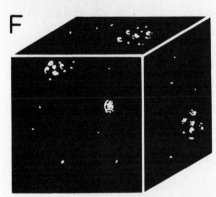

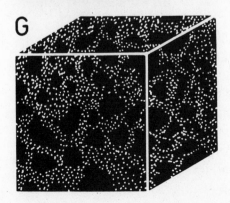

**A** Cube side 950au (0.015ly)
Contains the whole solar system.

**B** Cube side 1½ly
Contains the solar system surrounded by the Oort cloud of comets. This cloud is believed to be the original source of many of the comets that pass through the solar system. It surrounds the Sun at an average distance of 40,000au (2/3ly).

**C** Cube side 150ly
Contains the solar system and the nearer stars.

**D** Cube side 15,000ly
Contains the nearer spiral arms of our Galaxy.

**E** Cube side 1,500,000ly
Contains the whole of our Galaxy, the Large and Small Magellanic Clouds and other nearby galaxies in the Local Group.

**F** Cube side 150 million ly
Contains the whole of the Local Group and the Pisces, Cancer and Virgo clusters of galaxies.

**G** Cube side 15 billion ly
Contains all the known clusters and superclusters of galaxies and all other known objects in space, and represents the limits of our current knowledge of the size of the universe.

# Unmanned space flight (1)

**Satellite numbers** Over 5000 artificial satellites are now orbiting Earth, and about 150 more are launched each year. Most of these satellites are launched by the USA and USSR, but China, Japan, India and the European Space Agency (ESA) also have their own satellite launching programs.

## Satellite use

Here we look at some ways in which artificial satellites are used.
Communications: used to relay radio, telephone, television and other signals around the world.
Meteorology: these weather satellites send back details of clouds, winds, temperatures, etc.
Navigation: these send out radio signals that allow ships to plot their positions accurately.
Earth survey: used to study the way land is used, to find possible sources of oil and minerals, etc.
Research: used to discover more about the Sun, stars, comets, etc than can be discovered from Earth.
Military and reconnaissance: used for secret military purposes.

## Oldest satellite

The oldest artificial satellite in space is probably the third satellite launched, Explorer 1. Although it sent back signals for only 112 days, it is still believed to be in orbit. The first two satellites launched were in orbit for much shorter periods: Sputnik 1, 92 days; Sputnik 2, 163 days.

## Some satellite firsts (facing page)

First artificial satellite: Sputnik 1 (**a**), launched by USSR on October 4, 1957.
First animal in space: the dog Laika in Sputnik 2 (**b**), launched by USSR on November 3, 1957.
First American satellite: Explorer 1 (**c**), launched on February 1, 1958.
First Earth survey satellite: Vanguard1 (**d**), launched by USA on March 17, 1958. (It showed Earth's shape for the first time.)
First research satellite: Sputnik 3 (**e**), launched by USSR on May 15, 1958. (It was used to study Earth's magnetic field, radiation from the Sun, etc.)
First weather satellite: Tiros 1 (**f**), launched by USA on April 1, 1960.
First American navigation satellite: Transit 1B (**g**), launched on April 13, 1960.
First reported American reconnaissance satellite: Samos 2, launched on January 31, 1961.
First British satellite: Ariel 1 (**h**), launched by USA on April 26, 1962.
First communications satellite relaying live television across the Atlantic: Telstar 1 (**i**), launched by USA on July 10, 1962.

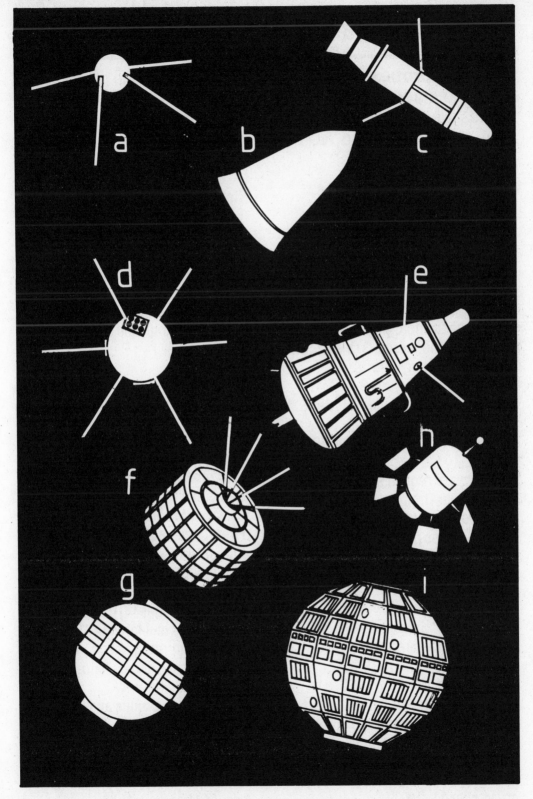

# Unmanned space flight (2)

**Planetary probes** These travel to the Moon and the planets and send photographs and other information back to Earth. Some probes are designed to observe a planet as they fly past it; others are designed to "soft-land" on a planet's surface to make close-up observations.

## Some Moon probe firsts

First Moon probe: Luna 1 (**a**), USSR, launched January 2, 1958. It missed its target.

First probe to reach the Moon: Luna 2, USSR, launched September 12, 1959. Crash-landed.

First probe to photograph the far side of the Moon: Luna 3 (**b**), USSR, launched October 4, 1959.

First soft-landing: Luna 9 (**c**), USSR, launched January 31, 1966.

First American soft-landing: Surveyor 1 (**d**), launched May 30, 1966.

First series of probes to map the Moon: Lunar Orbiters 1–5 (**e**), USA, launched August 10, 1966 – August 1, 1967. These probes mapped 99% of the Moon's surface.

## Some Venus probe firsts

First successful: Mariner 2 (**f**), USA, flew past on December 14, 1962.

First landing: Venera 3, USSR, crash-landed March 1, 1966.

First soft-landing: Venera 7, USSR, soft-landed on December 15, 1970 and survived for 23 minutes.

First photograph of surface: Venera 9, USSR, sent back one photograph on October 21, 1975.

## Some Mars probe firsts

First successful: Mariner 4 (**g**), USA. Sent back 22 photographs on July 14 and 15, 1965.

First landing: Mars 2, USSR, crash-landed on November 27, 1971.

First soft-landing: Viking 1 (**h**), USA, soft-landed on June 20, 1976.

## Other planets

First successful probe to Mercury: Mariner 10, USA, first flew past on March 29, 1974.

First successful probe to Jupiter: Pioneer 10 (**i**), USA, flew past on December 3, 1973. (Also first probe to leave the solar system.)

First successful probe to Saturn: Pioneer 11, USA, first flew past on September 1, 1979.

First successful probe to Jupiter's moons: Voyager 1 (**j**), USA, flew past Jupiter on March 5, 1979, and sent back information on the moons Io, Ganymede and Callisto. It went on to fly past Saturn.

First probe to Uranus and Neptune: Voyager 2, USA, launched August 20, 1977, is intended to reach Neptune in 1989. It has already been to Jupiter and Saturn and passed Uranus in 1986.

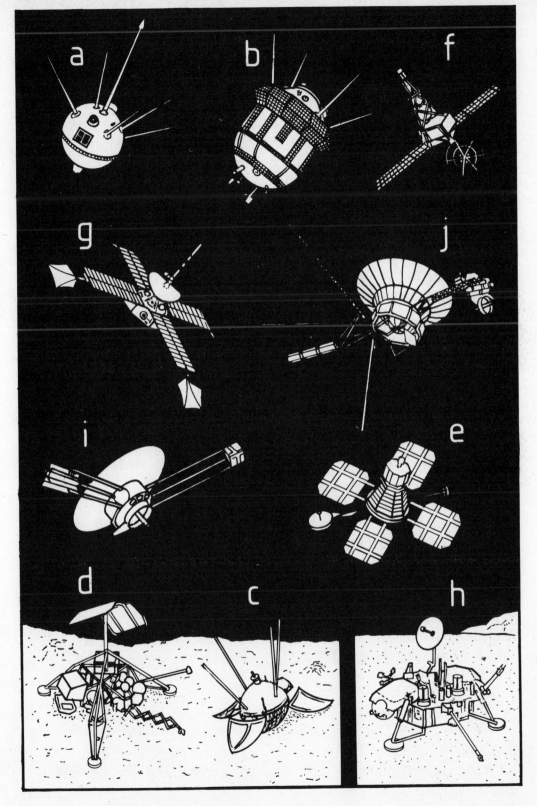

# Manned space flight (1)

**Choosing astronauts** The first men in space had to meet strict standards. A would-be astronaut had to be under 40 years old, less than 6ft tall and in perfect physical condition. He was expected to have majored in engineering and to be a trained test pilot with over 1500 hours flying experience.

## Some manned space flight firsts

First manned space flight: Yuri Gagarin in Vostok 1, launched by USSR on April 12, 1961. Completed one orbit of Earth.

First American manned space flight: Alan Shepard in the Mercury capsule "Freedom 7", launched on May 5, 1961. 15 minute suborbital flight.

First American orbital flight: John Glenn in the Mercury capsule "Friendship 7", launched on February 20, 1962. Completed three orbits of Earth.

First woman in space: Valentina Tereshkova in Vostok 6, launched by USSR on June 16, 1973. Completed 48 orbits of Earth.

First space walk: Alexei Leonov from Voskhod 2, launched by USSR on March 18, 1965. Walk lasted 10 min.

First American space walk: Edward White from Gemini 4, launched on June 3, 1965. Walk lasted 21 min.

First joint USA/USSR space mission: Apollo-Soyuz Test Project (ASTP). Apollo 18, launched by USA on July 15, 1975, docked with Soyuz 19, launched by USSR on same date. Crew members exchanged visits.

## Moon landings

The first landing was made by the Apollo 11 mission. The Apollo lunar module "Eagle" landed on the Moon's surface on July 20, 1969, and Neil Armstrong became the first man on the Moon. The other crew members were Buzz Aldrin and Michael Collins. Listed below are the crews and launch dates of the other five successful moon landings.

Apollo 12: Conrad, Gordon, Bean; November 14, 1969
Apollo 14: Shepard, Mitchell, Roosa; January 31, 1971
Apollo 15: Scott, Irwin, Worden; July 26, 1971
Apollo 16: Young, Duke, Mattingley; April 16, 1972
Apollo 17: Cernan, Schmitt, Evans; December 7, 1972

**Space craft** (facing page)
1  Vostok capsule (USSR)
2  Mercury capsule (USA)
3  Voskhod capsule (USSR)
4  Gemini capsule (USA)
5  Soyuz capsule (USSR)
6  Apollo capsule (USA)
7  Lunar module (USA)
8  Lunar roving vehicle (USA)
9  Apollo 18 docked with Soyuz 19

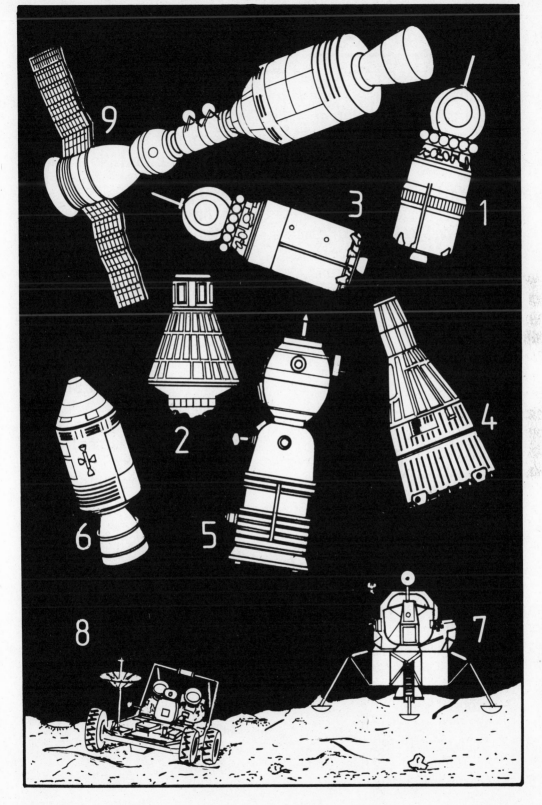

# Manned space flight (2)

**Reusable space craft** The USA and USSR have developed craft that can be used many times. Space laboratories and stations – like the USA's Skylab and USSR's Salyut – remain in orbit while crews come and go. The USA's space shuttle orbiter is a reusable vehicle launched like a rocket and landed like an aircraft.

### Skylab (A)

This was damaged when it was launched on May 14, 1973. Repair attempts were made by three crews. The first crew spent 28 days on board, the second crew 59 days and the third crew 84 days. Skylab was then abandoned and fell to Earth. It broke up as it entered Earth's atmosphere on July 11, 1979.

### Salyut

Salyut 1 was the first in a series of Salyut space stations. It was launched unmanned on April 19, 1971. A manned Soyuz capsule docked with it three days later (**B**). Salyut crews may spend several months on board. Here we list the records for the longest manned space flight set between June 1978 and June 1984.

Soyuz 29/Salyut 6: 140 days, June 15–November 2, 1978

Soyuz 32/Salyut 6: 175 days, February 25–August 19, 1979

Soyuz 35/Salyut 6: 185 days, April 9–October 11, 1980

Soyuz T5/Salyut 7: 211 days, May 13–December 10, 1982

Soyuz T9/Salyut 7: 212 days, June 28–December 23, 1983

### Space shuttle

The first space shuttle orbiter to be tested in flight was the Enterprise (**C**). Below we list some other shuttle firsts up to June 1984. Future plans for the shuttle include up to 24 flights a year using five orbiters. The first four of these orbiters were Columbia, Challenger, Discovery and Atlantis.

First full shuttle mission: STS 1/ Columbia, launched April 12, 1981

First commercial shuttle mission: STS 5/Columbia, launched November 11, 1982

First space walk from an orbiter: STS 6/Challenger, launched April 4, 1983

First American woman in space: Sally Ride in STS 7/Challenger, launched June 18, 1983

First night landing by an orbiter: STS 8/Challenger, launched August 30, 1983

First flight of the space laboratory "Spacelab": STS 9/Columbia, launched November 28, 1983

First use of the MMU (Manned Maneuvering Unit): 41B/ Challenger, launched February 3, 1984 (**D**)

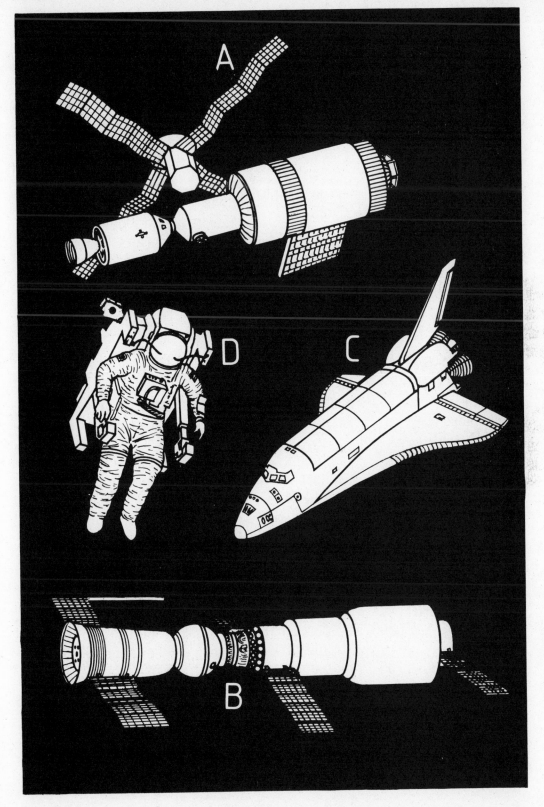

Where several page numbers are given, the reference in **bold** type is the most detailed.

Two page numbers followed by the word *passim* means that although the indexed word does not appear on every page, there are frequent references.

315